SMOKE AND STEEL

SLABS OF THE SUNBURNT WEST

GOOD MORNING, AMERICA

CARL SANDBURG

SMOKE AND STEEL

SLABS OF THE SUNBURNT WEST

GOOD MORNING, AMERICA

EASTERN NATIONAL ● FORT WASHINGTON, PENNSYLVANIA

ISBN 1-59091-020-6

2004 edition published by Eastern National. Eastern National
provides quality educational products and services to
America's national parks and other public trusts.

Eastern National
Serving America's National Parks
and Other Public Trusts

PREFACE

These three books published in the years 1920-1928 are now gathered into one volume. The first one, *Smoke and Steel,* had one intention of chanting and evoking industrial America and some of its human elements— and it was written in the aftermath of the first World War, carrying something heavy and brooding in the air of the years 1918, 1919, 1920. The second book, *Slabs of the Sunburnt West,* deals with a Grand Canyon of Arizona that varies little in a thousand years and a Windy City (Chicago) which changes its slang, proverbs, building and transportation styles with every generation. The third book, *Good Morning, America,* runs a wide gamut in its program. Written during the peak prosperity years, published in 1928 and exhibiting even in its typography the tendencies of the period, it voices little of that America which sank into its darkest economic depression a few years later. Nor does it edge into the terrible curtain raisers in China, Spain and Czecho-Slovakia and the fateful drama of the second World War though there are passages in the title-piece "Good Morning, America" which do not lack timing for America and its role in the second world conflict.

A man writes the best he can about what moves him

deeply. Once his writing gets published as a book he loses control over it. Time and the human family do what they want to with it. It may have periods of wide reading and acclamation, other periods of condemnation, decline, neglect—then a complete fadeout—or maybe a revival. And what revives in later years is often what was neglected when new. This happens. In literature and other arts—it happens.

Of course there are plenty of pieces in these books that I would write in a different way if I had them before me now as manuscripts for revision and re-writing. And more than that there are a few pieces I would throw away or lay by as experimental curiosities. A few such there are, though the titles of them are my own private memoranda and nobody's business just now. However, I could say in confidence that several items herein had become worn out for me and had arrived where I would rate them zero—and just about then came along this person and that saying these particular items were tops, were the goods, had what it takes. Or again, certain favorites of mine, so it seemed, were not being read by others as I read them—and I was almost of a notion that these favorites had some personal appeal for me and others were not getting the drift of them. Then after many years would come the surprise of a dancer wishing to build a program number around one of them or a composer wanting one for a song or a musical setting or an author for use in a

Preface

book. I have sat unaware at a radio set and suddenly heard a musical composition or a dramatic sketch or a campaign speech using lines of mine or an entire free verse piece which for me had long ago gone where the woodbine twineth and the lizards sleep on sunny slabs of inanimate stone.

Often in my travels with a guitar and a program of readings I have met the man or woman saying, "I don't get your poetry, Mr. Sandburg, but my son enjoys it and I wonder if I'm old-fashioned," or, "I've tried to read your poetry, Mr. Sammer, and it doesn't mean anything to me but my daughter studied you at college and she has all your books and is trying to tell me what they are about." The head of the St. Louis public library, Mr. Charles Compton, once made a survey around the question, "Who reads Sandburg?" and found that beyond a certain array of intellectuals, persons who socially and professionally are strong for Culture with a capital C, there were policemen, taxi drivers, stenographers, beauty parlor workers, machinists, and a wide range of plain people who could not afford to buy books but were regularly drawing out "the Sandburg poetry books" from the public library and finding in those books something close to their lives, something that sang to them.

Authors, like any others who do their best in some field of art, are in danger of being tricked and fooled by what their audiences do to them. Many an author would better have shut his ears to all that was ever said or written about him—so much of it was polite conversation or shallow in feeling or washed in malice or prejudice or misunderstanding. I have usually taken time to read such reviews and comments as came my way without particular effort on my part, having seen no less than three well known authors suffer the pangs of hell from what arrived in the mail through a clipping service they paid for.

That a large body of English teachers in high schools, colleges and universities have been kindly and favorable to my work in the field of free verse, more than occasionally one of them mentioning this or that student saying, "Until we got into Sandburg, I was never interested in poetry"—this I do not forget. That some of the professional reviewers and critics have been both kindly and eloquent toward my work as a verse writer—this too I do not forget.

Recently a poet was quoted as saying he would as soon play tennis without a net as to write free verse. This is almost as though a zebra should say to a leopard, "I would rather have stripes than spots," or as though a leopard should inform a zebra, "I prefer spots to stripes."

The poet without imagination or folly enough to play tennis by serving and returning the ball over an invisible net may see himself as highly disciplined. There have been poets who could and did play more than one

Preface

game of tennis with unseen rackets, volleying airy and fantastic balls over an insubstantial net, on a frail moonlit fabric of a court.

The arguments against free verse are old. They are not, however, as old as free verse itself. When primitive and prehistoric man first spoke with cadence or color, making either musical meaning or melodic nonsense worth keeping and repeating for its definite and intrinsic values, then free verse was born, ages before the sonnet, the ballad, the verse forms wherein the writer or singer must be acutely conscious, even exquisitely aware, of how many syllables are to be arithmetically numbered per line.

The matter should not be argued. Those who make poems and hope their poems are not bad may find readers or listeners—and again they may not. The affair should rest there. Nothing can be proved except that some poets have one kind of readers or listeners—and other poets have other kinds. The mortal and finite role of the poet is the same as that of the mathematician who said that after any equation you can write, "Make the sign of infinity and pass on." And all adverse critics of any work not yet tested by time come near falling headfirst into the category of the man who enjoys his personal habit of exclaiming to any and all who vocalize, "Would you just as soon sing as make that noise?"

To every poet of reputation come the young ones, the beginners, asking, "Will you look over my poems and tell me whether they are good or not?" And usually, if the beginner is told his poems are bad or not so good or he needs more practice, he gets sore and takes his manuscripts to still other poets of reputation, hoping to find someone who says he has what it takes. Often I have told a nice lad who considered it important to know whether he was wasting his time, "If you're going to be a poet, you don't care a hoot what I say or what anybody but yourself says. If you're afraid you're wasting your time you probably are." Quite a case can be made out that Shakespeare wrote his plays and poems because in the time it took him to do them he couldn't think of anything else he would rather be doing.

"Nothing much in the way of advice is going to help you," I once wrote to an inquirer. "You go your own way. You ride whatever horses you want to. You will go here and there and see what the best and the worst have in style, technic, themes . . . and after that go your own way.

"You will be in danger very likely at any time you listen seriously to dese dose and dem, saying you must looksee about dis or dat. Listen, yes, and listen again and do a lot of listening and rebuke yourself about your listening and pray often that you may be a better listener. You may be advised you must not, for instance, listen to shadows, for how can shadows speak? This is where the eyes must join the ears for listening, for the eyes gather the pantomimes of the shadows and there have been rolling thunders issue from a few crooks and crosses of singing fingers. And anyhow and ennyhoo shadows deal in whispers. Successful contradiction of this thesis cannot be maintained. The fact stands. And the fact is immeasurably important can it be verified. On this the poets and politicians can have a bowl of chile in peace and understanding. Shadows deal in whispers. Bluebirds burnish their wings with worms they eat. Poets cry their hearts out. If they don't they ain't poets.

"Subsistence won from sharing grief is what? Sorrows blend themselves with sorrows and wryly and bitterly shoot the works of sorrow. Out of it once in a while comes music, companionship, stately consolations. Every good Bach listener is a miniature Bach. Else Bach couldn't get by. You have much to go on. You are licensed to the latest slang; 'is everything under control?' Beware of proud words, sweet gal. On this road you go on lonely and at cost. My prayers are that many strengths be yours, new and harder thongs for the old always."

"You are vivid. Go on so. It will cost . . . but go on. Work hard . . . they all do when they are any good at all. The sense of futility will ride you often . . . and this is not too bad, for usually it means a requisite humility is operating. When you are too sure you are good then pray god help your vain little heart.

Preface

Write much. Write every day. Lay the pieces by. See what happens later."

Once a college student spoke his anxiety about whether to write his poetry in rhyme or not. The best I could do for him was the advice: "If it jells into free verse, all right. If it jells into rhyme, all right."

Any counselor should go slow about being certain as to what a beginner may or may not have. The more original a piece of writing is the less likely an adviser or critic is to find what is original. Some of the greatest poetry had to go through many tests of time before it came to be accepted. The early American poet, McDonald Clarke, wrote of this factor:

> 'Tis vain for present fame to wish,
> Our persons first must be forgotten;
> For poets are like stinking fish,
> They never shine until they're rotten.

CARL SANDBURG

Chikaming Goat Farm
Harbert, Michigan
September 30, 1941

SMOKE AND STEEL

TO

COL. EDWARD J. STEICHEN

PAINTER OF NOCTURNES AND FACES, CAMERA ENGRAVER
OF GLINTS AND MOMENTS, LISTENER TO BLUE
EVENING WINDS AND NEW YELLOW ROSES,
DREAMER AND FINDER, RIDER OF GREAT
MORNINGS IN GARDENS, VALLEYS,
BATTLES.

SMOKE AND STEEL

SMOKE NIGHTS

SMOKE AND STEEL	3
FIVE TOWNS ON THE B. & O.	11
WORK GANGS	12
PENNSYLVANIA	14
WHIRLS	15

PEOPLE WHO MUST

PEOPLE WHO MUST	19
ALLEY RATS	20
ELEVENTH AVENUE RACKET	21
HOME FIRES	22
HATS	23
THEY ALL WANT TO PLAY HAMLET	24
THE MAYOR OF GARY	25
OMAHA	26
GALOOTS	27
CRABAPPLE BLOSSOMS	28
REAL ESTATE NEWS	30
MANUAL SYSTEM	31
STRIPES	32
HONKY TONK IN CLEVELAND, OHIO	33
CRAPSHOOTERS	34
SOUP	35
CLINTON SOUTH OF POLK	36
BLUE ISLAND INTERSECTION	37
RED-HEADED RESTAURANT CASHIER	38
BOY AND FATHER	39
CLEAN CURTAINS	41
CRIMSON CHANGES PEOPLE	42
NEIGHBORS	44
CAHOOTS	45
BLUE MAROONS	46
THE HANGMAN AT HOME	47
MAN, THE MAN-HUNTER	48
THE SINS OF KALAMAZOO	49

BROKEN-FACE GARGOYLES

BROKEN-FACE GARGOYLES	57
APRONS OF SILENCE	59

DEATH SNIPS PROUD MEN   60
GOOD-NIGHT   61
SHIRT   62
JAZZ FANTASIA   63
DO YOU WANT AFFIDAVITS?   64
OLD-FASHIONED REQUITED LOVE   65
PURPLE MARTINS   66
BRASS KEYS   68
PICK OFFS   69
MANUFACTURED GODS   70
MASK   71

PLAYTHINGS OF THE WIND

FOUR PRELUDES ON PLAYTHINGS OF THE WIND   75
BROKEN TABERNACLES   78
OSSAWATOMIE   79
LONG GUNS   81
DUSTY DOORS   82
FLASH CRIMSON   83
THE LAWYERS KNOW TOO MUCH   85
LOSERS   87
PLACES   88
THREES   89
THE LIARS   90
PRAYERS AFTER WORLD WAR   93
A. E. F.   94
BAS-RELIEF   95
CARLOVINGIAN DREAMS   96
BRONZES   97
LET LOVE GO ON   98
KILLERS   99
CLEAN HANDS   100
THREE GHOSTS   102
PENCILS   103
JUG   105
AND THIS WILL BE ALL?   106
HOODLUMS   107
YES, THE DEAD SPEAK TO US   109

MIST FORMS

CALLS   115
SEA-WASH   116

SILVER WIND   117
EVENING WATERFALL   118
CRUCIBLE   119
SUMMER STARS   120
THROW ROSES   121
JUST BEFORE APRIL CAME   122
STARS, SONGS, FACES   123
SANDPIPERS   124
THREE VIOLINS   125
THE WIND SINGS WELCOME IN EARLY SPRING   126
TAWNY   127
SLIPPERY   128
HELGA   129
BABY TOES   130
PEOPLE WITH PROUD CHINS   131
WINTER MILK   132
SLEEPYHEADS   133
SUMACH AND BIRDS   134
WOMEN WASHING THEIR HAIR   135
PEACH BLOSSOMS   136
HALF MOON IN A HIGH WIND   137
REMORSE   138
RIVER MOONS   139
SAND SCRIBBLINGS   140
HOW YESTERDAY LOOKED   141
PAULA   142
LAUGHING BLUE STEEL   143
THEY ASK EACH OTHER WHERE THEY CAME FROM   144
HOW MUCH?   145
THROWBACKS   146
WIND SONG   147
THREE SPRING NOTATIONS ON BIPEDS   148
SANDHILL PEOPLE   150
FAR ROCKAWAY NIGHT TILL MORNING   151
HUMMING BIRD WOMAN   152
BUCKWHEAT   153
BLUE RIDGE   154
VALLEY SONG   155
MIST FORMS   156
PIGEON   157
CHASERS   158
HORSE FIDDLE   159

TIMBER WINGS 161
NIGHT STUFF 162
SPANISH 163
SHAGBARK HICKORY 164
THE SOUTH WIND SAY SO 165

ACCOMPLISHED FACTS

ACCOMPLISHED FACTS 169
GRIEG BEING DEAD 170
CHORDS 171
DOGHEADS 172
TRINITY PLACE 173
PORTRAIT 174
POTOMAC RIVER MIST 175
JACK LONDON AND O. HENRY 176
HIS OWN FACE HIDDEN 177
CUPS OF COFFEE 178

PASSPORTS

SMOKE ROSE GOLD 181
TANGIBLES 182
NIGHT MOVEMENT—NEW YORK 183
NORTH ATLANTIC 184
FOG PORTRAIT 188
FLYING FISH 189
HOME THOUGHTS 190
IN THE SHADOW OF THE PALACE 191
TWO ITEMS 192
STREETS TOO OLD 193
SAVOIR FAIRE 194
MOHAMMED BEK HADJETLACHE 196
HIGH CONSPIRATORIAL PERSONS 197
BALTIC FOG NOTES 198

CIRCLES OF DOORS

CIRCLES OF DOORS 203
HATE 204
TWO STRANGERS BREAKFAST 205
SNOW 206
DANCER 207
PLASTER 208
CURSE OF A RICH POLISH PEASANT ON HIS SISTER WHO
    RAN AWAY WITH A WILD MAN 209

WOMAN WITH A PAST   210
WHITE HANDS   211
AN ELECTRIC SIGN GOES DARK   212
THEY BUY WITH AN EYE TO LOOKS   214
PROUD AND BEAUTIFUL   215
TELEGRAM   216
GLIMMER   217
WHITE ASH   218
TESTIMONY REGARDING A GHOST   219
PUT OFF THE WEDDING FIVE TIMES AND NOBODY
    COMES TO IT   220
BABY VAMPS   222
VAUDEVILLE DANCER   223
BALLOON FACES   224

HAZE

HAZE   229
CADENZA   232
MEMORANDA   233
POTOMAC TOWN IN FEBRUARY   234
BUFFALO DUSK   235
CORN HUT TALK   236
BRANCHES   238
RUSTY CRIMSON   239
LETTER S   240
WEEDS   241
NEW FARM TRACTOR   242
PODS   243
HARVEST SUNSET   244
NIGHTS NOTHINGS AGAIN   245

PANELS

PANELS   253
DAN   254
WHIFFLETREE   255
MASCOTS   256
THE SKYSCRAPER LOVES NIGHT   257
NEVER BORN   258
THIN STRIPS   259
FIVE CENT BALLOONS   260
MY PEOPLE   261
TWIRL   262

WISTFUL	263
BASKET	264
FIRE PAGES	265
FINISH	266
FOR YOU	267

SMOKE NIGHTS

SMOKE AND STEEL

Smoke of the fields in spring is one,
Smoke of the leaves in autumn another.
Smoke of a steel-mill roof or a battleship funnel,
They all go up in a line with a smokestack,
Or they twist . . . in the slow twist . . . of the wind.

If the north wind comes they run to the south.
If the west wind comes they run to the east.
    By this sign
    all smokes
    know each other.
Smoke of the fields in spring and leaves in autumn,
Smoke of the finished steel, chilled and blue,
By the oath of work they swear: " I know you."

Hunted and hissed from the center
Deep down long ago when God made us over,
Deep down are the cinders we came from—
You and I and our heads of smoke.

   . . . .

Some of the smokes God dropped on the job
Cross on the sky and count our years
And sing in the secrets of our numbers;
Sing their dawns and sing their evenings,
Sing an old log-fire song:

You may put the damper up,
You may put the damper down,
The smoke goes up the chimney just the same.

Smoke of a city sunset skyline,
Smoke of a country dusk horizon—
They cross on the sky and count our years.

. . . .

Smoke of a brick-red dust
Winds on a spiral
Out of the stacks
For a hidden and glimpsing moon.
This, said the bar-iron shed to the blooming mill,
This is the slang of coal and steel.
The day-gang hands it to the night-gang,
The night-gang hands it back.

Stammer at the slang of this—
Let us understand half of it.
In the rolling mills and sheet mills,
In the harr and boom of the blast fires,
The smoke changes its shadow
And men change their shadow;
A nigger, a wop, a bohunk changes.

A bar of steel—it is only
Smoke at the heart of it, smoke and the blood of a man.
A runner of fire ran in it, ran out, ran somewhere else,
And left—smoke and the blood of a man
And the finished steel, chilled and blue.

So fire runs in, runs out, runs somewhere else again,
And the bar of steel is a gun, a wheel, a nail, a shovel,
A rudder under the sea, a steering-gear in the sky;
And always dark in the heart and through it,
        Smoke and the blood of a man.
Pittsburg, Youngstown, Gary—they make their steel
    with men.

In the blood of men and the ink of chimneys
The smoke nights write their oaths:
Smoke into steel and blood into steel;
Homestead, Braddock, Birmingham, they make their
    steel with men.
Smoke and blood is the mix of steel.

        The birdmen drone
        in the blue; it is steel
        a motor sings and zooms.

            .   .   .   .

Steel barb-wire around The Works.
Steel guns in the holsters of the guards at the gates of
    The Works.
Steel ore-boats bring the loads clawed from the earth
    by steel, lifted and lugged by arms of steel, sung
    on its way by the clanking clam-shells.
The runners now, the handlers now, are steel; they dig
    and clutch and haul; they hoist their automatic
    knuckles from job to job; they are steel making
    steel.

Fire and dust and air fight in the furnaces; the pour is
    timed, the billets wriggle; the clinkers are dumped:
Liners on the sea, skyscrapers on the land; diving steel
    in the sea, climbing steel in the sky.

.   .   .   .

Finders in the dark, you Steve with a dinner bucket,
    you Steve clumping in the dusk on the sidewalks
    with an evening paper for the woman and kids,
    you Steve with your head wondering where we
    all end up—
Finders in the dark, Steve: I hook my arm in cinder
    sleeves; we go down the street together; it is all
    the same to us; you Steve and the rest of us end
    on the same stars; we all wear a hat in hell
    together, in hell or heaven.

Smoke nights now, Steve.
Smoke, smoke, lost in the sieves of yesterday;
Dumped again to the scoops and hooks today.
Smoke like the clocks and whistles, always.
    Smoke nights now.
    To-morrow something else.

.   .   .   .

Luck moons come and go:
Five men swim in a pot of red steel.
Their bones are kneaded into the bread of steel:
Their bones are knocked into coils and anvils
And the sucking plungers of sea-fighting turbines.
Look for them in the woven frame of a wireless station.

So ghosts hide in steel like heavy-armed men in
mirrors.
Peepers, skulkers—they shadow-dance in laughing
tombs.
They are always there and they never answer.

One of them said: "I like my job, the company is
good to me, America is a wonderful country."
One: "Jesus, my bones ache; the company is a liar;
this is a free country, like hell."
One: "I got a girl, a peach; we save up and go on a
farm and raise pigs and be the boss ourselves."
And the others were roughneck singers a long ways
from home.
Look for them back of a steel vault door.

They laugh at the cost.
They lift the birdmen into the blue.
It is steel a motor sings and zooms.

In the subway plugs and drums,
In the slow hydraulic drills, in gumbo or gravel,
Under dynamo shafts in the webs of armature spiders.
They shadow-dance and laugh at the cost.

. . . .

The ovens light a red dome.
Spools of fire wind and wind.
Quadrangles of crimson sputter.
The lashes of dying maroon let down.
Fire and wind wash out the slag.
Forever the slag gets washed in fire and wind.

The anthem learned by the steel is:
> Do this or go hungry.

Look for our rust on a plow.
Listen to us in a threshing-engine razz.
Look at our job in the running wagon wheat.

. . . .

Fire and wind wash at the slag.
Box-cars, clocks, steam-shovels, churns, pistons, boilers,
    scissors—
Oh, the sleeping slag from the mountains, the slag-
    heavy pig-iron will go down many roads.
Men will stab and shoot with it, and make butter and
    tunnel rivers, and mow hay in swaths, and slit
    hogs and skin beeves, and steer airplanes across
    North America, Europe, Asia, round the world.

Hacked from a hard rock country, broken and baked
    in mills and smelters, the rusty dust waits
Till the clean hard weave of its atoms cripples and
    blunts the drills chewing a hole in it.
The steel of its plinths and flanges is reckoned, O God,
    in one-millionth of an inch.

. . . .

Once when I saw the curves of fire, the rough scarf
    women dancing,
Dancing out of the flues and smoke-stacks—flying hair
    of fire, flying feet upside down;
Buckets and baskets of fire exploding and chortling,
    fire running wild out of the steady and fastened
    ovens;

Sparks cracking a harr-harr-huff from a solar-plexus
    of rock-ribs of the earth taking a laugh for them-
    selves;
Ears and noses of fire, gibbering gorilla arms of fire,
    gold mud-pies, gold bird-wings, red jackets riding
    purple mules, scarlet autocrats tumbling from the
    humps of camels, assassinated czars straddling
    vermillion balloons;
I saw then the fires flash one by one: good-by: then
    smoke, smoke;
And in the screens the great sisters of night and cool
    stars, sitting women arranging their hair,
Waiting in the sky, waiting with slow easy eyes, wait-
    ing and half-murmuring:
      " Since you know all
      and I know nothing,
      tell me what I dreamed last night."

      . . . .

Pearl cobwebs in the windy rain,
in only a flicker of wind,
are caught and lost and never known again.

A pool of moonshine comes and waits,
but never waits long: the wind picks up
loose gold like this and is gone.

A bar of steel sleeps and looks slant-eyed
on the pearl cobwebs, the pools of moonshine;
sleeps slant-eyed a million years,

sleeps with a coat of rust, a vest of moths,
a shirt of gathering sod and loam.

The wind never bothers . . . a bar of steel.
The wind picks only . . pearl cobwebs . . pools
of moonshine.

FIVE TOWNS ON THE B. AND O.

By day . . . tireless smokestacks . . . hungry smoky
shanties hanging to the slopes . . . crooning:
We get by, that's all.

By night . . . all lit up . . . fire-gold bars, fire-gold
flues . . . and the shanties shaking in clumsy
shadows . . almost the hills shaking . . . all
crooning: By God, we're going to find out or
know why.

WORK GANGS

Box cars run by a mile long.
And I wonder what they say to each other
When they stop a mile long on a sidetrack.
    Maybe their chatter goes:
I came from Fargo with a load of wheat up to the
    danger line.
I came from Omaha with a load of shorthorns and
    they splintered my boards.
I came from Detroit heavy with a load of flivvers.
I carried apples from the Hood river last year and this
    year bunches of bananas from Florida; they look
    for me with watermelons from Mississippi next
    year.

Hammers and shovels of work gangs sleep in shop
    corners
when the dark stars come on the sky and the night
    watchmen walk and look.

Then the hammer heads talk to the handles,
then the scoops of the shovels talk,
how the day's work nicked and trimmed them,
how they swung and lifted all day,
how the hands of the work gangs smelled of hope.

In the night of the dark stars
when the curve of the sky is a work gang handle,
in the night on the mile long sidetracks,
in the night where the hammers and shovels sleep in
   corners,
the night watchmen stuff their pipes with dreams—
and sometimes they doze and don't care for nothin',
and sometimes they search their heads for meanings,
   stories, stars.
   The stuff of it runs like this:
A long way we come; a long way to go; long rests and
   long deep sniffs for our lungs on the way.
Sleep is a belonging of all; even if all songs are old
   songs and the singing heart is snuffed out like a
   switchman's lantern with the oil gone, even if we
   forget our names and houses in the finish, the
   secret of sleep is left us, sleep belongs to all,
   sleep is the first and last and best of all.

People singing; people with song mouths connecting
   with song hearts; people who must sing or die;
   people whose song hearts break if there is no
   song mouth; these are my people.

PENNSYLVANIA

I HAVE been in Pennsylvania,
In the Monongahela and the Hocking Valleys.

In the blue Susquehanna
On a Saturday morning
I saw the mounted constabulary go by,
I saw boys playing marbles.
Spring and the hills laughed.

And in places
Along the Appalachian chain,
I saw steel arms handling coal and iron,
And I saw the white-cauliflower faces
Of miners' wives waiting for the men to come home
    from the day's work.

I made color studies in crimson and violet
Over the dust and domes of culm at sunset.

coal dust

WHIRLS

NEITHER rose leaves gathered in a jar—respectably in
Boston—these—nor drops of Christ blood for a
chalice—decently in Philadelphia or Baltimore.

Cinders—these—hissing in a marl and lime of Chicago
—also these—the howling of northwest winds
across North and South Dakota—or the spatter
of winter spray on sea rocks of Kamchatka.

PEOPLE WHO MUST

PEOPLE WHO MUST

I PAINTED on the roof of a skyscraper.
I painted a long while and called it a day's work.
The people on a corner swarmed and the traffic cop's
    whistle never let up all afternoon.
They were the same as bugs, many bugs on their way—
Those people on the go or at a standstill;
And the traffic cop a spot of blue, a splinter of brass,
Where the black tides ran around him
And he kept the street. I painted a long while
And called it a day's work.

ALLEY RATS

THEY were calling certain styles of whiskers by the
   name of "lilacs."
And another manner of beard assumed in their chatter
   a verbal guise
Of "mutton chops," "galways," "feather dusters."

Metaphors such as these sprang from their lips while
   other street cries
Sprang from sparrows finding scattered oats among
   interstices of the curb.
Ah-hah these metaphors—and Ah-hah these boys—
   among the police they were known
As the Dirty Dozen and their names took the front
   pages of newspapers
And two of them croaked on the same day at a "neck-
   tie party" . . . if we employ the metaphors of
   their lips.

ELEVENTH AVENUE RACKET

THERE is something terrible
about a hurdy-gurdy,
a gipsy man and woman,
and a monkey in red flannel
all stopping in front of a big house
with a sign " For Rent " on the door
and the blinds hanging loose
and nobody home.
I never saw this.
I hope to God I never will.

Whoop-de-doodle-de-doo.
Hoodle-de-harr-de-hum.
Nobody home? Everybody home.
Whoop-de-doodle-de-doo.
Mamie Riley married Jimmy Higgins last night: Eddie
Jones died of whooping cough: George Hacks got
a job on the police force: the Rosenheims bought
a brass bed: Lena Hart giggled at a jackie: a
pushcart man called to*may*toes, to*may*toes.
Whoop-de-doodle-de-doo.
Hoodle-de-harr-de-hum.
Nobody home? Everybody home.

HOME FIRES

In a Yiddish eating place on Rivington Street . . .
faces . . . coffee spots . . . children kicking at
the night stars with bare toes from bare buttocks.
They know it is September on Rivington when the red
tomaytoes cram the pushcarts,
Here the children snozzle at milk bottles, children who
have never seen a cow.
Here the stranger wonders how so many people re-
member where they keep home fires.

HATS

HATS, where do you belong?
what is under you?

On the rim of a skyscraper's forehead
I looked down and saw: hats: fifty thousand hats:
Swarming with a noise of bees and sheep, cattle and
waterfalls,
Stopping with a silence of sea grass, a silence of
prairie corn.
Hats: tell me your high hopes.

THEY ALL WANT TO PLAY HAMLET

THEY all want to play Hamlet.
They have not exactly seen their fathers killed
Nor their mothers in a frame-up to kill,
Nor an Ophelia dying with a dust gagging the heart,
Not exactly the spinning circles of singing golden
　　　spiders,
Not exactly this have they got at nor the meaning of
　　　flowers—O flowers, flowers slung by a dancing
　　　girl—in the saddest play the inkfish, Shakespeare,
　　　ever wrote;
Yet they all want to play Hamlet because it is sad
　　　like all actors are sad and to stand by an open
　　　grave with a joker's skull in the hand and then
　　　to say over slow and say over slow wise, keen,
　　　beautiful words masking a heart that's breaking,
　　　breaking,
This is something that calls and calls to their blood.
They are acting when they talk about it and they know
　　　it is acting to be particular about it and yet: They
　　　all want to play Hamlet.

THE MAYOR OF GARY

I ASKED the Mayor of Gary about the 12-hour day
and the 7-day week.

And the Mayor of Gary answered more workmen steal
time on the job in Gary than any other place in
the United States.

" Go into the plants and you will see men sitting
around doing nothing—machinery does every-
thing," said the Mayor of Gary when I asked
him about the 12-hour day and the 7-day week.

And he wore cool cream pants, the Mayor of Gary,
and white shoes, and a barber had fixed him up
with a shampoo and a shave and he was easy
and imperturbable though the government weather
bureau thermometer said 96 and children were
soaking their heads at bubbling fountains on the
street corners.

And I said good-by to the Mayor of Gary and I went
out from the city hall and turned the corner into
Broadway.

And I saw workmen wearing leather shoes scruffed
with fire and cinders, and pitted with little holes
from running molten steel,

And some had bunches of specialized muscles around
their shoulder blades hard as pig iron, muscles
of their fore-arms were sheet steel and they looked
to me like men who had been somewhere.

Gary, Indiana, 1915.

OMAHA

RED barns and red heifers spot the green
grass circles around Omaha—the farmers
haul tanks of cream and wagon loads of
cheese.

Shale hogbacks across the river at Council
Bluffs—and shanties hang by an eyelash to
the hill slants back around Omaha.

A span of steel ties up the kin of Iowa and
Nebraska across the yellow, big-hoofed Missouri
River.

Omaha, the roughneck, feeds armies,
Eats and swears from a dirty face.
Omaha works to get the world a breakfast.

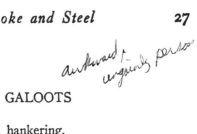

GALOOTS

Galoots, you hairy, hankering,
Snousle on the bones you eat, chew at the gristle and
  lick the last of it.
Grab off the bones in the paws of other galoots—hook
  your claws in their sleazy mouths—snap and run.
If long-necks sit on their rumps and sing wild cries
  to the winter moon, chasing their tails to the
  flickers of foolish stars . . . let 'em howl.
Galoots fat with too much, galoots lean with too little,
  galoot millions and millions, snousle and snicker
  on, plug your exhausts, hunt your snacks of fat
  and lean, grab off yours.

CRABAPPLE BLOSSOMS

SOMEBODY'S little girl—how easy to make a sob
    story over who she was once and who she is
    now.
Somebody's little girl—she played once under a crab-
    apple tree in June and the blossoms fell on the
    dark hair.

It was somewhere on the Erie line and the town was
    Salamanca or Painted Post or Horse's Head.
And out of her hair she shook the blossoms and went
    into the house and her mother washed her face
    and her mother had an ache in her heart at a rebel
    voice, " I don't want to."

Somebody's little girl—forty little girls of somebodies
    splashed in red tights forming horseshoes, arches,
    pyramids—forty little show girls, ponies, squabs.
How easy a sob story over who she once was and who
    she is now—and how the crabapple blossoms fell
    on her dark hair in June.

Let the lights of Broadway spangle and splatter—and
    the taxis hustle the crowds away when the show
    is over and the street goes dark.

Let the girls wash off the paint and go for their mid-
night sandwiches—let 'em dream in the morning
sun, late in the morning, long after the morning
papers and the milk wagons—

Let 'em dream long as they want to . . . of June
somewhere on the Erie line . . . and crabapple
blossoms.

REAL ESTATE NEWS

ARMOUR AVENUE was the name of this street and door
    signs on empty houses read " The Silver Dollar,"
    " Swede Annie " and the Christian names of
    madams such as " Myrtle " and " Jenny."
Scrap iron, rags and bottles fill the front rooms hither
    and yon and signs in Yiddish say Abe Kaplan &
    Co. are running junk shops in whore houses of
    former times.
The segregated district, the Tenderloin, is here no
    more; the red-lights are gone; the ring of shovels
    handling scrap iron replaces the banging of pianos
    and the bawling songs of pimps.
Chicago, 1915.

MANUAL SYSTEM

Mary has a thingamajig clamped on her ears
And sits all day taking plugs out and sticking plugs in.
Flashes and flashes—voices and voices
                    calling for ears to pour words in
Faces at the ends of wires asking for other faces
                    at the ends of other wires:
All day taking plugs out and sticking plugs in,
Mary has a thingamajig clamped on her ears.

STRIPES

POLICEMAN in front of a bank 3 A.M. . . . lonely.
Policeman State and Madison . . . high noon . . .
    mobs . . . cars . . . parcels . . . lonely.

Woman in suburbs . . . keeping night watch on a
    sleeping typhoid patient . . . only a clock to talk
    to . . . lonesome.
Woman selling gloves . . . bargain day department
    store . . . furious crazy-work of many hands
    slipping in and out of gloves . . . lonesome.

HONKY TONK IN CLEVELAND, OHIO

It's a jazz affair, drum crashes and cornet razzes.
The trombone pony neighs and the tuba jackass snorts.
The banjo tickles and titters too **awful**.
The chippies talk about the funnies in the papers.
    The cartoonists weep in their beer.
    Ship riveters talk with their feet
    To the feet of floozies under the tables.
A quartet of white hopes mourn with interspersed
    snickers:
        " I got the blues.
        I got the blues.
        I got the blues."
And . . . as we said earlier:
    The cartoonists weep in their beer.

CRAPSHOOTERS

SOMEBODY loses whenever somebody wins.
This was known to the Chaldeans long ago.
And more: somebody wins whenever somebody loses.
This too was in the savvy of the Chaldeans.

They take it heaven's hereafter is an eternity of crap
    games where they try their wrists years and years
    and no police come with a wagon; the game goes
    on forever.
The spots on the dice are the music signs of the songs
    of heaven here.
God is Luck: Luck is God: we are all bones the
    High Thrower rolled: some are two spots, some
    double sixes.

The myths are Phoebe, Little Joe, Big Dick.
Hope runs high with a: Huh, seven—huh, come seven
This too was in the savvy of the Chaldeans.

SOUP

I SAW a famous man eating soup.
I say he was lifting a fat broth
Into his mouth with a spoon.
His name was in the newspapers that day
Spelled out in tall black headlines
And thousands of people were talking about him.

When I saw him,
He sat bending his head over a plate
Putting soup in his mouth with a spoon.

CLINTON SOUTH OF POLK *

I WANDER down on Clinton street south of Polk
And listen to the voices of Italian children quarreling.
It is a cataract of coloratura
And I could sleep to their musical threats and accusa-
    tions.

BLUE ISLAND INTERSECTION

Six street ends come together here.
They feed people and wagons into the center.
In and out all day horses with thoughts of nose-bags,
Men with shovels, women with baskets and baby
    buggies.
Six ends of streets and no sleep for them all day.
The people and wagons come and go, out and in.
Triangles of banks and drug stores watch.
The policemen whistle, the trolley cars bump:
Wheels, wheels, feet, feet, all day.

In the false dawn when the chickens blink
And the east shakes a lazy baby toe at to-morrow,
And the east fixes a pink half-eye this way,
In the time when only one milk wagon crosses
These three streets, these six street ends,
It is the sleep time and they rest.
The triangle banks and drug stores rest.
The policeman is gone, his star and gun sleep.
The owl car blutters along in a sleep-walk.

RED-HEADED RESTAURANT CASHIER

SHAKE back your hair, O red-headed girl.
Let go your laughter and keep your two proud freckles
on your chin.
Somewhere is a man looking for a red-headed girl and
some day maybe he will look into your eyes for a
restaurant cashier and find a lover, maybe.
Around and around go ten thousand men hunting a
red headed girl with two freckles on her chin.
I have seen them hunting, hunting.
Shake back your hair; let go your laughter.

BOY AND FATHER

THE boy Alexander understands his father to be a
   famous lawyer.
The leather law books of Alexander's father fill a
   room like hay in a barn.
Alexander has asked his father to let him build a house
   like bricklayers build, a house with walls and
   roofs made of big leather law books.

> The rain beats on the windows
> And the raindrops run down the window glass
> And the raindrops slide off the green blinds
>   down the siding.

The boy Alexander dreams of Napoleon in John C.
   Abbott's history, Napoleon the grand and lonely
   man wronged, Napoleon in his life wronged and
   in his memory wronged.
The boy Alexander dreams of the cat Alice saw, the
   cat fading off into the dark and leaving the teeth
   of its Cheshire smile lighting the gloom.

Buffaloes, blizzards, way down in Texas, in the pan-
   handle of Texas snuggling close to New Mexico,
These creep into Alexander's dreaming by the window
   when his father talks with strange men about
   land down in Deaf Smith County.

Alexander's father tells the strange men: Five years
    ago we ran a Ford out on the prairie and chased
    antelopes.

Only once or twice in a long while has Alexander heard
    his father say "my first wife" so-and-so and
    such-and-such.
A few times softly the father has told Alexander,
    "Your mother . . . was a beautiful woman . . .
    but we won't talk about her."
Always Alexander listens with a keen listen when he
    hears his father mention "my first wife" or "Al-
    exander's mother."

Alexander's father smokes a cigar and the Episcopal
    rector smokes a cigar and the words come often:
    mystery of life, mystery of life.
These two come into Alexander's head blurry and gray
    while the rain beats on the windows and the rain-
    drops run down the window glass and the rain-
    drops slide off the green blinds and down the
    siding.
These and: There is a God, there must be a God, how
    can there be rain or sun unless there is a God?

So from the wrongs of Napoleon and the Cheshire cat
    smile on to the buffaloes and blizzards of Texas
    and on to his mother and to God, so the blurry
    gray rain dreams of Alexander have gone on five
    minutes, maybe ten, keeping slow easy time to the
    raindrops on the window glass and the raindrops
    sliding off the green blinds and down the siding.

CLEAN CURTAINS

NEW neighbors came to the corner house at Congress and Green streets.

The look of their clean white curtains was the same as the rim of a nun's bonnet.

One way was an oyster pail factory, one way they made candy, one way paper boxes, strawboard cartons.

The warehouse trucks shook the dust of the ways loose and the wheels whirled dust—there was dust of hoof and wagon wheel and rubber tire— dust of police and fire wagons—dust of the winds that circled at midnights and noon listening to no prayers.

" O mother, I know the heart of you," I sang passing the rim of a nun's bonnet—O white curtains—and people clean as the prayers of Jesus here in the faded ramshackle at Congress and Green.

Dust and the thundering trucks won—the barrages of the street wheels and the lawless wind took their way—was it five weeks or six the little mother, the new neighbors, battled and then took away the white prayers in the windows?

CRIMSON CHANGES PEOPLE

DID I see a crucifix in your eyes
and nails and Roman soldiers
and a dusk Golgotha?

Did I see Mary, the changed woman,
washing the feet of all men,
clean as new grass
when the old grass burns?

Did I see moths in your eyes, lost moths,
with a flutter of wings that meant:
we can never come again.

Did I see No Man's Land in your eyes
and men with lost faces, lost loves,
and you among the stubs crying?

Did I see you in the red death jazz of war
losing moths among lost faces,
speaking to the stubs who asked you
to speak of songs and God and dancing,
of bananas, northern lights or Jesus,
any hummingbird of thought whatever
flying away from the red death jazz of war?

Did I see your hand make a useless gesture
trying to say with a code of five fingers
something the tongue only stutters?
did I see a dusk Golgotha?

NEIGHBORS

ON Forty First Street
near Eighth Avenue
a frame house wobbles.

If houses went on crutches
this house would be
one of the cripples.

A sign on the house:
Church of the Living God
And Rescue Home for Orphan Children.

From a Greek coffee house
Across the street
A cabalistic jargon
Jabbers back.
        And men at tables
        Spill Peloponnesian syllables
        And speak of shovels for street work.
        And the new embankments of the Erie Railroad
        At Painted Post, Horse's Head, Salamanca.

CAHOOTS

PLAY it across the table.
What if we steal this city blind?
If they want any thing let 'em nail it down.

Harness bulls, dicks, front office men,
And the high goats up on the bench,
Ain't they all in cahoots?
Ain't it fifty-fifty all down the line,
Petemen, dips, boosters, stick-ups and guns—
        what's to hinder?

        Go fifty-fifty.
If they nail you call in a mouthpiece.
Fix it, you gazump, you slant-head, fix it.
        Feed 'em. . . .

Nothin' ever sticks to my fingers, nah, nah,
        nothin' like that,
But there ain't no law we got to wear mittens—
        huh—is there?
Mittens, that's a good one—mittens!
There oughta be a law everybody wear mittens.

BLUE MAROONS

"You slut," he flung at her.
It was more than a hundred times
He had thrown it into her face
And by this time it meant nothing to her.
She said to herself upstairs sweeping,
"Clocks are to tell time with, pitchers
Hold milk, spoons dip out gravy, and a
Coffee pot keeps the respect of those
Who drink coffee—I am a woman whose
Husband gives her a kiss once for ten
Times he throws it in my face, 'You slut.'
If I go to a small town and him along
Or if I go to a big city and him along,
What of it? Am I better off?" She swept
The upstairs and came downstairs to fix
Dinner for the family.

THE HANGMAN AT HOME

WHAT does the hangman think about
When he goes home at night from work?
When he sits down with his wife and
Children for a cup of coffee and a
Plate of ham and eggs, do they ask
Him if it was a good day's work
And everything went well or do they
Stay off some topics and talk about
The weather, base ball, politics
And the comic strips in the papers
And the movies? Do they look at his
Hands when he reaches for the coffee
Or the ham and eggs? If the little
Ones say, Daddy, play horse, here's
A rope—does he answer like a joke:
I seen enough rope for today?
Or does his face light up like a
Bonfire of joy and does he say:
It's a good and dandy world we live
In. And if a white face moon looks
In through a window where a baby girl
Sleeps and the moon gleams mix with
Baby ears and baby hair—the hangman—
How does he act then? It must be easy
For him. Anything is easy for a hangman,
I guess.

MAN, THE MAN-HUNTER

I saw Man, the man-hunter,
Hunting with a torch in one hand
And a kerosene can in the other,
Hunting with guns, ropes, shackles.

I listened
And the high cry rang,
The high cry of Man, the man-hunter:
We'll get you yet,   you   sbxyzch!

I listened later.
The high cry rang:
Kill him!   kill him!   the sbxyzch!

In the morning the sun saw
Two butts of something, a smoking rump,
And a warning in charred wood:
                    Well, we got him,
                    the   sbxyzch.

THE SINS OF KALAMAZOO

THE sins of Kalamazoo are neither scarlet nor crimson.
The sins of Kalamazoo are a convict gray, a dishwater
drab.
And the people who sin the sins of Kalamazoo are
neither scarlet nor crimson.
They run to drabs and grays—and some of them sing
they shall be washed whiter than snow—and
some: We should worry.

Yes, Kalamazoo is a spot on the map
And the passenger trains stop there
And the factory smokestacks smoke
And the grocery stores are open Saturday nights
And the streets are free for citizens who vote
And inhabitants counted in the census.
Saturday night is the big night.
> Listen with your ears on a Saturday night in
> Kalamazoo
> And say to yourself: I hear America, I hear,
> *what* do I hear?

Main street there runs through the middle of the town
And there is a dirty postoffice
And a dirty city hall
And a dirty railroad station

And the United States flag cries, cries the Stars and
　　Stripes to the four winds on Lincoln's birthday
　　and the Fourth of July.

Kalamazoo kisses a hand to something far off.

Kalamazoo calls to a long horizon, to a shivering silver
　　angel, to a creeping mystic what-is-it.

" We're here because we're here," is the song of Kala-
　　mazoo.

" We don't know where we're going but we're on our
　　way," are the words.

There are hound dogs of bronze on the public square,
　　hound dogs looking far beyond the public square.

Sweethearts there in Kalamazoo

Go to the general delivery window of the postoffice

And speak their names and ask for letters

And ask again, " Are you sure there is nothing for me?

I wish you'd look again—there must be a letter for
　　me."

And sweethearts go to the city hall

And tell their names and say, " We want a license."

And they go to an installment house and buy a bed on
　　time and a clock

And the children grow up asking each other, " What
　　can we do to kill time?"

They grow up and go to the railroad station and buy
　　tickets for Texas, Pennsylvania, Alaska.

" Kalamazoo is all right," they say.   " But I want to
　　see the world."

And when they have looked the world over they come
    back saying it is all like Kalamazoo.

The trains come in from the east and hoot for the
    crossings,
And buzz away to the peach country and Chicago to
    the west
Or they come from the west and shoot on to the Battle
    Creek breakfast bazaars
And the speedbug heavens of Detroit.

" I hear America, I hear, *what* do I hear?"
Said a loafer lagging along on the sidewalks of Kal-
    amazoo,
Lagging along and asking questions, reading signs.

Oh yes, there is a town named Kalamazoo,
A spot on the map where the trains hesitate.
I saw the sign of a five and ten cent store there
And the Standard Oil Company and the International
    Harvester
And a graveyard and a ball grounds
And a short order counter where a man can get a
    stack of wheats
And a pool hall where a rounder leered confidential
    like and said:
" Lookin' for a quiet game?"

The loafer lagged along and asked,
" Do you make guitars here?
Do you make boxes the singing wood winds ask to
    sleep in?

Do you rig up strings the singing wood winds sift over
    and sing low?"
The answer: "We manufacture musical instruments
    here."

Here I saw churches with steeples like hatpins,
Undertaking rooms with sample coffins in the show
    window
And signs everywhere satisfaction is guaranteed,
Shooting galleries where men kill imitation pigeons,
And there were doctors for the sick,
And lawyers for people waiting in jail,
And a dog catcher and a superintendent of streets,
And telephones, water-works, trolley cars,
And newspapers with a splatter of telegrams from
    sister cities of Kalamazoo the round world over.

And the loafer lagging along said:
Kalamazoo, you ain't in a class by yourself;
I seen you before in a lot of places.
If you are nuts America is nuts.
       And lagging along he said bitterly:
       Before I came to Kalamazoo I was silent.
       Now I am gabby, God help me, I am gabby.

Kalamazoo, both of us will do a fadeaway.
I will be carried out feet first
And time and the rain will chew you to dust
And the winds blow you away.
And an old, old mother will lay a green moss cover
    on my bones

And a green moss cover on the stones of your post-
    office and city hall.

    Best of all
I have loved your kiddies playing run-sheep-run
And cutting their initials on the ball ground fence.
They knew every time I fooled them who was fooled
    and how.

    Best of all
I have loved the red gold smoke of your sunsets;
I have loved a moon with a ring around it
Floating over your public square;
I have loved the white dawn frost of early winter
    silver
And purple over your railroad tracks and lumber
    yards.

    The wishing heart of you I loved, Kalamazoo.
    I sang bye-lo, bye-lo to your dreams.
I sang bye-lo to your hopes and songs.
I wished to God there were hound dogs of bronze on
    your public square,
Hound dogs with bronze paws looking to a long
    horizon with a shivering silver angel,
    a creeping mystic what-is-it.

BROKEN-FACE GARGOYLES

BROKEN-FACE GARGOYLES

ALL I can give you is broken-face gargoyles.
It is too early to sing and dance at funerals,
Though I can whisper to you I am looking for an
    undertaker humming a lullaby and throwing his
    feet in a swift and mystic buck-and-wing, now
    you see it and now you don't.

Fish to swim a pool in your garden flashing a speckled
    silver,
A basket of wine-saps filling your room with flame-
    dark for your eyes and the tang of valley orchards
    for your nose,
Such a beautiful pail of fish, such a beautiful peck
    of apples, I cannot bring you now.
It is too early and I am not footloose yet.

I shall come in the night when I come with a hammer
    and saw.
I shall come near your window, where you look out
    when your eyes open in the morning,
And there I shall slam together bird-houses and bird-
    baths for wing-loose wrens and hummers to live
    in, birds with yellow wing tips to blur and buzz
    soft all summer,

So I shall make little fool homes with doors, always
   open doors for all and each to run away when
   they want to.
I shall come just like that even though now it is early
   and I am not yet footloose,
Even though I am still looking for an undertaker with
   a raw, wind-bitten face and a dance in his feet.
I make a date with you (put it down) for six o'clock
   in the evening a thousand years from now.

All I can give you now is broken-face gargoyles.
All I can give you now is a double gorilla head with
   two fish mouths and four eagle eyes hooked on a
   street wall, spouting water and looking two ways
   to the ends of the street for the new people, the
   young strangers, coming, coming, always coming.

It is early.
I shall yet be footloose.

APRONS OF SILENCE

MANY things I might have said today.
And I kept my mouth shut.
So many times I was asked
To come and say the same things
Everybody was saying, no end
To the yes-yes, yes-yes,
    me-too, me-too.

The aprons of silence covered me.
A wire and hatch held my tongue.
I spit nails into an abyss and listened.
I shut off the gabble of Jones, Johnson, Smith,
All whose names take pages in the city directory.

I fixed up a padded cell and lugged it around.
I locked myself in and nobody knew it.
Only the keeper and the kept in the hoosegow
Knew it—on the streets, in the postoffice,
On the cars, into the railroad station
Where the caller was calling, "All a-board,
All a-board for . . Blaa-blaa . . Blaa-blaa,
Blaa-blaa . . and all points northwest . . all a-board."
Here I took along my own hoosegow
And did business with my own thoughts.
Do you see? It must be the aprons of silence.

DEATH SNIPS PROUD MEN

DEATH is stronger than all the governments because
the governments are men and men die and then
death laughs: Now you see 'em, now you don't.

Death is stronger than all proud men and so death
snips proud men on the nose, throws a pair of
dice and says: Read 'em and weep.

Death sends a radiogram every day: When I want
you I'll drop in—and then one day he comes with a
master-key and lets himself in and says: We'll
go now.

Death is a nurse mother with big arms: 'Twon't hurt
you at all; it's your time now; you just need a
long sleep, child; what have you had anyhow
better than sleep?

GOOD NIGHT

MANY ways to spell good night.

Fireworks at a pier on the Fourth of July
    spell it with red wheels and yellow spokes.
They fizz in the air, touch the water and quit.
Rockets make a trajectory of gold-and-blue
    and then go out.

Railroad trains at night spell with a smokestack
    mushrooming a white pillar.

Steamboats turn a curve in the Mississippi crying
    in a baritone that crosses lowland cottonfields
    to a razorback hill.

It is easy to spell good night.
                    Many ways to spell good night.

SHIRT

My shirt is a token and symbol,
more than a cover for sun and rain,
my shirt is a signal,
and a teller of souls.

I can take off my shirt and tear it,
and so make a ripping razzly noise,
and the people will say,
"Look at him tear his shirt."

I can keep my shirt on.
I can stick around and sing like a little bird
and look 'em all in the eye and never be fazed.
I can keep my shirt on.

JAZZ FANTASIA

DRUM on your drums, batter on your banjoes,
sob on the long cool winding saxophones.
Go to it, O jazzmen.

Sling your knuckles on the bottoms of the happy
tin pans, let your trombones ooze, and go husha-
husha-hush with the slippery sand-paper.

Moan like an autumn wind high in the lonesome tree-
tops, moan soft like you wanted somebody terrible,
cry like a racing car slipping away from a motorcycle
cop, bang-bang! you jazzmen, bang altogether drums,
traps, banjoes, horns, tin cans—make two people fight
on the top of a stairway and scratch each other's eyes
in a clinch tumbling down the stairs.

Can the rough stuff . . . now a Mississippi steamboat
pushes up the night river with a hoo-hoo-hoo-oo . . .
and the green lanterns calling to the high soft stars
. . . a red moon rides on the humps of the low river
hills . . . go to it, O jazzmen.

DO YOU WANT AFFIDAVITS?

THERE'S a hole in the bottom of the sea.
>   Do you want affidavits?
There's a man in the moon with money for you.
>   Do you want affidavits?
There are ten dancing girls in a sea-chamber off Nan-
        tucket waiting for you.
There are tall candles in Timbuctoo burning penance
        for you.
There are—anything else?
Speak now—for now we stand amid the great wishing
        windows—and the law says we are free to be
        wishing all this week at the windows.
Shall I raise my right hand and swear to you in the
        monotone of a notary public? this is "the truth,
        the whole truth, and nothing but the truth."

"OLD-FASHIONED REQUITED LOVE"

I HAVE ransacked the encyclopedias
And slid my fingers among topics and titles
Looking for you.

And the answer comes slow.
There seems to be no answer.

I shall ask the next banana peddler the who and the
    why of it.

Or—the iceman with his iron tongs gripping a clear
    cube in summer sunlight—maybe he will know.

PURPLE MARTINS

IF we were such and so, the same as these,
maybe we too would be slingers and sliders,
tumbling half over in the water mirrors,
tumbling half over at the horse heads of the sun,
tumbling our purple numbers.

Twirl on, you and your satin blue.
Be water birds, be air birds.
Be these purple tumblers you are.

    Dip and get away
From loops into slip-knots,
Write your own ciphers and figure eights.
It is your wooded island here in Lincoln park.
Everybody knows this belongs to you.

    Five fat geese
Eat grass on a sod bank
And never count your slinging ciphers,
                  your sliding figure eights,

A man on a green paint iron bench,
Slouches his feet and sniffs in a book,
And looks at you and your loops and slip-knots,
And looks at you and your sheaths of satin blue,
And slouches again and sniffs in the book,
And mumbles: It is an idle and a doctrinaire exploit.

Go on tumbling half over in the water mirrors.
Go on tumbling half over at the horse heads of the sun.
    Be water birds, be air birds.
    Be these purple tumblers you are.

BRASS KEYS

Joy . . . weaving two violet petals for a coat lapel . . . painting on a slab of night sky a Christ face . . . slipping new brass keys into rusty iron locks and shouldering till at last the door gives and we are in a new room . . . forever and ever violet petals, slabs, the Christ face, brass keys and new rooms.

are we near or far? . . . is there anything else? . . . who comes back? . . . and why does love ask nothing and give all? and why is love rare as a tailed comet shaking guesses out of men at telescopes ten feet long? why does the mystery sit with its chin on the lean forearm of women in gray eyes and women in hazel eyes?

are any of these less proud, less important, than a cross-examining lawyer? are any of these less perfect than the front page of a morning newspaper?

the answers are not computed and attested in the back of an arithmetic for the verifications of the lazy

there is no authority in the phone book for us to call and ask the why, the wherefore, and the howbeit it's . . . a riddle . . . by God

PICK-OFFS

THE telescope picks off star dust
on the clean steel sky and sends it to me.

The telephone picks off my voice and
sends it cross country a thousand miles.

The eyes in my head pick off pages of
Napoleon memoirs . . . a rag handler,
a head of dreams walks in a sheet of
mist . . . the palace panels shut in no-
bodies drinking nothings out of silver
helmets . . . in the end we all come to a
rock island and the hold of the sea-walls.

MANUFACTURED GODS

THEY put up big wooden gods.
Then they burned the big wooden gods
And put up brass gods and
Changing their minds suddenly
Knocked down the brass gods and put up
A doughface god with gold earrings.
The poor mutts, the pathetic slant heads,
They didn't know a little tin god
Is as good as anything in the line of gods
Nor how a little tin god answers prayer
And makes rain and brings luck
The same as a big wooden god or a brass
God or a doughface god with golden
Earrings.

MASK

To have your face left overnight
Flung on a board by a crazy sculptor;
To have your face drop off a board
And fall to pieces on a floor
Lost among lumps all finger-marked
      —How now?

To be calm and level, placed high,
Looking among perfect women bathing
And among bareheaded long-armed men,
Corner dreams of a crazy sculptor,
And then to fall, drop clean off the board,
Four o'clock in the morning and not a dog
Nor a policeman anywhere—

      Hoo hoo!
   had it been my laughing face
   maybe I would laugh with you,
   but my lover's face, the face I give
   women and the moon and the sea!

PLAYTHINGS OF THE WIND

FOUR PRELUDES ON PLAYTHINGS OF THE WIND

" The past is a bucket of ashes."

1

THE woman named To-morrow
sits with a hairpin in her teeth
and takes her time
and does her hair the way she wants it
and fastens at last the last braid and coil
and puts the hairpin where it belongs
and turns and drawls: Well, what of it?
My grandmother, Yesterday, is gone.
What of it? Let the dead be dead.

2

The doors were cedar
and the panels strips of gold
and the girls were golden girls
and the panels read and the girls chanted:
    We are the greatest city,
    the greatest nation:
    nothing like us ever was.

The doors are twisted on broken hinges.
Sheets of rain swish through on the wind
    where the golden girls ran and the panels
      read:
    We are the greatest city,
    the greatest nation,
    nothing like us ever was.

3

It has happened before.
Strong men put up a city and got
    a nation together,
And paid singers to sing and women
    to warble: We are the greatest city,
      the greatest nation,
      nothing like us ever was.

And while the singers sang
and the strong men listened
and paid the singers well
and felt good about it all,
    there were rats and lizards who listened
    . . . and the only listeners left now
    . . . are . . . the rats . . . and the lizards.

And there are black crows
crying, " Caw, caw,"
bringing mud and sticks
building a nest

over the words carved
on the doors where the panels were cedar
and the strips on the panels were gold
and the golden girls came singing:
> We are the greatest city,
> the greatest nation:
> nothing like us ever was.

The only singers now are crows crying, " Caw, caw,"
And the sheets of rain whine in the wind and doorways.
And the only listeners now are . . . the rats . . . and
the lizards.

4

The feet of the rats
scribble on the door sills;
the hieroglyphs of the rat footprints
chatter the pedigrees of the rats
and babble of the blood
and gabble of the breed
of the grandfathers and the great-grandfathers
of the rats.

And the wind shifts
and the dust on a door sill shifts
and even the writing of the rat footprints
tells us nothing, nothing at all
about the greatest city, the greatest nation
where the strong men listened
and the women warbled: Nothing like us ever
was.

BROKEN TABERNACLES

HAVE I broken the smaller tabernacles, O Lord?
And in the destruction of these set up the greater and
    massive, the everlasting tabernacles?
I know nothing today, what I have done and why,
    O Lord, only I have broken and broken taber-
    nacles.
They were beautiful in a way, these tabernacles torn
    down by strong hands swearing—
They were beautiful—why did the hypocrites carve
    their own names on the corner-stones? why did
    the hypocrites keep on singing their own names
    in their long noses every Sunday in these taber-
    nacles?
Who lays any blame here among the split corner-
    stones?

OSSAWATOMIE

I DON'T know how he came,
shambling, dark, and strong.

He stood in the city and told men:
My people are fools, my people are young and strong,
     my people must learn, my people are terrible
     workers and fighters.
Always he kept on asking: Where did that blood come
     from?

    They said: You for the fool killer,
           you for the booby hatch
           and a necktie party.

    They hauled him into jail.
    They sneered at him and spit on him,
    And he wrecked their jails,
    Singing, "God damn your jails,"
    And when he was most in jail
    Crummy among the crazy in the dark
    Then he was most of all out of jail
    Shambling, dark, and strong,
Always asking: Where did that blood come from?

They laid hands on him
And the fool killers had a laugh
And the necktie party was a go, by God.
They laid hands on him and he was a goner.
They hammered him to pieces and he stood up.
They buried him and he walked out of the grave, by God,
Asking again: Where did that blood come from?

LONG GUNS

THEN came, Oscar, the time of the guns.
And there was no land for a man, no land for a
    country,
        Unless guns sprang up
        And spoke their language.
The how of running the world was all in guns.

The law of a God keeping sea and land apart,
The law of a child sucking milk,
The law of stars held together,
        They slept and worked in the heads of men
        Making twenty mile guns, sixty mile guns,
        Speaking their language
        Of no land for a man, no land for a country
Unless . . . guns . . . unless . . . guns.

There was a child wanted the moon shot off the sky,
        asking a long gun to get the moon,
        to conquer the insults of the moon,
        to conquer something, anything,
        to put it over and win the day,
To show them the running of the world was all in guns.
There was a child wanted the moon shot off the sky.
They dreamed . . . in the time of the guns . . . of guns.

DUSTY DOORS

CHILD of the Aztec gods,
how long must we listen here,
how long before we go?

The dust is deep on the lintels.
The dust is dark on the doors.
If the dreams shake our bones,
     what can we say or do?

Since early morning we waited.
Since early, early morning, child.
There must be dreams on the way now.
There must be a song for our bones.

The dust gets deeper and darker.
Do the doors and lintels shudder?
   How long must we listen here?
   How long before we go?

FLASH CRIMSON

I SHALL cry God to give me a broken foot.

I shall ask for a scar and a slashed nose.

I shall take the last and the worst.

I shall be eaten by gray creepers in a bunkhouse where
no runners of the sun come and no dogs live.

And yet—of all "and yets" this is the bronze strong-
est—

I shall keep one thing better than all else; there is the
blue steel of a great star of early evening in it;
it lives longer than a broken foot or any scar.

The broken foot goes to a hole dug with a shovel or
the bone of a nose may whiten on a hilltop—and
yet—"and yet"—

There is one crimson pinch of ashes left after all;
and none of the shifting winds that whip the grass
and none of the pounding rains that beat the dust,
know how to touch or find the flash of this crim-
son.

I cry God to give me a broken foot, a scar, or a lousy
   death.

I who have seen the flash of this crimson, I ask God
   for the last and worst.

THE LAWYERS KNOW TOO MUCH

THE lawyers, Bob, know too much.
They are chums of the books of old John Marshall.
They know it all, what a dead hand wrote,
A stiff dead hand and its knuckles crumbling,
The bones of the fingers a thin white ash.
 The lawyers know
 a dead man's thoughts too well.

In the heels of the higgling lawyers, Bob,
Too many slippery ifs and buts and howevers,
Too much hereinbefore provided whereas,
Too many doors to go in and out of.

 When the lawyers are through
 What is there left, Bob?
 Can a mouse nibble at it
 And find enough to fasten a tooth in?

 Why is there always a secret singing
 When a lawyer cashes in?
 Why does a hearse horse snicker
 Hauling a lawyer away?

86 *The Lawyers Know Too Much*

The work of a bricklayer goes to the blue.
The knack of a mason outlasts a moon.
The hands of a plasterer hold a room together.
The land of a farmer wishes him back again.
    Singers of songs and dreamers of plays
    Build a house no wind blows over.
The lawyers—tell me why a hearse horse snickers
    hauling a lawyer's bones.

LOSERS

If I should pass the tomb of Jonah
I would stop there and sit for awhile;
Because I was swallowed one time deep in the dark
And came out alive after all.

If I pass the burial spot of Nero
I shall say to the wind, " Well, well ! "—
I who have fiddled in a world on fire,
I who have done so many stunts not worth doing.

I am looking for the grave of Sinbad too.
I want to shake his ghost-hand and say,
" Neither of us died very early, did we? "

And the last sleeping-place of Nebuchadnezzar—
When I arrive there I shall tell the wind:
" You ate grass; I have eaten crow—
Who is better off now or next year? "

Jack Cade, John Brown, Jesse James,
There too I could sit down and stop for awhile.
I think I could tell their headstones:
" God, let me remember all good losers."

I could ask people to throw ashes on their heads
In the name of that sergeant at Belleau Woods,
Walking into the drumfires, calling his men,
" Come on, you . . . Do you want to live forever? "

PLACES

Roses and gold
For you today,
And the flash of flying flags.

I will have
Ashes,
Dust in my hair,
Crushes of hoofs.

Your name
Fills the mouth
Of rich man and poor.
Women bring
Armfuls of flowers
And throw on you.

I go hungry
Down in dreams
And loneliness,
Across the rain
To slashed hills
Where men wait and hope for me.

THREES

I was a boy when I heard three red words
a thousand Frenchmen died in the streets
for: Liberty, Equality, Fraternity—I asked
why men die for words.

I was older; men with mustaches, sideburns,
lilacs, told me the high golden words are:
Mother, Home, and Heaven—other older men with
face decorations said: God, Duty, Immortality
—they sang these threes slow from deep lungs.

Years ticked off their say-so on the great clocks
of doom and damnation, soup and nuts: meteors flashed
their say-so: and out of great Russia came three
dusky syllables workmen took guns and went out to die
for: Bread, Peace, Land.

And I met a marine of the U. S. A., a leatherneck with
a girl on his knee for a memory in ports circling the
earth and he said: Tell me how to say three things
and I always get by—gimme a plate of ham and eggs—
how much?—and—do you love me, kid?

THE LIARS
(*March, 1919*)

A LIAR goes in fine clothes.
A liar goes in rags.
A liar is a liar, clothes or no clothes.
A liar is a liar and lives on the lies he tells
        and dies in a life of lies.
And the stonecutters earn a living—with lies—
        on the tombs of liars.

A liar looks 'em in the eye
And lies to a woman,
Lies to a man, a pal, a child, a fool.
And he is an old liar; we know him many years back.

  A liar lies to nations.
  A liar lies to the people.
A liar takes the blood of the people
And drinks this blood with a laugh and a lie,
  A laugh in his neck,
  A lie in his mouth.
And this liar is an old one; we know him many years.
  He is straight as a dog's hind leg.
  He is straight as a corkscrew.
He is white as a black cat's foot at midnight.

The Liars

The tongue of a man is tied on this,
On the liar who lies to nations,
The liar who lies to the people.
The tongue of a man is tied on this
And ends: To hell with 'em all.
           To hell with 'em all.

It's a song hard as a riveter's hammer,
    Hard as the sleep of a crummy hobo,
    Hard as the sleep of a lousy doughboy,
Twisted as a shell-shock idiot's gibber.

The liars met where the doors were locked.
They said to each other: Now for war.
The liars fixed it and told 'em: Go.

Across their tables they fixed it up,
Behind their doors away from the mob.
And the guns did a job that nicked off millions.
The guns blew seven million off the map,
The guns sent seven million west.
Seven million shoving up the daisies.
Across their tables they fixed it up,
           The liars who lie to nations.

   And now
   Out of the butcher's job
   And the boneyard junk the maggots have cleaned,
   Where the jaws of skulls tell the jokes of war ghosts,
Out of this they are calling now: Let's go back where
       we were.
           Let us run the world again, us, us.

Where the doors are locked the liars say: Wait and
we'll cash in again.

So I hear The People talk.
I hear them tell each other:
Let the strong men be ready.
Let the strong men watch.
Let your wrists be cool and your head clear.
Let the liars get their finish,
The liars and their waiting game, waiting a day again
To open the doors and tell us: War! get out to your
war again.

So I hear The People tell each other:
Look at to-day and to-morrow.
Fix this clock that nicks off millions
When The Liars say it's time.
Take things in your own hands.
            To hell with 'em all,
The liars who lie to nations,
The liars who lie to The People.

PRAYER AFTER WORLD WAR

WANDERING oversea dreamer,
Hunting and hoarse, Oh daughter and mother,
Oh daughter of ashes and mother of blood,
Child of the hair let down, and tears,
Child of the cross in the south
And the star in the north,
Keeper of Egypt and Russia and France,
Keeper of England and Poland and Spain,
Make us a song for to-morrow.
Make us one new dream, us who forget,
Out of the storm let us have one star.

    Struggle, Oh anvils, and help her.
Weave with your wool, Oh winds and skies.
Let your iron and copper help,
        Oh dirt of the old dark earth.

Wandering oversea singer,
Singing of ashes and blood,
Child of the scars of fire,
    Make us one new dream, us who forget.
    Out of the storm let us have one star.

A. E. F.

THERE will be a rusty gun on the wall, sweetheart,
The rifle grooves curling with flakes of rust.
A spider will make a silver string nest in the
          darkest, warmest corner of it.
The trigger and the range-finder, they too will be rusty.
And no hands will polish the gun, and it will hang
    on the wall.
Forefingers and thumbs will point absently and casu-
    ally toward it.
It will be spoken among half-forgotten, wished-to-be-
    forgotten things.
They will tell the spider: Go on, you're doing good
    work.

BAS-RELIEF

FIVE geese deploy mysteriously.
Onward proudly with flagstaffs,
Hearses with silver bugles,
Bushels of plum-blossoms dropping
For ten mystic web-feet—
Each his own drum-major,
Each charged with the honor
Of the ancient goose nation,
Each with a nose-length surpassing
The nose-lengths of rival nations.
Somberly, slowly, unimpeachably,
Five geese deploy mysteriously.

CARLOVINGIAN DREAMS

COUNT these reminiscences like money.
The Greeks had their picnics under another name.
The Romans wore glad rags and told their neighbors,
    "What of it?"
The Carlovingians hauling logs on carts, they too
Stuck their noses in the air and stuck their thumbs to
    their noses
And tasted life as a symphonic dream of fresh eggs
    broken over a frying pan left by an uncle who
    killed men with spears and short swords.
Count these reminiscences like money.

        Drift, and drift on, white ships.
Sailing the free sky blue, sailing and changing and
    sailing,
Oh, I remember in the blood of my dreams how they
    sang before me.
Oh, they were men and women who got money for
    their work, money or love or dreams.
            Sail on, white ships.
            Let me have spring dreams.
Let me count reminiscences like money; let me count
    picnics, glad rags and the great bad manners of
    the Carlovingians breaking fresh eggs in the cop-
    per pans of their proud uncles.

BRONZES

THEY ask me to handle bronzes
Kept by children in China
Three thousand years
Since their fathers
Took fire and molds and hammers
And made these.

The Ming, the Chou,
And other dynasties,
Out, gone, reckoned in ciphers,
Dynasties dressed up
In old gold and old yellow—
They saw these.

Let the wheels
Of three thousand years
Turn, turn, turn on.

Let one poet then
(One will be enough)
Handle these bronzes
And mention the dynasties
And pass them along.

LET LOVE GO ON

LET it go on; let the love of this hour be poured out
till all the answers are made, the last dollar spent
and the last blood gone.

Time runs with an ax and a hammer, time slides down
the hallways with a pass-key and a master-key,
and time gets by, time wins.

Let the love of this hour go on; let all the oaths and
children and people of this love be clean as a
washed stone under a waterfall in the sun.

Time is a young man with ballplayer legs, time runs
a winning race against life and the clocks, time
tickles with rust and spots.

Let love go on; the heartbeats are measured out with
a measuring glass, so many apiece to gamble with,
to use and spend and reckon; let love go on.

KILLERS

I AM put high over all others in the city today.
I am the killer who kills for those who wish a killing
today.

Here is a strong young man who killed.
There was a driving wind of city dust and horse dung
blowing and he stood at an intersection of five
sewers and there pumped the bullets of an auto-
matic pistol into another man, a fellow citizen.
Therefore, the prosecuting attorneys, fellow citizens,
and a jury of his peers, also fellow citizens, lis-
tened to the testimony of other fellow citizens,
policemen, doctors, and after a verdict of guilty,
the judge, a fellow citizen, said: I sentence you
to be hanged by the neck till you are dead.

So there is a killer to be killed and I am the killer of
the killer for today.
I don't know why it beats in my head in the lines I
read once in an old school reader: I'm to be queen
of the May, mother, I'm to be queen of the May.
Anyhow it comes back in language just like that today.

I am the high honorable killer today.
There are five million people in the state, five million
killers for whom I kill
I am the killer who kills today for five million killers
who wish a killing.

CLEAN HANDS

It is something to face the sun and know you are free.
To hold your head in the shafts of daylight slanting
the earth
And know your heart has kept a promise and the blood
runs clean:
It is something.
To go one day of your life among all men with clean
hands,
Clean for the day book today and the record of the
after days,
Held at your side proud, satisfied to the last, and ready,
So to have clean hands:
God, it is something,
One day of life so
And a memory fastened till the stars sputter out
And a love washed as white linen in the noon
drying.
Yes, go find the men of clean hands one day and see
the life, the memory, the love they have, to stay
longer than the plunging sea wets the shores or
the fires heave under the crust of the earth.
O yes, clean hands is the chant and only one man
knows its sob and its undersong and he dies
clenching the secret more to him than any woman
or chum.

And O the great brave men, the silent little brave
men, proud of their hands—clutching the knuckles
of their fingers into fists ready for death and the
dark, ready for life and the fight, the pay and the
memories—O the men proud of their hands.

THREE GHOSTS

THREE tailors of Tooley Street wrote: We, the People.
The names are forgotten.   It is a joke in ghosts.

Cutters or bushelmen or armhole basters, they sat
cross-legged stitching, snatched at scissors, stole each
other thimbles.

Cross-legged, working for wages, joking each other
as misfits cut from the cloth of a Master Tailor,
they sat and spoke their thoughts of the glory of
The People, they met after work and drank beer to
The People.

Faded off into the twilights the names are forgotten.
It is a joke in ghosts.   Let it ride.   They wrote: We,
The People.

PENCILS

PENCILS
telling where the wind comes from
    open a story.

Pencils
telling where the wind goes
    end a story.

    These eager pencils
    come to a stop
    . . only . . when the stars high over
    come to a stop.   *— secret society's doctrines*
Out of (cabalistic) to-morrows
come cryptic babies calling life
a strong and a lovely thing.

I have seen neither these
nor the stars high over
come to a stop.

Neither these nor the sea horses
running with the clocks of the moon.
Nor even a shooting star
snatching a pencil of fire
writing a curve of gold and white.

Like you . . I counted the shooting stars of a
winter night and my head was dizzy with all
of them calling one by one:

Look for us again.

JUG

THE shale and water thrown together so-so first of all,
Then a potter's hand on the wheel and his fingers shap-
　　ing the jug; out of the mud a mouth and a handle;
Slimpsy loose and ready to fall at a touch, fire plays
　　on it, slow fire coaxing all the water out of the
　　shale mix.
Dipped in glaze more fire plays on it till a molasses lava
　　runs in waves, rises and retreats, a varnish of
　　volcanoes.
Take it now; out of mud now here is a mouth and
　　handle; out of this now mothers will pour milk
　　and maple syrup and cider, vinegar, apple juice,
　　and sorghum.
There is nothing proud about this; only one out of
　　many; the potter's wheel slings them out and the
　　fires harden them hours and hours thousands and
　　thousands.
" Be good to me, put me down easy on the floors of
　　the new concrete houses; I was poured out like a
　　concrete house and baked in fire too."

AND THIS WILL BE ALL?

AND this will be all?
And the gates will never open again?
And the dust and the wind will play around the rusty
    door hinges and the songs of October moan, Why-
    oh, why-oh?

And you will look to the mountains
And the mountains will look to you
And you will wish you were a mountain
And the mountain will wish nothing at all?
        This will be all?
The gates will never-never open again?

The dust and the wind only
And the rusty door hinges and moaning October
And Why-oh, why-oh, in the moaning dry leaves,
        This will be all?

Nothing in the air but songs
And no singers, no mouths to know the songs?
You tell us a woman with a heartache tells you it is so?
        This will be all?

HOODLUMS

I AM a hoodlum, you are a hoodlum, we and all of us
are a world of hoodlums—maybe so.

I hate and kill better men than I am, so do you, so
do all of us—maybe—maybe so.

In the ends of my fingers the itch for another man's
neck, I want to see him hanging, one of dusk's
cartoons against the sunset.

This is the hate my father gave me, this was in my
mother's milk, this is you and me and all of us
in a world of hoodlums—maybe so.

Let us go on, brother hoodlums, let us kill and kill, it
has always been so, it will always be so, there is
nothing more to it.

Let us go on, sister hoodlums, kill, kill, and kill, the
torsoes of the world's mother's are tireless and the
loins of the world's fathers are strong—so go on
—kill, kill, kill.

Lay them deep in the dirt, the stiffs we fixed, the
cadavers bumped off, lay them deep and let the
night winds of winter blizzards howl their burial
service.

The night winds and the winter, the great white sheets
of northern blizzards, who can sing better for the
lost hoodlums the old requiem, " Kill him! kill
him! . . ."

Today my son, to-morrow yours, the day after your
   next door neighbor's—it is all in the wrists of
   the gods who shoot craps—it is anybody's guess
   whose eyes shut next.

Being a hoodlum now, you and I, being all of us a
   world of hoodlums, let us take up the cry when
   the mob sluffs by on a thousand shoe soles, let
   us too yammer, "Kill him! kill him! . . ."

Let us do this now . . . for our mothers . . . for our
   sisters and wives . . . let us kill, kill, kill—for
   the torsoes of the women are tireless and the
   loins of the men are strong.

Chicago, July 29, 1919.

YES, THE DEAD SPEAK TO US

Yes, the Dead speak to us.
This town belongs to the Dead, to the Dead and to
the Wilderness.

Back of the clamps on a fireproof door they hold the
papers of the Dead in a house here
And when two living men fall out, when one says the
Dead spoke a Yes, and the other says the Dead
spoke a No, they go then together to this house.

They loosen the clamps and haul at the hasps and try
their keys and curse at the locks and the combina-
tion numbers.
For the teeth of the rats are barred and the tongues
of the moths are outlawed and the sun and the
air of wind is not wanted.

They open a box where a sheet of paper shivers, in a
dusty corner shivers with the dry inkdrops of the
Dead, the signed names.
Here the ink testifies, here we find the say-so, here
we learn the layout, now we know where the
cities and farms belong.

Dead white men and dead red men
tested each other with shot and
knives: they twisted each others'
necks: land was yours if you took and
kept it.

How are the heads the rain seeps
in, the rain-washed knuckles in
sod and gumbo?

Where the sheets of paper shiver,
Back of the hasps and handles,
Back of the fireproof clamps,
They read what the fingers scribbled, who the land
belongs to now—it is herein provided, it is hereby
stipulated—the land and all appurtenances thereto and
all deposits of oil and gold and coal and silver, and
all pockets and repositories of gravel and diamonds,
dung and permanganese, and all clover and bumblebees,
all bluegrass, johnny-jump-ups, grassroots, springs of
running water or rivers or lakes or high spreading
trees or hazel bushes or sumach or thorn-apple branches
or high in the air the bird nest with spotted blue eggs
shaken in the roaming wind of the treetops—
So it is scrawled here,
"I direct and devise
So and so and such and such,"
And this is the last word.
There is nothing more to it.

In a shanty out in the Wilderness, ghosts of to-morrow
    sit, waiting to come and go, to do their job.
They will go into the house of the Dead and take the
    shivering sheets of paper and make a bonfire and
    dance a deadman's dance over the hissing crisp.
In a slang their own the dancers out of the Wilderness
    will write a paper for the living to read and sign:
The dead need peace, the dead need sleep, let the dead
    have peace and sleep, let the papers of the Dead
    who fix the lives of the Living, let them be a
    hissing crisp and ashes, let the young men and the
    young women forever understand we are through
    and no longer take the say-so of the Dead;
Let the dead have honor from us with our thoughts
    of them and our thoughts of land and all appur-
    tenances thereto and all deposits of oil and gold
    and coal and silver, and all pockets and repositories
    of gravel and diamonds, dung and permanganese,
    and all clover and bumblebees, all bluegrass,
    johnny-jump-ups, grassroots, springs of running
    water or rivers or lakes or high spreading trees
    or hazel bushes or sumach or thornapple branches
    or high in the air the bird nest with spotted blue
    eggs shaken in the roaming wind of the treetops.

And so, it is a shack of ghosts, a lean-to they have in
    the Wilderness, and they are waiting and they
    have learned strange songs how easy it is to wait
    and how anything comes to those who wait long
    enough and how most of all it is easy to wait for
    death, and waiting, dream of new cities.

MIST FORMS

CALLS

Because I have called to you
as the flame flamingo calls,
or the want of a spotted hawk
is called—
             because in the dusk
the warblers shoot the running
waters of short songs to the
homecoming warblers—
                      because
the cry here is wing to wing
and song to song—

I am waiting,
waiting with the flame flamingo,
the spotted hawk, the running water
warbler—
          waiting for you.

SEA-WASH

THE sea-wash never ends.
The sea-wash repeats, repeats.
Only old songs? Is that all the sea knows?
     Only the old strong songs?
     Is that all?
The sea-wash repeats, repeats.

SILVER WIND

Do you know how the dream looms? how if summer
    misses one of us the two of us miss summer—
Summer when the lungs of the earth take a long
    breath for the change to low contralto singing
    mornings when the green corn leaves first break
    through the black loam—
And another long breath for the silver soprano melody
    of the moon songs in the light nights when the
    earth is lighter than a feather, the iron mountains
    lighter than a goose down—
So I shall look for you in the light nights then, in the
    laughter of slats of silver under a hill hickory.
In the listening tops of the hickories, in the wind
    motions of the hickory shingle leaves, in the imi-
    tations of slow sea water on the shingle silver
    in the wind—
        I shall look for you.

EVENING WATERFALL

WHAT was the name you called me? —
And why did you go so soon?

The crows lift their caw on the wind,
And the wind changed and was lonely.

The warblers cry their sleepy-songs
Across the valley gloaming,
Across the cattle-horns of early stars.

Feathers and people in the crotch of a treetop
Throw an evening waterfall of sleepy-songs.

What was the name you called me?—
And why did you go so soon?

CRUCIBLE

Hot gold runs a winding stream on the inside of a
green bowl.

Yellow trickles in a fan figure, scatters a line of
skirmishers, spreads a chorus of dancing girls,
performs blazing ochre evolutions, gathers the
whole show into one stream, forgets the past and
rolls on.

The sea-mist green of the bowl's bottom is a dark
throat of sky crossed by quarreling forks of
umber and ochre and yellow changing faces.

SUMMER STARS

BEND low again, night of summer stars.
So near you are, sky of summer stars,
So near, a long arm man can pick off stars,
Pick off what he wants in the sky bowl,
So near you are, summer stars,
So near, strumming, strumming,
       So lazy and hum-strumming.

THROW ROSES

THROW roses on the sea where the dead went down.
      The roses speak to the sea,
      And the sea to the dead.
Throw roses, O lovers—
      Let the leaves wash on the salt in the sun.

JUST BEFORE APRIL CAME

THE snow piles in dark places are gone.
Pools by the railroad tracks shine clear.
The gravel of all shallow places shines.
A white pigeon reels and somersaults.

Frogs plutter and squdge—and frogs beat
  the air with a recurring thin
  steel sliver of melody.
Crows go in fives and tens; they march their
  black feathers past a blue pool; they
  celebrate an old festival.
A spider is trying his webs, a pink bug sits
  on my hand washing his forelegs.
I might ask: Who are these people?

STARS, SONGS, FACES

GATHER the stars if you wish it so.
Gather the songs and keep them.
Gather the faces of women.
Gather for keeping years and years.
       And then . . .
Loosen your hands, let go and say good-by.
    Let the stars and songs go.
    Let the faces and years go.
    Loosen your hands and say good-by.

SANDPIPERS

TEN miles of flat land along the sea.
Sandland where the salt water kills the
    sweet potatoes.
Homes for sandpipers—the script of their
    feet is on the sea shingles—they write
    in the morning, it is gone at noon—they
    write at noon, it is gone at night.
Pity the land, the sea, the ten mile flats,
    pity anything but the sandpiper's wire
    legs and feet.

THREE VIOLINS

THREE violins are trying their hearts.
The piece is MacDowell's Wild Rose.
   And the time of the wild rose
   And the leaves of the wild rose
And the dew-shot eyes of the wild rose
Sing in the air over three violins.
Somebody like you was in the heart of MacDowell.
Somebody like you is in three violins.

THE WIND SINGS WELCOME IN EARLY SPRING

(*For Paula*)

THE grip of the ice is gone now.
The silvers chase purple.
The purples tag silver.
        They let out their runners
Here where summer says to the lilies:
        " Wish and be wistful,
Circle this wind-hunted, wind-sung water."

Come along always, come along now.
You for me, kiss me, pull me by the ear.
Push me along with the wind push.
Sing like the whinnying wind.
Sing like the hustling obstreperous wind.

Have you ever seen deeper purple . . .
        this in my wild wind fingers?
Could you have more fun with a pony or a goat?
Have you seen such flicking heels before,
Silver jig heels on the purple sky rim?
        Come along always, come along now.

TAWNY

THESE are the tawny days: your face comes back.

The grapes take on purple: the sunsets redden
early on the trellis.

The bashful mornings hurl gray mist on the stripes
of sunrise.

Creep, silver on the field, the frost is welcome.

Run on, yellow balls on the hills, and you tawny
pumpkin flowers, chasing your lines of orange.

Tawny days: and your face again.

SLIPPERY

THE six month child
Fresh from the tub
Wriggles in our hands.
This is our fish child.
Give her a nickname: Slippery.

HELGA

THE wishes on this child's mouth
Came like snow on marsh cranberries;
The tamarack kept something for her;
The wind is ready to help her shoes.
The north has loved her; she will be
A grandmother feeding geese on frosty
Mornings; she will understand
Early snow on the cranberries
Better and better then.

BABY TOES

There is a blue star, Janet,
Fifteen years' ride from us,
If we ride a hundred miles an hour.

There is a white star, Janet,
Forty years' ride from us,
If we ride a hundred miles an hour.

Shall we ride
To the blue star
Or the white star?

PEOPLE WITH PROUD CHINS

I TELL them where the wind comes from,
Where the music goes when the fiddle is in the box.

Kids—I saw one with a proud chin, a sleepyhead,
And the moonline creeping white on her pillow.
   I have seen their heads in the starlight
   And their proud chins marching in a mist of stars.

They are the only people I never lie to.
   I give them honest answers,
Answers shrewd as the circles of white on brown
    chestnuts.

WINTER MILK

THE milk drops on your chin, Helga,
Must not interfere with the cranberry red of your
    cheeks
Nor the sky winter blue of your eyes.
Let your mammy keep hands off the chin.
This is a high holy spatter of white on the reds and
    blues.

Before the bottle was taken away,
Before you so proudly began today
Drinking your milk from the rim of a cup
They did not splash this high holy white on your chin.

There are dreams in your eyes, Helga.
Tall reaches of wind sweep the clear blue.
The winter is young yet, so young.
Only a little cupful of winter has touched your lips.
Drink on . . . milk with your lips . . . dreams with
    your eyes.

SLEEPYHEADS

SLEEP is a maker of makers. Birds sleep. Feet cling to a perch. Look at the balance. Let the legs loosen, the backbone untwist, the head go heavy over, the whole works tumbles a done bird off the perch.

Fox cubs sleep. The pointed head curls round into hind legs and tail. It is a ball of red hair. It is a muff waiting. A wind might whisk it in the air across pastures and rivers, a cocoon, a pod of seeds. The snooze of the black nose is in a circle of red hair.

Old men sleep. In chimney corners, in rocking chairs, at wood stoves, steam radiators. They talk and forget and nod and are out of talk with closed eyes. Forgetting to live. Knowing the time has come useless for them to live. Old eagles and old dogs run and fly in the dreams.

Babies sleep. In flannels the papoose faces, the bambino noses, and dodo, dodo the song of many matushkas. Babies—a leaf on a tree in the spring sun. A nub of a new thing sucks the sap of a tree in the sun, yes a new thing, a what-is-it? A left hand stirs, an eyelid twitches, the milk in the belly bubbles and gets to be blood and a left hand and an eyelid. Sleep is a maker of makers.

SUMACH AND BIRDS

If you never came with a pigeon rainbow purple
Shining in the six o'clock September dusk:
If the red sumach on the autumn roads
Never danced on the flame of your eyelashes:
If the red-haws never burst in a million
Crimson fingertwists of your heartcrying:
If all this beauty of yours never crushed me
Then there are many flying acres of birds for me,
Many drumming gray wings going home I shall see,
Many crying voices riding the north wind.

WOMEN WASHING THEIR HAIR

THEY have painted and sung
the women washing their hair,
and the plaits and strands in the sun,
and the golden combs
and the combs of elephant tusks
and the combs of buffalo horn and hoof.

The sun has been good to women,
drying their heads of hair
as they stooped and shook their shoulders
and framed their faces with copper
and framed their eyes with dusk or chestnut

The rain has been good to women.
If the rain should forget,
if the rain left off for a year—
the heads of women would wither,
the copper, the dusk and chestnuts, go.

They have painted and sung
the women washing their hair—
reckon the sun and rain in, too.

PEACH BLOSSOMS

WHAT cry of peach blossoms
   let loose on the air today
I heard with my face thrown
     in the pink-white of it all?
     in the red whisper of it all?

What man I heard saying:
   Christ, these are beautiful!

And Christ and Christ was in his mouth,
   over these peach blossoms?

HALF MOON IN A HIGH WIND

MONEY is nothing now, even if I had it,
O mooney moon, yellow half moon,
Up over the green pines and gray elms,
Up in the new blue.

     Streel, streel,
White lacey mist sheets of cloud,
Streel in the blowing of the wind,
Streel over the blue-and-moon sky,
Yellow gold half moon. It is light
On the snow; it is dark on the snow,
Streel, O lacey thin sheets, up in the new blue.

Come down, stay there, move on.
I want you, I don't, keep all.
There is no song to your singing.
I am hit deep, you drive far,
O mooney yellow half moon,
Steady, steady; or will you tip over?
Or will the wind and the streeling
Thin sheets only pass and move on
And leave you alone and lovely?
I want you, I don't, come down,
     Stay there, move on.
Money is nothing now, even if I had it.

REMORSE

THE horse's name was Remorse.
There were people said, " Gee, what a nag ! "
And they were Edgar Allan Poe bugs and so
They called him Remorse.
                           When he was a gelding
He flashed his heels to other ponies
And threw dust in the noses of other ponies
And won his first race and his second
And another and another and hardly ever
Came under the wire behind the other runners.

And so, Remorse, who is gone, was the hero of a play
By Henry Blossom, who is now gone.

What is there to a monicker?   Call me anything.
A nut, a cheese, something that the cat brought in.
    Nick me with any old name.
Class me up for a fish, a gorilla, a slant head, an egg,
    a ham.
Only . . . slam me across the ears sometimes . . .
    and hunt for a white star
In my forehead and twist the bang of my forelock
    around it.
Make a wish for me.   Maybe I will light out like a
    streak of wind.

RIVER MOONS

The double moon, one on the high back drop of the
west, one on the curve of the river face,
The sky moon of fire and the river moon of water,
I am taking these home in a basket, hung on an
elbow, such a teeny weeny elbow, in my head.
I saw them last night, a cradle moon, two horns of
a moon, such an early hopeful moon, such a child's
moon for all young hearts to make a picture of.
The river—I remember this like a picture—the river
was the upper twist of a written question mark.
I know now it takes many many years to write a river,
a twist of water asking a question.
And white stars moved when the moon moved, and
one red star kept burning, and the Big Dipper was
almost overhead.

SAND SCRIBBLINGS

THE wind stops, the wind begins.
The wind says stop, begin.

A sea shovel scrapes the sand floor.
The shovel changes, the floor changes.

The sandpipers, maybe they know.
Maybe a three-pointed foot can tell.
Maybe the fog moon they fly to, guesses.

The sandpipers cheep " Here " and get away.
Five of them fly and keep together flying.

Night hair of some sea woman
Curls on the sand when the sea leaves
The salt tide without a good-by.

Boxes on the beach are empty.
Shake 'em and the nails loosen.
They have been somewhere.

HOW YESTERDAY LOOKED

THE high horses of the sea broke their white riders
On the walls that held and counted the hours
The wind lasted.

Two landbirds looked on and the north and the east
Looked on and the wind poured cups of foam
And the evening began.

The old men in the shanties looked on and lit their
Pipes and the young men spoke of the girls
For a wild night like this.

The south and the west looked on and the moon came
When the wind went down and the sea was sorry
And the singing slow.

Ask how the sunset looked between the wind going
Down and the moon coming up and I would struggle
To tell the how of it.

I give you fire here, I give you water, I give you
The wind that blew them across and across,
The scooping, mixing wind.

PAULA

NOTHING else in this song—only your face.
Nothing else here—only your drinking, night-gray eyes.

The pier runs into the lake straight as a rifle barrel.
I stand on the pier and sing how I know you mornings.
It is not your eyes, your face, I remember.
It is not your dancing, race-horse feet.
It is something else I remember you for on the pier
   mornings.

Your hands are sweeter than nut-brown bread when
   you touch me.
Your shoulder brushes my arm—a south-west wind
   crosses the pier.
I forget your hands and your shoulder and I say again:

Nothing else in this song—only your face.
Nothing else here—only your drinking, night-gray
   eyes.

LAUGHING BLUE STEEL

Two fishes swimming in the sea,
Two birds flying in the air,
Two chisels on an anvil—maybe.
Beaten, hammered, laughing blue steel to each other
    —maybe.
Sure I would rather be a chisel with you
                     than a fish.
Sure I would rather be a chisel with you
                     than a bird.
Take these two chisel-pals, O God.
Take 'em and beat 'em, hammer 'em,
                 hear 'em laugh.

THEY ASK EACH OTHER WHERE THEY CAME FROM

Am I the river your white birds fly over?
Are you the green valley my silver channels roam?
The two of us a bowl of blue sky day time
            and a bowl of red stars night time?
      Who picked you
      out of the first great whirl of nothings
      and threw you here?

HOW MUCH?

How much do you love me, a million bushels?
Oh, a lot more than that, Oh, a lot more.

And to-morrow maybe only half a bushel?
To-morrow maybe not even a half a bushel.

And is this your heart arithmetic?
This is the way the wind measures the weather.

THROWBACKS

Somewhere you and I remember we came.
Stairways from the sea and our heads dripping.
Ladders of dust and mud and our hair snarled.
Rags of drenching mist and our hands clawing, climb-
ing.
You and I that snickered in the crotches and corners,
in the gab of our first talking.
Red dabs of dawn summer mornings and the rain
sliding off our shoulders summer afternoons.
Was it you and I yelled songs and songs in the nights
of big yellow moons?

WIND SONG

LONG ago I learned how to sleep,
In an old apple orchard where the wind swept by
counting its money and throwing it away,
In a wind-gaunt orchard where the limbs forked out
and listened or never listened at all,
In a passel of trees where the branches trapped the
wind into whistling, "Who, who are you?"
I slept with my head in an elbow on a summer after-
noon and there I took a sleep lesson.
There I went away saying: I know why they sleep,
I know how they trap the tricky winds.
Long ago I learned how to listen to the singing wind
and how to forget and how to hear the deep
whine,
Slapping and lapsing under the day blue and the night
stars:
Who, who are you?

Who can ever forget
listening to the wind go by
counting its money
and throwing it away?

THREE SPRING NOTATIONS ON BIPEDS

1

THE down drop of the blackbird,
The wing catch of arrested flight,
The stop midway and then off:
    off for triangles, circles, loops
    of new hieroglyphs—
This is April's way: a woman:
" O yes, I'm here again and your heart
    knows I was coming."

2

White pigeons rush at the sun,
A marathon of wing feats is on:
"Who most loves danger? Who most loves
    wings? Who somersaults for God's sake
    in the name of wing power
    in the sun and blue
    on an April Thursday."
So ten winged heads, ten winged feet,
    race their white forms over Elmhurst.
They go fast: once the ten together were
    a feather of foam bubble, a chrysanthemum
    whirl speaking to silver and azure.

3

The child is on my shoulders.
In the prairie moonlight the child's legs
  hang over my shoulders.
She sits on my neck and I hear her calling
  me a good horse.
She slides down—and into the moon silver of
  a prairie stream
She throws a stone and laughs at the clug-clug.

SANDHILL PEOPLE

I TOOK away three pictures.

One was a white gull forming a half-mile arch from the pines toward Waukegan.

One was a whistle in the little sandhills, a bird crying either to the sunset gone or the dusk come.

One was three spotted waterbirds, zigzagging, cutting scrolls and jags, writing a bird Sanscrit of wing points, half over the sand, half over the water, a half-love for the sea, a half-love for the land.

I took away three thoughts.

One was a thing my people call "love," a shut-in river hunting the sea, breaking white falls between tall clefs of hill country.

One was a thing my people call "silence," the wind running over the butter faced sand-flowers, running over the sea, and never heard of again.

One was a thing my people call "death," neither a whistle in the little sandhills, nor a bird Sanscrit of wing points, yet a coat all the stars and seas have worn, yet a face the beach wears between sunset and dusk.

FAR ROCKAWAY NIGHT TILL MORNING

WHAT can we say of the night?
The fog night, the moon night,
           the fog moon night last night?

There swept out of the sea a song.
There swept out of the sea—
           torn white plungers.
There came on the coast wind drive
In the spit of a driven spray,
On the boom of foam and rollers,
The cry of midnight to morning:
           Hoi-a-loa.
           Hoi-a-loa.
           Hoi-a-loa.

Who has loved the night more than I have?
Who has loved the fog moon night last night
           more than I have?

Out of the sea that song
           —can I ever forget it?
Out of the sea those plungers
           —can I remember anything else?
Out of the midnight morning cry: Hoi-a-loa:
           —how can I hunt any other songs now?

HUMMINGBIRD WOMAN

WHY should I be wondering
How you would look in black velvet and yellow?
in orange and green?
I who cannot remember whether it was a dash of blue
Or a whirr of red under your willow throat—
Why do I wonder how you would look in humming-
bird feathers?

BUCKWHEAT

1

THERE was a late autumn cricket,
And two smoldering mountain sunsets
Under the valley roads of her eyes.

There was a late autumn cricket,
A hangover of summer song,
Scraping a tune
Of the late night clocks of summer,
In the late winter night fireglow,
This in a circle of black velvet at her neck.

2

In pansy eyes a flash, a thin rim of white light, a
beach bonfire ten miles across dunes, a speck of
a fool star in night's half circle of velvet.

In the corner of the left arm a dimple, a mole, a
forget-me-not, and it fluttered a hummingbird
wing, a blur in the honey-red clover, in the honey-
white buckwheat.

BLUE RIDGE

Born a million years ago you stay here a million
    years . . . watching the women come and live
    and be laid away . . . you and they thin-gray
    thin-dusk lovely.
So it goes: either the early morning lights are lovely
    or the early morning star.
I am glad I have seen racehorses, women, mountains.

VALLEY SONG

THE sunset swept
To the valley's west, you remember.

The frost was on.
A star burnt blue
We were warm, you remember,
And counted the rings on a moon.

The sunset swept
To the valley's west
And was gone in a big dark door of stars.

MIST FORMS

THE sheets of night mist travel a long valley.
I know why you came at sundown in a scarf mist.

What was it we touched asking nothing and asking all?
How many times can death come and pay back what
we saw?

In the oath of the sod, the lips that swore,
In the oath of night mist, nothing and all,
A riddle is here no man tells, no woman.

PIGEON

The flutter of blue pigeon's wings
Under a river bridge
Hunting a clean dry arch,
A corner for a sleep—
This flutters here in a woman's hand.

A singing sleep cry,
A drunken poignant two lines of song,
Somebody looking clean into yesterday
And remembering, or looking clean into
To-morrow, and reading,—
This sings here as a woman's sleep cry sings.

Pigeon friend of mine,
Fly on, sing on.

CHASERS

THE sea at its worst drives a white foam up,
The same sea sometimes, so easy and rocking with
    green mirrors,
So you were there when the white foam was up
And the salt spatter and the rack and the dulse—
You were done fingering these, and high, higher and
    higher
Your feet went and it was your voice went, " Hai,
    hai, hai,"
Up where the rocks let nothing live and the grass was
    gone,
Not even a hank nor a wisp of sea moss hoping.
Here your feet and your same singing, " Hai, hai, hai."

Was there anything else to answer than, " Hai, hai,
    hai "?
Did I go up those same crags yesterday and the day
    before
Scruffing my shoe leather and scraping the tough
    gnomic stuff
Of stones woven on a cold criss-cross so long ago?
Have I not sat there . . . watching the white foam up,
The hoarse white lines coming to curve, foam, slip
    back?
Didn't I learn then how the call comes, " Hai, hai,
    hai "?

HORSE FIDDLE

First I would like to write for you a poem to be
shouted in the teeth of a strong wind.

Next I would like to write one for you to sit on a
hill and read down the river valley on a late
summer afternoon, reading it in less than a whis-
per to Jack on his soft wire legs learning to stand
up and preach, Jack-in-the-pulpit.

As many poems as I have written to the moon and
the streaming of the moon spinners of light, so
many of the summer moon and the winter moon I
would like to shoot along to your ears for nothing,
for a laugh, a song,
>   for nothing at all,
>   for one look from you,
>   for your face turned away
>   and your voice in one clutch
>   half way between a tree wind moan
>   and a night-bird sob.

Believe nothing of it all, pay me nothing, open your
window for the other singers and keep it shut
for me.

The road I am on is a long road and I can go hungry
again like I have gone hungry before.

What else have I done nearly all my life than go
hungry and go on singing?

Leave me with the hoot owl.
I have slept in a blanket listening.
He learned it, he must have learned it
From two moons, the summer moon,
And the winter moon
And the streaming of the moon spinners of light.

TIMBER WINGS

THERE was a wild pigeon came often to Hinkley's
    timber.
Gray wings that wrote their loops and triangles on
    the walnuts and the hazel.
        There was a wild pigeon.

There was a summer came year by year to Hinkley's
    timber.
Rainy months and sunny and pigeons calling and one
    pigeon best of all who came.
        There was a summer.

It is so long ago I saw this wild pigeon and listened.
It is so long ago I heard the summer song of the
    pigeon who told me why night comes, why death
    and stars come, why the whippoorwill remembers
    three notes only and always.
It is so long ago; it is like now and today; the gray
    wing pigeon's way of telling it all, telling it to the
    walnuts and hazel, telling it to me.
      So there is memory.
      So there is a pigeon, a summer, a gray wing
        beating my shoulder.

NIGHT STUFF

LISTEN a while, the moon is a lovely woman, a lonely
woman, lost in a silver dress, lost in a circus
rider's silver dress.

Listen a while, the lake by night is a lonely woman, a
lovely woman, circled with birches and pines mix-
ing their green and white among stars shattered
in spray clear nights.

I know the moon and the lake have twisted the roots
under my heart the same as a lonely woman, a
lovely woman, in a silver dress, in a circus rider's
silver dress.

SPANISH

FASTEN black eyes on me.
I ask nothing of you under the peach trees,
Fasten your black eyes in my gray
            with the spear of a storm.
The air under the peach blossoms is a haze of pink.

SHAG-BARK HICKORY

IN the moonlight under a shag-bark hickory **tree**
Watching the yellow shadows melt in hoof-pools,
Listening to the yes and the no of a woman's hands,
I kept my guess why the night was glad.

The night was lit with a woman's eyes.
The night was crossed with a woman's hands,
The night kept humming an undersong.

THE SOUTH WIND SAYS SO

If the oriole calls like last year
when the south wind sings in the oats,
if the leaves climb and climb on a bean pole
saying over a song learnt from the south wind,
if the crickets send up the same old lessons
found when the south wind keeps on coming,
we will get by, we will keep on coming,
we will get by, we will come along,
we will fix our hearts over,
the south wind says so.

ACCOMPLISHED FACTS

ACCOMPLISHED FACTS

EVERY year Emily Dickinson sent one friend
the first arbutus bud in her garden.

In a last will and testament Andrew Jackson
remembered a friend with the gift of George
Washington's pocket spy-glass.

Napoleon too, in a last testament, mentioned a silver
watch taken from the bedroom of Frederick the Great,
and passed along this trophy to a particular friend.

O. Henry took a blood carnation from his coat lapel
and handed it to a country girl starting work in a
bean bazaar, and scribbled: " Peach blossoms may or
may not stay pink in city dust."

So it goes. Some things we buy, some not.
Tom Jefferson was proud of his radishes, and Abe
Lincoln blacked his own boots, and Bismarck called
Berlin a wilderness of brick and newspapers.

So it goes. There are accomplished facts.
Ride, ride, ride on in the great new blimps—
Cross unheard-of oceans, circle the planet.
When you come back we may sit by five hollyhocks.
We might listen to boys fighting for marbles.
The grasshopper will look good to us.

So it goes . . .

GRIEG BEING DEAD

GRIEG being dead we may speak of him and his art.
Grieg being dead we can talk about whether he was
any good or not.
Grieg being with Ibsen, Björnson, Lief Ericson and
the rest,
Grieg being dead does not care a hell's hoot what
we say.

Morning, Spring, Anitra's Dance,
He dreams them at the doors of new stars.

? sketches ?

CHORDS

In the morning, a Sunday morning, shadows of sea
and adumbrants of rock in her eyes . . . horse-
back in leather boots and leather gauntlets by
the sea.

In the evening, a Sunday evening, a rope of pearls
on her white shoulders . . . and a speaking,
brooding black velvet, relapsing to the voiceless
. . . battering Russian marches on a piano . . .
drive of blizzards across Nebraska.

Yes, riding horseback on hills by the sea . . . sitting
at the ivory keys in black velvet, a rope of pearls
on white shoulders.

DOGHEADS

AMONG the grassroots
In the moonlight, who comes circling,
    red tongues and high noses?
Is one of 'em Buck and one of 'em
    White Fang?

In the moonlight, who are they, cross-legged,
    telling their stories over and over?
Is one of 'em Martin Eden and one of 'em Larsen
    the Wolf?

Let an epitaph read:
    He loved the straight eyes of dogs
    and the strong heads of men.

TRINITY PEACE

THE grave of Alexander Hamilton is in Trinity yard
    at the end of Wall Street.

The grave of Robert Fulton likewise is in Trinity
    yard where Wall Street stops.

And in this yard stenogs, bundle boys, scrubwomen,
    sit on the tombstones, and walk on the grass of
    graves, speaking of war and weather, of babies,
    wages and love.

An iron picket fence . . . and streaming thousands
    along Broadway sidewalks . . . straw hats,
    faces, legs . . . a singing, talking, hustling river
    . . . down the great street that ends with a Sea.

    . . . easy is the sleep of Alexander Hamilton.
    . . . easy is the sleep of Robert Fulton.
    . . . easy are the great governments and the great
        steamboats.

PORTRAIT

(*For S. A.*)

To write one book in five years
or five books in one year,
to be the painter and the thing painted,
. . . where are we, bo?

Wait—get his number.
The barber shop handling is here
and the tweeds, the cheviot, the Scotch Mist,
and the flame orange scarf.

Yet there is more—he sleeps under bridges
with lonely crazy men; he sits in country
jails with bootleggers; he adopts the children
of broken-down burlesque actresses; he has
cried a heart of tears for Windy MacPherson's
father; he pencils wrists of lonely women.

Can a man sit at a desk in a skyscraper in Chicago
and be a harnessmaker in a corn town in Iowa
and feel the tall grass coming up in June
and the ache of the cottonwood trees
singing with the prairie wind?

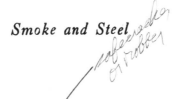

POTOMAC RIVER MIST

ALL the policemen, saloonkeepers and efficiency experts in Toledo knew Bern Dailey; secretary ten years when Whitlock was mayor.

Pickpockets, yeggs, three card men, he knew them all and how they flit from zone to zone, birds of wind and weather, singers, fighters, scavengers.

The Washington monument pointed to a new moon for us and a gang from over the river sang ragtime to a ukelele.

The river mist marched up and down the Potomac, we hunted the fog-swept Lincoln Memorial, white as a blond woman's arm.

We circled the city of Washington and came back home four o'clock in the morning, passing a sign: House Where Abraham Lincoln Died, Admission 25 Cents.

I got a letter from him in Sweden and I sent him a postcard from Norway . . every newspaper from America ran news of "the flu."

The path of a night fog swept up the river to the Lincoln Memorial when I saw it again and alone at a winter's end, the marble in the mist white as a blond woman's arm.

JACK LONDON AND O. HENRY

BOTH were jailbirds; no speechmakers at all;
speaking best with one foot on a brass rail;
a beer glass in the left hand and the right
hand employed for gestures.

And both were lights snuffed out . . . no warning
. . . no lingering:

Who knew the hearts of these boozefighters?

HIS OWN FACE HIDDEN

HOKUSAI's portrait of himself
Tells what his hat was like
And his arms and legs. The only faces
Are a river and a mountain
And two laughing farmers.

The smile of Hokusai
is under his hat.

CUPS OF COFFEE

THE haggard woman with a hacking cough **and a** deathless love whispers of white flowers . . . in your poem you pour like a cup of coffee, Gabriel.

The slim girl whose voice was lost in the waves of flesh piled on her bones . . . and the woman who sold to many men and saw her breasts shrivel . . . in two poems you pour these like a cup of coffee, Francois.

The woman whose lips are a thread of scarlet, the woman whose feet take hold on hell, the woman who turned to a memorial of salt looking at the lights of a forgotten city . . . in your affidavits, ancient Jews, you pour these like cups of coffee.

The woman who took men as snakes take rabbits, a rag and a bone and a hank of hair, she whose eyes called men to sea dreams and shark's teeth . . . in a poem you pour this like a cup of coffee, Kip.

Marching to the footlights in night robes with spots of blood, marching in white sheets muffling the faces, marching with heads in the air they come back and cough and cry and sneer: . . . in your poems, men, you pour these like cups of coffee.

PASSPORTS

SMOKE ROSE GOLD

THE dome of the capitol looks to the Potomac river.
       Out of haze over the sunset,
       Out of a smoke rose gold:
One star shines over the sunset.
Night takes the dome and the river, the sun and the
    smoke rose gold,
The haze changes from sunset to star.
The pour of a thin silver struggles against the dark.
A star might call: It's a long way across.

TANGIBLES

(Washington, August, 1918)

I HAVE seen this city in the day and the sun.
I have seen this city in the night and the moon.
And in the night and the moon I have seen a thing this
city gave me nothing of in the day and the sun.

The float of the dome in the day and the sun is one
thing.
The float of the dome in the night and the moon is
another thing.
In the night and the moon the float of the dome is a
dream-whisper, a croon of a hope: " Not today,
child, not today, lover; maybe tomorrow, child,
maybe tomorrow, lover."

Can a dome of iron dream deeper than living men?
Can the float of a shape hovering among tree-tops—
can this speak an oratory sad, singing and red
beyond the speech of the living men?

A mother of men, a sister, a lover, a woman past the
dreams of the living—
Does she go sad, singing and red out of the float of
this dome?

There is . . . something . . . here . . . men die for.

NIGHT MOVEMENT—NEW YORK

In the night, when the sea-winds take the city in their
   arms,
And cool the loud streets that kept their dust noon and
   afternoon;
In the night, when the sea-birds call to the lights of
   the city,
The lights that cut on the skyline their name of a city;
In the night, when the trains and wagons start from
   a long way off
For the city where the people ask bread and want
   letters;
In the night the city lives too—the day is not all.
In the night there are dancers dancing and singers
   singing,
And the sailors and soldiers look for numbers on doors.
In the night the sea-winds take the city in their arms.

NORTH ATLANTIC

When the sea is everywhere
from horizon to horizon . .
  when the salt and blue
  fill a circle of horizons . .
I swear again how I know
the sea is older than anything else
and the sea younger than anything else.

My first father was a landsman.
My tenth father was a sea-lover,
  a gipsy sea-boy, a singer of chanties.
  (Oh Blow the Man Down!)

The sea is always the same:
and yet the sea always changes.

    The sea gives all,
    and yet the sea keeps something back.

The sea takes without asking.
The sea is a worker, a thief and a loafer.
    Why does the sea let go so slow?
    Or never let go at all?

  The sea always the same
  day after day,
  the sea always the same

night after night,
fog on fog and never a star,
wind on wind and running white sheets,
bird on bird always a sea-bird—
so the days get lost:
it is neither Saturday nor Monday,
it is any day or no day,
it is a year, ten years.

Fog on fog and never a star,
what is a man, a child, a woman,
to the green and grinding sea?
The ropes and boards squeak and groan.

On the land they know a child they have named Today.
On the sea they know three children they have named:
                  Yesterday, Today, To-morrow.

I made a song to a woman:—it ran:
    I have wanted you.
    I have called to you
    on a day I counted a thousand years.

In the deep of a sea-blue noon
many women run in a man's head,
phantom women leaping from a man's forehead
    . . to the railings . . . into the sea . . . to the
    sea rim . . .
      . . a man's mother . . . a man's wife . . . other
    women . . .
I asked a sure-footed sailor how and he said:
    I have known many women but there is only one sea.

I saw the North Star once
and our old friend, The Big Dipper,
  only the sea between us:
    " Take away the sea
    and I lift The Dipper,
    swing the handle of it,
    drink from the brim of it."

I saw the North Star one night
and five new stars for me in the rigging ropes,
and seven old stars in the cross of the wireless
          plunging by night,
          plowing by night—
Five new cool stars, seven old warm stars.

I have been let down in a thousand graves
          by my kinfolk.
I have been left alone with the sea and the sea's
  wife, the wind, for my last friends
And my kinfolk never knew anything about it at all.

Salt from an old work of eating our graveclothes is
  here.
  The sea-kin of my thousand graves,
  The sea and the sea's wife, the wind,
They are all here to-night
          between the circle of horizons,
          between the cross of the wireless
          and the seven old warm stars.

Out of a thousand sea-holes I came yesterday.
Out of a thousand sea-holes I come to-morrow.

I am kin of the changer.
        I am a son of the sea
        and the sea's wife, the wind.

FOG PORTRAIT

Rings of iron gray smoke; a woman's steel face . . .
    looking . . . looking.
Funnels of an ocean liner negotiating a fog night;
    pouring a taffy mass down the wind; layers of
    soot on the top deck; a taffrail . . . and a
    woman's steel face . . . looking . . . looking.
Cliffs challenge humped; sudden arcs form on a gull's
    wing in the storm's vortex; miles of white horses
    plow through a stony beach; stars, clear sky, and
    everywhere free climbers calling; and a woman's
    steel face . . . looking . . . looking . . .

FLYING FISH

I HAVE lived in many half-worlds myself . . . and
so I know you.

I leaned at a deck rail watching a monotonous sea, the
same circling birds and the same plunge of fur-
rows carved by the plowing keel.

I leaned so . . . and you fluttered struggling between
two waves in the air now . . . and then under
the water and out again . . . a fish . . . a bird
. . . a fin thing . . . a wing thing.

Child of water, child of air, fin thing and wing thing
. . . I have lived in many half worlds myself . . .
and so I know you.

HOME THOUGHTS

THE sea rocks have a green moss.
The pine rocks have red berries.
I have memories of you.

. . . .

Speak to me of how you miss me.
Tell me the hours go long and slow.

Speak to me of the drag on your heart,
The iron drag of the long days.

I know hours empty as a beggar's tin cup on a rainy
day, empty as a soldier's sleeve with an arm lost.

Speak to me . . .

IN THE SHADOW OF THE PALACE

LET us go out of the fog, John, out of the filmy per-
   sistent drizzle on the streets of Stockholm, let
   us put down the collars of our raincoats, take
   off our hats and sit in the newspaper office.

Let us sit among the telegrams—clickety-click—the
   kaiser's crown goes into the gutter and the Hohen-
   zollern throne of a thousand years falls to pieces
   a one-hoss shay — *carriage*

It is a fog night out and the umbrellas are up and
   the collars of the raincoats—and all the steam-
   boats up and down the Baltic sea have their lights
   out and the wheelsmen sober.

Here the telegrams come—one king goes and another
   —butter is costly: there is no butter to buy for
   our bread in Stockholm—and a little patty of
   butter costs more than all the crowns of Germany.

Let us go out in the fog, John, let us roll up our
   raincoat collars and go on the streets where men
   are sneering at the kings.

TWO ITEMS

STRONG rocks hold up the riksdag bridge . . . always
strong river waters shoving their shoulders against
them . . .

In the riksdag to-night three hundred men are talking
to each other about more potatoes and bread for
the Swedish people to eat this winter.

In a boat among calm waters next to the running
waters a fisherman sits in the dark and I, leaning
at a parapet, see him lift a net and let it down
. . . he waits . . . the waters run . . . the
riksdag talks . . . he lifts the net and lets it
down . . .

Stars lost in the sky ten days of drizzle spread over
the sky saying yes-yes.

. . . .

Every afternoon at four o'clock fifteen apple women
who have sold their apples in Christiania meet
at a coffee house and gab.

Every morning at nine o'clock a girl wipes the win-
dows of a hotel across the street from the post-
office in Stockholm.

I have pledged them when I go to California next
summer and see the orange groves splattered with
yellow balls

I shall remember other people half way round the
world.

STREETS TOO OLD

I WALKED among the streets of an old city and the streets were lean as the throats of hard seafish soaked in salt and kept in barrels many years.

How old, how old, how old, we are:—the walls went on saying, street walls leaning toward each other like old women of the people, like old midwives tired and only doing what must be done.

The greatest the city could offer me, a stranger, was statues of the kings, on all corners bronzes of kings—ancient bearded kings who wrote books and spoke of God's love for all people—and young kings who took forth armies out across the frontiers splitting the heads of their opponents and enlarging their kingdoms.

Strangest of all to me, a stranger in this old city, was the murmur always whistling on the winds twisting out of the armpits and fingertips of the kings in bronze:—Is there no loosening? Is this for always?

In an early snowflurry one cried:—Pull me down where the tired old midwives no longer look at me, throw the bronze of me to a fierce fire and make me into neckchains for dancing children.

SAVOIR FAIRE

CAST a bronze of my head and legs and put them on
the king's street.

Set the cast of me here alongside Carl XII, making
two Carls for the Swedish people and the utlanders
to look at between the palace and the Grand
Hotel.

The summer sun will shine on both the Carls, and
November drizzles wrap the two, one in tall
leather boots, one in wool leggins.

Also I place it in the record: the Swedish people may
name boats after me or change the name of a
long street and give it one of my nicknames.

The old men who beset the soil of Sweden and own
the titles to the land—the old men who enjoy a
silken shimmer to their chin whiskers when they
promenade the streets named after old kings—
if they forget me—the old men whose varicose
veins stand more and more blue on the calves of
their legs when they take their morning baths
attended by old women born to the bath service
of old men and young—if these old men say
another King Carl should have a bronze on the
king's street rather than a Fool Carl—

Then I would hurl them only another fool's laugh—

I would remember last Sunday when I stood on a
jutland of fire-born red granite watching the
drop of the sun in the middle of the afternoon and
the full moon shining over Stockholm four o'clock
in the afternoon.

If the young men will read five lines of one of my
poems I will let the kings have all the bronze—
I ask only that one page of my writings be a
knapsack keepsake of the young men who are the
bloodkin of those who laughed nine hundred years
ago: We are afraid of nothing—only—the sky
may fall on us.

MOHAMMED BEK HADJETLACHE

THIS Mohammedan colonel from the Caucasus yells
    with his voice and wigwags with his arms.
The interpreter translates, "I was a friend of Korni-
    lov, he asks me what to do and I tell him."
A stub of a man, this Mohammedan colonel . . . a
    projectile shape . . . a bald head hammered . . .
"Does he fight or do they put him in a cannon and
    shoot him at the enemy?"
This fly-by-night, this bull-roarer who knows every-
    body.
"I write forty books, history of Islam, history of
    Europe, true religion, scientific farming, I am
    the Roosevelt of the Caucasus, I go to America
    and ride horses in the moving pictures for $500,-
    000, you get $50,000 . . ."
"I have 30,000 acres in the Caucasus, I have a stove
    factory in Petrograd the bolsheviks take from
    me, I am an old friend of the Czar, I am an old
    family friend of Clemenceau . . ."
These hands strangled three fellow workers for the
    czarist restoration, took their money, sent them
    in sacks to a river bottom . . . and scandalized
    Stockholm with his gang of strangler women.
Mid-sea strangler hands rise before me illustrating a
    wish, "I ride horses for the moving pictures in
    America, $500,000, and you get ten per cent . . ."
This rider of fugitive dawns. . . .

HIGH CONSPIRATORIAL PERSONS

Out of the testimony of such reluctant lips, out of
the oaths and mouths of such scrupulous liars,
out of perjurers whose hands swore by God to
the white sun before all men,

Out of a rag saturated with smears and smuts gath-
ered from the footbaths of kings and the loin
cloths of whores, from the scabs of Babylon and
Jerusalem to the scabs of London and New York,

From such a rag that has wiped the secret sores of
kings and overlords across the milleniums of
human marches and babblings,

From such a rag perhaps I shall wring one reluctant
desperate drop of blood, one honest-to-God spot
of red speaking a mother-heart.
December, 1918.
Christiania, Norway

BALTIC FOG NOTES

(Bergen)

SEVEN days all fog, all mist, and the turbines pound-
    ing through high seas.

I was a plaything, a rat's neck in the teeth of a scuffling
    mastiff.

Fog and fog and no stars, sun, moon.

Then an afternoon in fjords, low-lying lands scrawled
    in granite languages on a gray sky,

A night harbor, blue dusk mountain shoulders against
    a night sky,

And a circle of lights blinking: Ninety thousand
    people here.

>   Among the Wednesday night thousands in
>   goloshes and coats slickered for rain,
>   I learned how hungry I was for streets and
>   people.

.   .   .   .

I would rather be water than anything else.

I saw a drive of salt fog and mist in the North Atlantic
    and an iceberg dusky as a cloud in the gray of
    morning.

And I saw the dream pools of fjords in Norway . . .
    and the scarf of dancing water on the rocks and
    over the edges of mountain shelves.

.   .   .   .

Bury me in a mountain graveyard in Norway.
Three tongues of water sing around it with snow
    from the mountains.

Bury me in the North Atlantic.
A fog there from Iceland will be a murmur in gray
    over me and a long deep wind sob always.

Bury me in an Illinois cornfield.
The blizzards loosen their pipe organ voluntaries in
    winter stubble and the spring rains and the fall
    rains bring letters from the sea.

CIRCLES OF DOORS

CIRCLES OF DOORS

I LOVE him, I love him, ran the patter of her lips
And she formed his name on her tongue and sang
And she sent him word she loved him so much,
So much, and death was nothing; work, art, home,
All was nothing if her love for him was not first
Of all; the patter of her lips ran, I love him,
I love him; and he knew the doors that opened
Into doors and more doors, no end of doors,
And full length mirrors doubling and tripling
The apparitions of doors: circling corridors of
Looking glasses and doors, some with knobs, some
With no knobs, some opening slow to a heavy push,
And some jumping open at a touch and a hello.
And he knew if he so wished he could follow her
Swift running through circles of doors, hearing
Sometimes her whisper, I love him, I love him,
And sometimes only a high chaser of laughter
Somewhere five or ten doors ahead or five or ten
Doors behind, or chittering *h-st, h-st,* among corners
Of the tall full-length dusty looking glasses.
I love, I love, I love, she sang short and quick in
High thin beaten soprano and he knew the meanings,
The high chaser of laughter, the doors on doors
And the looking glasses, the room to room hunt,
The ends opening into new ends always.

HATE

ONE man killed another. The saying between them
had been " I'd give you the shirt off my back."

The killer wept over the dead. The dead if he looks
back knows the killer was sorry. It was a shot
in one second of hate out of ten years of love.

Why is the sun a red ball in the six o'clock mist?
Why is the moon a tumbling chimney? . . . tumbling
. . . tumbling . . . " I'd give you the shirt off
my back " . . . And I'll kill you if my head
goes wrong.

TWO STRANGERS BREAKFAST

THE law says you and I belong to each other, George.
The law says you are mine and I am yours, George.
And there are a million miles of white snowstorms, a
  million furnaces of hell,
Between the chair where you sit and the chair where
  I sit.
The law says two strangers shall eat breakfast together
  after nights on the horn of an Arctic moon.

SNOW

Snow took us away from the smoke valleys into white
   mountains, we saw velvet blue cows eating a
   vermillion grass and they gave us a pink milk.

Snow changes our bones into fog streamers caught
   by the wind and spelled into many dances.

Six bits for a sniff of snow in the old days bought
   us bubbles beautiful to forget floating long arm
   women across sunny autumn hills.

Our bones cry and cry, no let-up, cry their telegrams:
   More, more—a yen is on, a long yen and God only
   knows when it will end.

In the old days six bits got us snow and stopped the
   yen—now the government says: No, no, when our
   bones cry their telegrams: More, more.

The blue cows are dying, no more pink milk, no more
   floating long arm women, the hills are empty—
   us for the smoke valleys—sneeze and shiver and
   croak, you dopes—the government says: No, no.

DANCER

THE lady in red, she in the chile con carne red,
Brilliant as the shine of a pepper crimson in the
summer sun,
She behind a false-face, the much sought-after dancer,
the most sought-after dancer of all in this mas-
querade,
The lady in red sox and red hat, ankles of willow,
crimson arrow amidst the Spanish clashes of
music,

> I sit in a corner
> watching her dance first with one man
> and then another.

PLASTER

"I KNEW a real man once," says Agatha in the splendor of a shagbark hickory tree.

Did a man touch his lips to Agatha? Did a man hold her in his arms? Did a man only look at her and pass by?

Agatha, far past forty in a splendor of remembrance, says, "I knew a real man once."

CURSE OF A RICH POLISH PEASANT ON HIS SISTER WHO RAN AWAY WITH A WILD MAN

FELIKSOWA has gone again from our house and this time for good, I hope.

She and her husband took with them the cow father gave them, and they sold it.

She went like a swine, because she called neither on me, her brother, nor on her father, before leaving for those forests.

That is where she ought to live, with bears, not with men.

She was something of an ape before and there, with her wild husband, she became altogether an ape.

No honest person would have done as they did.

Whose fault is it? And how much they have cursed me and their father!

May God not punish them for it. They think only about money; they let the church go if they can only live fat on their money.

WOMAN WITH A PAST

THERE was a woman tore off a red velvet gown
And slashed the white skin of her right shoulder
And a crimson zigzag wrote a finger nail hurry.

There was a woman spoke six short words
And quit a life that was old to her
For a life that was new.

There was a woman swore an oath
And gave hoarse whisper to a prayer
And it was all over.

She was a thief and a whore and a kept woman,
She was a thing to be used and played with.
She wore an ancient scarlet sash.

The story is thin and wavering,
White as a face in the first apple blossoms,
White as a birch in the snow of a winter moon.

The story is never told.
There are white lips whisper alone.
There are red lips whisper alone.

In the cool of the old walls,
In the white of the old walls,
The red song is over.

WHITE HANDS

FOR the second time in a year this lady with the white hands is brought to the west room second floor of a famous sanatorium.

Her husband is a cornice manufacturer in an Iowa town and the lady has often read papers on Victorian poets before the local literary club.

Yesterday she washed her hands forty seven times during her waking hours and in her sleep moaned restlessly attempting to clean imaginary soiled spots off her hands.

Now the head physician touches his chin with a crooked forefinger.

AN ELECTRIC SIGN GOES DARK

Poland, France, Judea ran in her veins,
Singing to Paris for bread, singing to Gotham in a
fizz at the pop of a bottle's cork.

" Won't you come and play wiz me " she sang . . . and
" I just can't make my eyes behave."
" Higgeldy-Piggeldy," " Papa's Wife," " Follow Me "
were plays.

Did she wash her feet in a tub of milk? Was a strand
of pearls sneaked from her trunk? The news-
papers asked.
Cigarettes, tulips, pacing horses, took her name.

Twenty years old . . . thirty . . . forty . . .
Forty-five and the doctors fathom nothing, the doctors
quarrel, the doctors use silver tubes feeding
twenty-four quarts of blood into the veins, the
respects of a prize-fighter, a cab driver.
And a little mouth moans: It is easy to die when they
are dying so many grand deaths in France.

A voice, a shape, gone.
A baby bundle from Warsaw . . . legs, torso, head
. . . on a hotel bed at The Savoy.

The white chiselings of flesh that flung themselves in
    somersaults, straddles, for packed houses:
A memory, a stage and footlights out, an electric sign
    on Broadway dark.

She belonged to somebody, nobody.
No one man owned her, no ten nor a thousand.
She belonged to many thousand men, lovers of the
    white chiseling of arms and shoulders, the ivory
    of a laugh, the bells of song.

Railroad brakemen taking trains across Nebraska
    prairies, lumbermen jaunting in pine and tamarack
    of the Northwest, stock ranchers in the middle
    west, mayors of southern cities
Say to their pals and wives now: I see by the papers
    Anna Held is dead.

THEY BUY WITH AN EYE TO LOOKS

THE fine cloth of your love might be a fabric of Egypt,
Something Sinbad, the sailor, took away from robbers,
Something a traveler with plenty of money might
    pick up
And bring home and stick on the walls and say:
"There's a little thing made a hit with me
When I was in Cairo—I think I must see Cairo again
    some day."
So there are cornice manufacturers, chewing gum
    kings,
Young Napoleons who corner eggs or corner cheese,
Phenoms looking for more worlds to corner,
And still other phenoms who lard themselves in
And make a killing in steel, copper, permanganese,
And they say to random friends in for a call:
"Have you had a look at my wife? Here she is.
    Haven't I got her dolled up for fair?"
O-ee! the fine cloth of your love might be a fabric of
    Egypt.

PROUD AND BEAUTIFUL

AFTER you have spent all the money modistes and
    manicures and mannikins will take for fixing you
    over into a thing the people on the streets call
    proud and beautiful,

After the shops and fingers have worn out all they
    have and know and can hope to have and know
    for the sake of making you what the people on
    the streets call proud and beautiful,

After there is absolutely nothing more to be done for
    the sake of staging you as a great enigmatic bird
    of paradise and they must all declare you to be
    proud and beautiful,

After you have become the last word in good looks,
    insofar as good looks may be fixed and formu-
    lated, then, why then, there is nothing more to
    it then, it is then you listen and see how voices
    and eyes declare you to be proud and beautiful.

TELEGRAM

I saw a telegram handed a two hundred pound man
at a desk. And the little scrap of paper charged
the air like a set of crystals in a chemist's tube
to a whispering pinch of salt.

Cross my heart, the two hundred pound man had just
cracked a joke about a new hat he got his wife,
when the messenger boy slipped in and asked
him to sign. He gave the boy a nickel, tore the
envelope and read.

Then he yelled " Good God," jumped for his hat and
raincoat, ran for the elevator and took a taxi
to a railroad depot.

As I say, it was like a set of crystals in a chemist's
tube and a whispering pinch of salt.

I wonder what Diogenes who lived in a tub in the
sun would have commented on the affair.

I know a shoemaker who works in a cellar slamming
half-soles onto shoes, and when I told him, he
said: " I pay my bills, I love my wife, and I am
not afraid of anybody."

GLIMMER

LET down your braids of hair, lady.
Cross your legs and sit before the looking-glass
And gaze long on lines under your eyes.
Life writes, men dance.
        And you know how men pay women.

WHITE ASH

THERE is a woman on Michigan Boulevard keeps a parrot and goldfish and two white mice.

She used to keep a houseful of girls in kimonos and three pushbuttons on the front door.

Now she is alone with a parrot and goldfish and two white mice . . . but these are some of her thoughts:

The love of a soldier on furlough or a sailor on shore leave burns with a bonfire red and saffron.

The love of an emigrant workman whose wife is a thousand miles away burns with a blue smoke.

The love of a young man whose sweetheart married an older man for money burns with a sputtering uncertain flame.

And there is a love . . . one in a thousand . . . burns clean and is gone leaving a white ash. . . .

And this is a thought she never explains to the parrot and goldfish and two white mice.

TESTIMONY REGARDING A GHOST

THE roses slanted crimson sobs
On the night sky hair of the women,
And the long light-fingered men
Spoke to the dark-haired women,
"Nothing lovelier, nothing lovelier."
How could he sit there among us all
Guzzling blood into his guts,
Goblets, mugs, buckets—
Leaning, toppling, laughing
With a slobber on his mouth,
A smear of red on his strong raw lips,
How could he sit there
And only two or three of us see him?
There was nothing to it.
He wasn't there at all, of course.

The roses leaned from the pots.
The sprays snot roses gold and red
And the roses slanted crimson sobs
In the night sky hair
And the voices chattered on the way
To the frappe, speaking of pictures,
Speaking of a strip of black velvet
Crossing a girlish woman's throat,
Speaking of the mystic music flash
Of pots and sprays of roses,
"Nothing lovelier, nothing lovelier."

short,
pithy
saying

PUT OFF THE WEDDING FIVE TIMES AND NOBODY COMES TO IT

(Handbook for Quarreling Lovers)

I THOUGHT of offering you apothegms.

I might have said, "Dogs bark and the wind carries it away."

I might have said, "He who would make a door of gold must knock a nail in every day."

So easy, so easy it would have been to inaugurate a high impetuous moment for you to look on before the final farewells were spoken.

You who assumed the farewells in the manner of people buying newspapers and reading the headlines—and all peddlers of gossip who buttonhole each other and wag their heads saying, "Yes, I heard all about it last Wednesday."

I considered several apothegms.

"There is no love but service," of course, would only initiate a quarrel over who has served and how and when.

"Love stands against fire and flood and much bitterness," would only initiate a second misunderstanding, and bickerings with lapses of silence.

What is there in the Bible to cover our case, or Shakespere? What poetry can help? Is there any left but Epictetus?

Since you have already chosen to interpret silence for
    language and silence for despair and silence for
    contempt and silence for all things but love,
Since you have already chosen to read ashes where
    God knows there was something else than ashes,
Since silence and ashes are two identical findings for
    your eyes and there are no apothegms worth
    handing out like a hung jury's verdict for a record
    in our own hearts as well as the community at
    large,
I can only remember a Russian peasant who told me
    his grandfather warned him: If you ride too good
    a horse you will not take the straight road to
    town.

It will always come back to me in the blur of that
    hokku: The heart of a woman of thirty is like
    the red ball of the sun seen through a mist.
Or I will remember the witchery in the eyes of a girl
    at a barn dance one winter night in Illinois saying:
        Put off the wedding five times and nobody
        comes to it.

BABY VAMPS

BABY vamps, is it harder work than it used to be?
Are the new soda parlors worse than the old time
    saloons?
  Baby vamps, do you have jobs in the day time
          or is this all you do?
          do you come out only at night?
In the winter at the skating rinks, in the summer at the
    roller coaster parks,
Wherever figure eights are carved, by skates in winter,
    by roller coasters in summer,
Wherever the whirligigs are going and chicken spanish
    and hot dog are sold,
There you come, giggling baby vamp, there you come
    with your blue baby eyes, saying:
        Take me along.

VAUDEVILLE DANCER

ELSIE FLIMMERWON, you got a job now with a jazz outfit in vaudeville.

The houses go wild when you finish the act shimmying a fast shimmy to The Livery Stable Blues.

It is long ago, Elsie Flimmerwon, I saw your mother over a washtub in a grape arbor when your father came with the locomotor ataxia shuffle.

It is long ago, Elsie, and now they spell your name with an electric sign.

Then you were a little thing in checked gingham and your mother wiped your nose and said: You little fool, keep off the streets.

Now you are a big girl at last and streetfuls of people read your name and a line of people shaped like a letter S stand at the box office hoping to see you shimmy.

BALLOON FACES

THE balloons hang on wires in the Marigold Gardens.
They spot their yellow and gold, they juggle their blue
and red, they float their faces on the face of the
sky.

Balloon face eaters sit by hundreds reading the eat
cards, asking, "What shall we eat?"—and the
waiters, "Have you ordered?" they are sixty
ballon faces sifting white over the tuxedoes.

Poets, lawyers, ad men, mason contractors, smart-
alecks discussing "educated jackasses," here they
put crabs into their balloon faces.

Here sit the heavy balloon face women lifting crimson
lobsters into their crimson faces, lobsters out of
Sargossa sea bottoms.

Here sits a man cross-examining a woman, "Where
were you last night? What do you do with all
your money? Who's buying your shoes now,
anyhow?"

So they sit eating whitefish, two balloon faces swept
on God's night wind.

And all the time the balloon spots on the wires, a little
mile of festoons, they play their own silence play
of film yellow and film gold, bubble blue and bub-
ble red.

The wind crosses the town, the wind from the west
side comes to the banks of marigolds boxed in the
Marigold Gardens.

Night moths fly and fix their feet in the leaves and
eat and are seen by the eaters.

The jazz outfit sweats and the drums and the saxo-
phones reach for the ears of the eaters.

The chorus brought from Broadway works at the fun
and the slouch of their shoulders, the kick of their
ankles, reach for the eyes of the eaters.

These girls from Kokomo and Peoria, these hungry
girls, since they are paid-for, let us look on and
listen, let us get their number.

Why do I go again to the balloons on the wires, some-
thing for nothing, kin women of the half-moon,
dream women?

And the half-moon swinging on the wind crossing the
town—these two, the half-moon and the wind—
this will be about all, this will be about all.

Eaters, go to it; your mazuma pays for it all; it's a
knockout, a classy knockout—and payday always
comes.

The moths in the marigolds will do for me, the half-
moon, the wishing wind and the little mile of
balloon spots on wires—this will be about all, this
will be about all.

HAZE

HAZE

KEEP a red heart of memories
Under the great gray rain sheds of the sky,
Under the open sun and the yellow gloaming embers.
Remember all paydays of lilacs and songbirds;
All starlights of cool memories on storm paths.

Out of this prairie rise the faces of dead men.
They speak to me. I can not tell you what they say.

Other faces rise on the prairie.
                              They are the unborn. The future.

Yesterday and to-morrow cross and mix on the sky-
      line
The two are lost in a purple haze. One forgets. One
      waits.

In the yellow dust of sunsets, in the meadows of
      vermilion eight o'clock June nights . . . the
      dead men and the unborn children speak to me
      . . . I can not tell you what they say . . . you
      listen and you know.

I don't care who you are, man:
I know a woman is looking for you
and her soul is a corn-tassel kissing a south-west wind.

(The farm-boy whose face is the color of brick-dust,
is calling the cows; he will form the letter X with
crossed streams of milk from the teats; he will
beat a tattoo on the bottom of a tin pail with X's
of milk.)

I don't care who you are, man:
I know sons and daughters looking for you
And they are gray dust working toward star paths
And you see them from a garret window when you
    laugh
At your luck and murmur, "I don't care."

I don't care who you are, woman:
I know a man is looking for you
And his soul is a south-west wind kissing a corn-
    tassel.

(The kitchen girl on the farm is throwing oats to the
    chickens and the buff of their feathers says hello
    to the sunset's late maroon.)

I don't care who you are, woman:
I know sons and daughters looking for you
And they are next year's wheat or the year after
    hidden in the dark and loam.

My love is a yellow hammer spinning circles in Ohio,
    Indiana. My love is a redbird shooting flights
    in straight lines in Kentucky and Tennessee. My
    love is an early robin flaming an ember of copper

on her shoulders in March and April. My love
is a graybird living in the eaves of a Michigan
house all winter. Why is my love always a crying
thing of wings?

On the Indiana dunes, in the Mississippi marshes, I
have asked: Is it only a fishbone on the beach?
Is it only a dog's jaw or a horse's skull whitening in
the sun? Is the red heart of man only ashes?
Is the flame of it all a white light switched off
and the power house wires cut?

Why do the prairie roses answer every summer? Why
do the changing repeating rains come back out
of the salt sea wind-blown? Why do the stars
keep their tracks? Why do the cradles of the
sky rock new babies?

CADENZA

THE knees
   of this proud woman
are bone.

The elbows
   of this proud woman
are bone.

The summer-white stars
   and the winter-white stars
never stop circling
   around this proud woman.

The bones
   of this proud woman
answer the vibrations
   of the stars.

   In summer
the stars speak deep thoughts
   In the winter
the stars repeat summer speeches.

The knees
   of this proud woman
know these thoughts
   and know these speeches
of the summer and winter stars.

MEMORANDA

THIS handful of grass, brown, says little. This quarter mile field of it, waving seeds ripening in the sun, is a lake of luminous firefly lavender.

. . . .

Prairie roses, two of them, climb down the sides of a road ditch. In the clear pool they find their faces along stiff knives of grass, and cat-tails who speak and keep thoughts in beaver brown.

. . . .

These gardens empty; these fields only flower ghosts; these yards with faces gone; leaves speaking as feet and skirts in slow dances to slow winds; I turn my head and say good-by to no one who hears; I pronounce a useless good-by.

POTOMAC TOWN IN FEBRUARY

THE bridge says: Come across, try me; see how good
   I am.
The big rock in the river says: Look at me; learn
   how to stand up.
The white water says: I go on; around, under, over,
   I go on.
A kneeling, scraggly pine says: I am here yet; they
   nearly got me last year.
A sliver of moon slides by on a high wind calling: I
   know why; I'll see you to-morrow; I'll tell you
   everything to-morrow.

BUFFALO DUSK

THE buffaloes are gone.
And those who saw the buffaloes are gone.
Those who saw the buffaloes by thousands and how
    they pawed the prairie sod into dust with their
    hoofs, their great heads down pawing on in a
    great pageant of dusk,
Those who saw the buffaloes are gone.
And the buffaloes are gone.

CORN HUT TALK

WRITE your wishes
  on the door
  and come in.

Stand outside
  in the pools of the harvest moon.

Bring in
  the handshake of the pumpkins.

There's a wish
  for every hazel nut?
There's a hope
  for every corn shock?
There's a kiss
  for every clumsy climbing shadow?

  Clover and the bumblebees once,
  high winds and November rain now.

Buy shoes
  for rough weather in November.
Buy shirts
  to sleep outdoors when May comes.

Buy me
something useless to remember you by.
   Send me
a sumach leaf from an Illinois hill.

In the faces marching in the firelog flickers,
In the fire music of wood singing to winter,
Make my face march through the purple and ashes.
Make me one of the fire singers to winter.

BRANCHES

THE dancing girls here . . . after a long night of
it . . .
The long beautiful night of the wind and rain in April,
The long night hanging down from the drooping
branches of the top of a birch tree,
Swinging, swaying, to the wind for a partner, to the
rain for a partner.
What is the humming, swishing thing they sing in
the morning now?
The rain, the wind, the swishing whispers of the long
slim curve so little and so dark on the western
morning sky . . . these dancing girls here on an
April early morning . . .
They have had a long cool beautiful night of it with
their partners learning this year's song of April.

RUSTY CRIMSON

(*Christmas Day*, 1917)

THE five o'clock prairie sunset is a strong man going to sleep after a long day in a cornfield.

The red dust of a rusty crimson is fixed with two fingers of lavender. A hook of smoke, a woman's nose in charcoal and . . . nothing.

The timberline turns in a cover of purple. A grain elevator humps a shoulder. One steel star whisks out a pointed fire. Moonlight comes on the stubble.

. . . .

"Jesus in an Illinois barn early this morning, the baby Jesus . . . in flannels . . ."

LETTER S

The river is gold under a sunset of Illinois.
It is a molten gold someone pours and changes.
A woman mixing a wedding cake of butter and eggs
Knows what the sunset is pouring on the river here.
The river twists in a letter S.
    A gold S now speaks to the Illinois sky.

WEEDS

FROM the time of the early radishes
To the time of the standing corn
Sleepy Henry Hackerman hoes.

There are laws in the village against weeds.
The law says a weed is wrong and shall be killed.
The weeds say life is a white and lovely thing
And the weeds come on and on in irrepressible regi-
    ments.
Sleepy Henry Hackerman hoes; and the village law
    uttering a ban on weeds is unchangeable law.

NEW FARM TRACTOR

SNUB nose, the guts of twenty mules are in your cylinders and transmission.

The rear axles hold the kick of twenty Missouri jackasses.

It is in the records of the patent office and the ads there is twenty horse power pull here.

The farm boy says hello to you instead of twenty mules—he sings to you instead of ten span of mules.

A bucket of oil and a can of grease is your hay and oats.

Rain proof and fool proof they stable you anywhere in the fields with the stars for a roof.

I carve a team of long ear mules on the steering wheel —it's good-by now to leather reins and the songs of the old mule skinners.

PODS

PEA pods cling to stems.
Neponset the village,
Clings to the Burlington railway main line.
Terrible midnight limiteds roar through
Hauling sleepers to the Rockies and Sierras.
The earth is slightly shaken
And Neponset trembles slightly in its sleep.

HARVEST SUNSET

Red gold of pools,
Sunset furrows six o'clock,
And the farmer done in the fields
And the cows in the barns with bulging udders.

Take the cows and the farmer,
Take the barns and bulging udders.
Leave the red gold of pools
And sunset furrows six o'clock.
The farmer's wife is singing.
The farmer's boy is whistling.
I wash my hands in red gold of pools.

NIGHT'S NOTHINGS AGAIN

WHO knows what I know
when I have asked the night questions
and the night has answered nothing
only the old answers?

something written in code

Who picked a crimson cryptogram,
the tail light of a motor car turning a corner,
or the midnight sign of a chile con carne place,
or a man out of the ashes of false dawn muttering
    " hot-dog " to the night watchmen:
Is there a spieler who has spoken the word or taken
    the number of night's nothings? am I the spieler?
    or you?

Is there a tired head
the night has not fed and rested
and kept on its neck and shoulders?

Is there a wish
of man to woman
and woman to man
the night has not written
and signed its name under?

Does the night forget
as a woman forgets?
and remember
as a woman remembers?

Who gave the night
this head of hair,
this gipsy head
calling: Come-on?

Who gave the night anything at all
and asked the night questions
and was laughed at?

Who asked the night
for a long soft kiss
and lost the half-way lips?
who picked a red lamp in a mist?

Who saw the night
fold its Mona Lisa hands
and sit half-smiling, half-sad,
nothing at all,
and everything,
all the world?

Who saw the night
let down its hair
and shake its bare shoulders
and blow out the candles of the moon,
whispering, snickering,
cutting off the snicker . . and sobbing . .
out of pillow-wet kisses and tears?

Is the night woven of anything else
than the secret wishes of women,
the stretched empty arms of women?
the hair of women with stars and roses?

I asked the night these questions.
I heard the night asking me these questions.

I saw the night
put these whispered nothings
across the city dust and stones,
across a single yellow sunflower,
one stalk strong as a woman's wrist;

And the play of a light rain,
the jig-time folly of a light rain,
the creepers of a drizzle on the sidewalks
for the policemen and the railroad men,
for the home-goers and the homeless,
silver fans and funnels on the asphalt,
the many feet of a fog mist that crept away;

I saw the night
put these nothings across
and the night wind came saying: Come-on:
and the curve of sky swept off white clouds
and swept on white stars over Battery to Bronx,
scooped a sea of stars over Albany, Dobbs Ferry, Cape
    Horn, Constantinople.

I saw the night's mouth and lips
strange as a face next to mine on a pillow
and now I know . . . as I knew always . . .
the night is a lover of mine . . .
I know the night is . . . everything.
I know the night is . . . all the world.

I have seen gold lamps in a lagoon
play sleep and murmur
with never an eyelash,
never a glint of an eyelid,
quivering in the water-shadows.

A taxi whizzes by, an owl car clutters, passengers yawn
    reading street signs, a bum on a park bench shifts,
    another bum keeps his majesty of stone stillness,
    the forty-foot split rocks of Central Park sleep
    the sleep of stone whalebacks, the cornices of the
    Metropolitan Art mutter their own nothings to the
    men with rolled-up collars on the top of a bus:
Breaths of the sea salt Atlantic, breaths of two rivers,
    and a heave of hawsers and smokestacks, the
    swish of multiplied sloops and war dogs, the hesi-
    tant hoo-hoo of coal boats: among these I listen
    to Night calling:
I give you what money can never buy: all other lovers
    change: all others go away and come back and go
    away again:
        I am the one you slept with last night.
        I am the one you sleep with tonight and
            tomorrow night.
        I am the one whose passion kisses
            keep your head wondering
            and your lips aching
            to sing one song
            never sung before
            at night's gipsy head
            calling: Come-on.

These hands that slid to my neck and held me,
these fingers that told a story,
this gipsy head of hair calling: Come-on:
can anyone else come along now
and put across night's nothings again?

I have wanted kisses my heart stuttered at asking,
I have pounded at useless doors and called my people
    fools.
I have staggered alone in a winter dark making
    mumble songs
to the sting of a blizzard that clutched and swore.

    It was the night in my blood:
        open dreaming night,
        night of tireless sheet-steel blue:
    The hands of God washing something,
        feet of God walking somewhere.

PANELS

signal

PANELS

THE west window is a panel of marching onions.
Five new lilacs nod to the wind and fence boards.
The rain dry fence boards, the stained knot holes,
        heliograph a peace.
(How long ago the knee drifts here and a blizzard
        howling at the knot holes,
        whistling winter war drums?)

DAN

EARLY May, after cold rain the sun baffling cold wind.
Irish setter pup finds a corner near the cellar door,
          all sun and no wind,
Cuddling there he crosses forepaws and lays his skull
Sideways on this pillow, dozing in a half-sleep,
Browns of hazel nut, mahogany, rosewood, played off
          against each other on his paws
          and head.

WHIFFLETREE

GIVE me your anathema.
Speak new damnations on my head.
The evening mist in the hills is soft.
The boulders on the road say communion.
The farm dogs look out of their eyes and keep thoughts
    from the corn cribs.
Dirt of the reeling earth holds horseshoes.
The rings in the whiffletree count their secrets.
Come on, you.

MASCOTS

I WILL keep you and bring hands to hold you against
a great hunger.
I will run a spear in you for a great gladness to die
with.
I will stab you between the ribs of the left side with
a great love worth remembering.

THE SKYSCRAPER LOVES NIGHT

ONE by one lights of a skyscraper fling their checker-
ing cross work on the velvet gown of night.
I believe the skyscraper loves night as a woman and
brings her playthings she asks for, brings her a
velvet gown,
And loves the white of her shoulders hidden under
the dark feel of it all.

The masonry of steel looks to the night for somebody
it loves,
He is a little dizzy and almost dances . . . waiting
. . . dark . . .

NEVER BORN

THE time has gone by.
The child is dead.
The child was never even born.
Why go on? Why so much as begin?
How can we turn the clock back now
And not laugh at each other
As ashes laugh at ashes?

THIN STRIPS

In a jeweler's shop I saw a man beating
out thin sheets of gold.   I heard a woman
laugh many years ago.

Under a peach tree I saw petals scattered
. . torn strips of a bride's dress.   I heard
a woman laugh many years ago.

FIVE CENT BALLOONS

Pietro has twenty red and blue balloons on a string.
They flutter and dance pulling Pietro's arm.
A nickel apiece is what they sell for.

Wishing children tag Pietro's heels.

He sells out and goes the streets alone.

MY PEOPLE

My people are gray,
    pigeon gray, dawn gray, storm gray.
I call them beautiful,
    and I wonder where they are going.

SWIRL

A swirl in the air where your head was once, here.
You walked under this tree, spoke to a moon for me
I might almost stand here and believe you alive.

WISTFUL

WISHES left on your lips
The mark of their wings.
Regrets fly kites in your eyes.

BASKET

SPEAK, sir, and be wise.
Speak choosing your words, sir,
    like an old woman over a bushel
    of apples.

FIRE PAGES

I WILL read ashes for you, if you ask me.
I will look in the fire and tell you from the gray lashes
And out of the red and black tongues and stripes,
I will tell how fire comes
And how fire runs far as the sea.

FINISH

DEATH comes once, let it be easy.
Ring one bell for me once, let it go at that.
Or ring no bell at all, better yet.

Sing one song if I die.
Sing John Brown's Body or Shout All Over God's
    Heaven.
Or sing nothing at all, better yet.

Death comes once, let it be easy.

FOR YOU

THE peace of great doors be for you.
Wait at the knobs, at the panel oblongs.
Wait for the great hinges.

The peace of great churches be for you,
Where the players of loft pipe organs
Practice old lovely fragments, alone.

The peace of great books be for you,
Stains of pressed clover leaves on pages,
Bleach of the light of years held in leather.

The peace of great prairies be for you.
Listen among windplayers in cornfields,
The wind learning over its oldest music.

The peace of great seas be for you.
Wait on a hook of land, a rock footing
For you, wait in the salt wash.

The peace of great mountains be for you,
The sleep and the eyesight of eagles,
Sheet mist shadows and the long look across.

The peace of great hearts be for you,
Valves of the blood of the sun,
Pumps of the strongest wants we cry.

The peace of great silhouettes be for you,
Shadow dancers alive in your blood now,
Alive and crying, " Let us out, let us out."

The peace of great changes be for you.
Whisper, Oh beginners in the hills.
Tumble, Oh cubs—to-morrow belongs to you.

The peace of great loves be for you.
Rain, soak these roots; wind, shatter the dry rot.
Bars of sunlight, grips of the earth, hug these.

The peace of great ghosts be for you,
Phantoms of night-gray eyes, ready to go
To the fog-star dumps, to the fire-white doors.

Yes, the peace of great phantoms be for you,
Phantom iron men, mothers of bronze,
Keepers of the lean clean breeds.

SLABS
OF THE SUNBURNT WEST

SLABS OF THE SUNBURNT WEST

THE WINDY CITY	3
WASHINGTON MONUMENT BY NIGHT	18
AND SO TO-DAY	20
BLACK HORIZONS	28
SEA SLANT	29
UPSTREAM	30
FOUR STEICHEN PRINTS	31
FINS	32
BEAT, OLD HEART	33
MOON RIDERS	34
AT THE GATES OF TOMBS	37
HAZARDOUS OCCUPATIONS	39
PROPS	40
GYPSY MOTHER	41
GOLD MUD	43
CROSSING THE PACES	45
COUPLES	46
CALIGARI	47
FEATHER LIGHTS	48
PEARL HORIZONS	49
HOOF DUSK	50
HARSK, HARSK	51
BRANCUSI	53
AMBASSADORS OF GRIEF	55
WITHOUT THE CANE AND THE DERBY	56
THE RAKEOFF AND THE GETAWAY	60
TWO HUMPTIES	62
IMPROVED FARM LAND	63
HELL ON THE WABASH	64
THIS—FOR THE MOON—YES?	65
PRIMER LESSON	66
SLABS OF THE SUNBURNT WEST	67

THE WINDY CITY

THE lean hands of wagon men
put out pointing fingers here,
picked this crossway, put it on a map,
set up their sawbucks, fixed their shotguns,
found a hitching place for the pony express,
made a hitching place for the iron horse,
the one-eyed horse with the fire-spit head,
found a homelike spot and said, " Make a home,"
saw this corner with a mesh of rails, shuttling
    people, shunting cars, shaping the junk of
    the earth to a new city.

The hands of men took hold and tugged
And the breaths of men went into the junk
And the junk stood up into skyscrapers and asked:
Who am I? Am I a city? And if I am what is my name?
And once while the time whistles blew and blew again
The men answered: Long ago we gave you a name,
Long ago we laughed and said: You? Your name is
    Chicago.

Early the red men gave a name to a river,
    the place of the skunk,
    the river of the wild onion smell,
    Shee-caw-go.

Out of the payday songs of steam shovels,
Out of the wages of structural iron rivets,
The living lighted skyscrapers tell it now as a name,
Tell it across miles of sea blue water, gray blue land:
I am Chicago, I am a name given out by the breaths of
     working men, laughing men, a child, a belonging.

So between the Great Lakes,
The Grand De Tour, and the Grand Prairie,
The living lighted skyscrapers stand,
Spotting the blue dusk with checkers of yellow,
     streamers of smoke and silver,
     parallelograms of night-gray watchmen,
Singing a soft moaning song: I am a child, a belonging.

2

How should the wind songs of a windy city go?
Singing in a high wind the dirty chatter gets blown
     away on the wind—the clean shovel,
               the clean pickax,
               lasts.

It is easy for a child to get breakfast and pack off
     to school with a pair of roller skates,
     buns for lunch, and a geography.
Riding through a tunnel under a river running backward,
     to school to listen . . . how the Pottawattamies . . .
     and the Blackhawks . . . ran on moccasins . . .
     between Kaskaskia, Peoria, Kankakee, and Chicago.

It is easy to sit listening to a boy babbling
    of the Pottawattamie moccasins in Illinois,
    how now the roofs and smokestacks cover miles
    where the deerfoot left its writing
    and the foxpaw put its initials
    in the snow . . . for the early moccasins . . . to
        read.

It is easy for the respectable taxpayers to sit in the
    street cars and read the papers, faces of burglars,
    the prison escapes, the hunger strikes, the cost of
    living, the price of dying, the shop gate battles of
    strikers and strikebreakers, the strikers killing
    scabs and the police killing strikers—the strongest,
    the strongest, always the strongest.

It is easy to listen to the haberdasher customers hand
    each other their easy chatter—it is easy to die
    alive—to register a living thumbprint and be dead
    from the neck up.
And there are sidewalks polished with the footfalls of
    undertakers' stiffs, greased mannikins, wearing up-to-
    the-minute sox, lifting heels across doorsills,
    shoving their faces ahead of them—dead from the
    neck up—proud of their sox—their sox are the last
    word—dead from the neck up—it is easy.

3

Lash yourself to the bastion of a bridge
and listen while the black cataracts of people go by,
　　　　baggage, bundles, balloons,
　　　　listen while they jazz the classics:

　　　" Since when did you kiss yourself in
　　　　And who do you think you are?
　　　　Come across, kick in, loosen up.
　　　　Where do you get that chatter? "

　　　" Beat up the short change artists.
　　　　They never did nothin' for you.
　　　　How do you get that way?
　　　　Tell me and I'll tell the world.
　　　　I'll say so, I'll say it is."

　　　" You're trying to crab my act.
　　　　You poor fish, you mackerel,
　　　　You ain't got the sense God
　　　　Gave an oyster—it's raining—
　　　　What you want is an umbrella."

　　　　" Hush baby—
　　　I don't know a thing.
　　　I don't know a thing.
　　　　Hush baby."

　　　　" Hush baby,
　　　It ain't how old you are,

It's how old you look.
It ain't what you got,
It's what you can get away with."

    " Bring home the bacon.
Put it over, shoot it across.
    Send 'em to the cleaners.
What we want is results, re-sults
    And damn the consequences.
            Sh . . . sh. . . .
You can fix anything
If you got the right fixers."

" Kid each other, you cheap skates.
    Tell each other you're all to the mustard—
    You're the gravy."

    " Tell 'em, honey.
Ain't it the truth, sweetheart?
    Watch your step.
    You said it.
    You said a mouthful.
We're all a lot of damn fourflushers."

    " Hush baby!
    Shoot it,
    Shoot it all!
    Coo coo, coo coo "—
This is one song of Chicago.

4

It is easy to come here a stranger and show the whole
    works, write a book, fix it all up—it is easy to come
    and go away a muddle-headed pig, a bum and a
    bag of wind.

Go to it and remember this city fished from its
        depths a text: " independent as a hog on ice."
Venice is a dream of soft waters, Vienna and Bagdad
        recollections of dark spears and wild turbans; Paris
        is a thought in Monet gray on scabbards, fabrics,
        façades; London is a fact in a fog filled with the
        moaning of transatlantic whistles; Berlin sits amid
        white scrubbed quadrangles and torn arithmetics and
        testaments; Moscow brandishes a flag and repeats a
        dance figure of a man who walks like a bear.
Chicago fished from its depths a text: Independent
        as a hog on ice.

5

Forgive us if the monotonous houses go mile on mile
Along monotonous streets out to the prairies—
If the faces of the houses mumble hard words
At the streets—and the street voices only say:
" Dust and a bitter wind shall come."

Forgive us if the lumber porches and doorsteps
Snarl at each other—
And the brick chimneys cough in a close-up of
Each other's faces—
And the ramshackle stairways watch each other
As thieves watch—
And dooryard lilacs near a malleable iron works
Long ago languished
In a short whispering purple.

And if the alley ash cans
Tell the garbage wagon drivers
The children play the alley is Heaven
And the streets of Heaven shine
With a grand dazzle of stones of gold
And there are no policemen in Heaven—
Let the rag-tags have it their way.

And if the geraniums
In the tin cans of the window sills
Ask questions not worth answering—
And if a boy and a girl hunt the sun
With a sieve for sifting smoke—
Let it pass—let the answer be—
" Dust and a bitter wind shall come."

Forgive us if the jazz timebeats
Of these clumsy mass shadows
Moan in saxophone undertones,

And the footsteps of the jungle,
The fang cry, the rip claw hiss,
The sneak-up and the still watch,
The slant of the slit eyes waiting—
If these bother respectable people
  with the right crimp in their napkins
  reading breakfast menu cards—
  forgive us—let it pass—let be.

If cripples sit on their stumps
And joke with the newsies bawling,
" Many lives lost! many lives lost!
Ter-ri-ble ac-ci-dent! many lives lost! "—
If again twelve men let a woman go,
" He done me wrong; I shot him "—
Or the blood of a child's head
Spatters on the hub of a motor truck—
Or a 44-gat cracks and lets the skylights
Into one more bank messenger—
Or if boys steal coal in a railroad yard
And run with humped gunnysacks
While a bull picks off one of the kids
And the kid wriggles with an ear in cinders
And a mother comes to carry home
A bundle, a limp bundle,
To have his face washed, for the last time,
Forgive us if it happens—and happens again—
And happens again.

  Forgive the jazz timebeat
  of clumsy mass shadows,

footsteps of the jungle,
the fang cry, the rip claw hiss,
the slant of the slit eyes waiting.

Forgive us if we work so hard
And the muscles bunch clumsy on us
And we never know why we work so hard—
If the big houses with little families
And the little houses with big families
Sneer at each other's bars of misunderstanding;
Pity us when we shackle and kill each other
And believe at first we understand
And later say we wonder why.

Take home the monotonous patter
Of the elevated railroad guard in the rush hours:
"Watch your step. Watch your step. Watch your step."
Or write on a pocket pad what a pauper said
To a patch of purple asters at a whitewashed wall:
"Let every man be his own Jesus—that's enough."

6

The wheelbarrows grin, the shovels and the mortar
    hoist an exploit.
The stone shanks of the Monadnock, the Transportation,
    the People's Gas Building, stand up and scrape
    at the sky.
The wheelbarrows sing, the bevels and the blue prints
    whisper.

The library building named after Crerar, naked
    as a stock farm silo, light as a single eagle
    feather, stripped like an airplane propeller,
    takes a path up.
Two cool new rivets say, " Maybe it is morning,"
    " God knows."

Put the city up; tear the city down;
    put it up again; let us find a city.
Let us remember the little violet-eyed
    man who gave all, praying, " Dig and
    dream, dream and hammer, till your
    city comes."

Every day the people sleep and the city dies;
    every day the people shake loose, awake and
    build the city again.

The city is a tool chest opened every day,
    a time clock punched every morning,
    a shop door, bunkers and overalls
    counting every day.

The city is a balloon and a bubble plaything
    shot to the sky every evening, whistled in
    a ragtime jig down the sunset.

The city is made, forgotten, and made again,
    trucks hauling it away haul it back
    steered by drivers whistling ragtime
    against the sunsets.

Every day the people get up and carry the city,
    carry the bunkers and balloons of the city,
    lift it and put it down.

      " I will die as many times
        as you make me over again,
        says the city to the people,
" I am the woman, the home, the family,
I get breakfast and pay the rent;
I telephone the doctor, the milkman, the undertaker;
      I fix the streets
      for your first and your last ride—
" Come clean with me, come clean or dirty,
I am stone and steel of your sleeping numbers;
      I remember all you forget.
      I will die as many times
      as you make me over again."

Under the foundations,
Over the roofs,
The bevels and the blue prints talk it over.
The wind of the lake shore waits and wanders.
The heave of the shore wind hunches the sand piles.
The winkers of the morning stars count out cities
And forget the numbers.

7

At the white clock-tower
lighted in night purples
over the boulevard link bridge
only the blind get by without acknowledgments.

The passers-by, factory punch-clock numbers,
   hotel girls out for the air, teameoes,
   coal passers, taxi drivers, window washers,
   paperhangers, floorwalkers, bill collectors,
   burglar alarm salesmen, massage students,
   manicure girls, chiropodists, bath rubbers,
   booze runners, hat cleaners, armhole basters,
   delicatessen clerks, shovel stiffs, work plugs—
They all pass over the bridge, they all look up
   at the white clock-tower
   lighted in night purples
   over the boulevard link bridge—
   And sometimes one says, " Well, we hand it to 'em."

Mention proud things, catalogue them.
The jack-knife bridge opening, the ore boats,
   the wheat barges passing through.
Three overland trains arriving the same hour,
   one from Memphis and the cotton belt,
   one from Omaha and the corn belt,
   one from Duluth, the lumberjack and the iron range.
Mention a carload of shorthorns taken off the valleys
   of Wyoming last week, arriving yesterday, knocked in
   the head, stripped, quartered, hung in ice boxes
   to-day, mention the daily melodrama of this hum-
   drum, rhythms of heads, hides, heels, hoofs hung up.

8

It is wisdom to think the people are the city.
It is wisdom to think the city would fall to pieces
   and die and be dust in the wind.

If the people of the city all move away and leave no
    people at all to watch and keep the city.
It is wisdom to think no city stood here at all until
    the working men, the laughing men, came.
It is wisdom to think to-morrow new working men, new
    laughing men, may come and put up a new city—
Living lighted skyscrapers and a night lingo of lanterns
    testify to-morrow shall have its own say-so.

9

Night gathers itself into a ball of dark yarn.
Night loosens the ball and it spreads.
The lookouts from the shores of Lake Michigan
    find night follows day, and ping! ping! across
    sheet gray the boat lights put their signals.
Night lets the dark yarn unravel, Night speaks and
    the yarns change to fog and blue strands.

The lookouts turn to the city.
The canyons swarm with red sand lights
    of the sunset.
The atoms drop and sift, blues cross over,
    yellows plunge.
Mixed light shafts stack their bayonets,
    pledge with crossed handles.
So, when the canyons swarm, it is then the
    lookouts speak
Of the high spots over a street . . . mountain language
Of skyscrapers in dusk, the Railway Exchange,
The People's Gas, the Monadnock, the Transportation,
Gone to the gloaming.

The river turns in a half circle.
The Goose Island bridges curve
    over the river curve.
      Then the river panorama
      performs for the bridge,
      dots . . . lights . . . dots . . . lights,
      sixes and sevens of dots and lights,
      a lingo of lanterns and searchlights,
      circling sprays of gray and yellow.

10

A man came as a witness saying:
" I listened to the Great Lakes
And I listened to the Grand Prairie,
And they had little to say to each other,
A whisper or so in a thousand years.
' Some of the cities are big,' said one.
' And some not so big,' said another.
' And sometimes the cities are all gone,'
Said a black knob bluff to a light green sea."

Winds of the Windy City, come out of the prairie,
    all the way from Medicine Hat.
Come out of the inland sea blue water, come where
    they nickname a city for you.

Corn wind in the fall, come off the black lands,
    come off the whisper of the silk hangers,
    the lap of the flat spear leaves.

Blue water wind in summer, come off the blue miles
    of lake, carry your inland sea blue fingers,
    carry us cool, carry your blue to our homes.

White spring winds, come off the bag wool clouds,
    come off the running melted snow, come white
    as the arms of snow-born children.

Gray fighting winter winds, come along on the tear-
    ing blizzard tails, the snouts of the hungry
    hunting storms, come fighting gray in winter.

Winds of the Windy City,
Winds of corn and sea blue,
Spring wind white and fighting winter gray,
Come home here—they nickname a city for you.

The wind of the lake shore waits and wanders.
The heave of the shore wind hunches the sand piles.
The winkers of the morning stars count out cities
And forget the numbers.

WASHINGTON MONUMENT BY NIGHT

1

THE stone goes straight.
A lean swimmer dives into night sky,
Into half-moon mist.

2

Two trees are coal black.
This is a great white ghost between.
It is cool to look at.
Strong men, strong women, come here.

3

Eight years is a long time
To be fighting all the time.

4

The republic is a dream.
Nothing happens unless first a dream.

5

The wind bit hard at Valley Forge one Christmas.
Soldiers tied rags on their feet.

Red footprints wrote on the snow . . .
. . . and stone shoots into stars here
. . . into half-moon mist to-night.

6

Tongues wrangled dark at a man.
He buttoned his overcoat and stood alone.
In a snowstorm, red hollyberries, thoughts,
    he stood alone.

7

Women said: He is lonely
. . . fighting . . . fighting . . . eight years . . .

8

The name of an iron man goes over the world.
It takes a long time to forget an iron man.

9

. . .   .
. . .   . °

AND SO TO-DAY

AND so to-day—they lay him away—
the boy nobody knows the name of—
the buck private—the unknown soldier—
the doughboy who dug under and died
when they told him to—that's him.

Down Pennsylvania Avenue to-day the riders go,
men and boys riding horses, roses in their teeth,
stems of roses, rose leaf stalks, rose dark leaves—
the line of the green ends in a red rose flash.

Skeleton men and boys riding skeleton horses,
the rib bones shine, the rib bones curve,
shine with savage, elegant curves—
a jawbone runs with a long white slant,
a skull dome runs with a long white arch,
bone triangles click and rattle,
elbows, ankles, white line slants—
shining in the sun, past the White House,
past the Treasury Building, Army and Navy Buildings,
on to the mystic white Capitol Dome—
so they go down Pennsylvania Avenue to-day,
skeleton men and boys riding skeleton horses,
stems of roses in their teeth,

And So To-day 21

rose dark leaves at their white jaw slants—
and a horse laugh question nickers and whinnies,
moans with a whistle out of horse head teeth:
why? who? where?

  (" The big fish—eat the little fish—
     the little fish—eat the shrimps—
     and the shrimps—eat mud."—
     said a cadaverous man—with a black umbrella—
     spotted with white polka dots—with a missing
     ear—with a missing foot and arms—
     with a missing sheath of muscles
      singing to the silver sashes of the sun.)

And so to-day—they lay him away—
the boy nobody knows the name of—
the buck private—the unknown soldier—
the doughboy who dug under and died
when they told him to—that's him.

If he picked himself and said, " I am ready to die,"
if he gave his name and said, " My country, take me,"
then the baskets of roses to-day are for the Boy,
the flowers, the songs, the steamboat whistles,
the proclamations of the honorable orators,
they are all for the Boy—that's him.

If the government of the Republic picked him saying,
" You are wanted, your country takes you "—
if the Republic put a stethoscope to his heart
and looked at his teeth and tested his eyes and said,

" You are a citizen of the Republic and a sound animal
in all parts and functions—the Republic takes you "—
then to-day the baskets of flowers are all for the Republic,
the roses, the songs, the steamboat whistles,
the proclamations of the honorable orators—
they are all for the Republic.

And so to-day—they lay him away—
and an understanding goes—his long sleep shall be
under arms and arches near the Capitol Dome—
there is an authorization—he shall have tomb com-
    panions—
the martyred presidents of the Republic—
the buck private—the unknown soldier—that's him.

The man who was war commander of the armies of the
    Republic
rides down Pennsylvania Avenue—
The man who is peace commander of the armies of the
    Republic
rides down Pennsylvania Avenue—
for the sake of the Boy, for the sake of the Republic.

   (And the hoofs of the skeleton horses
    all drum soft on the asphalt footing—
    so soft is the drumming, so soft the roll call
    of the grinning sergeants calling the roll call—
    so soft is it all—a camera man murmurs, " Moon-
      shine.")

Look—who salutes the coffin—
lays a wreath of remembrance
on the box where a buck private
sleeps a clean dry sleep at last—
look—it is the highest ranking general
of the officers of the armies of the Republic.

   (Among pigeon corners of the Congressional Library
   —they file documents quietly, casually, all in a day's
   work—this human document, the buck private
   nobody knows the name of—they file away in gran-
   ite and steel—with music and roses, salutes, proc-
   lamations of the honorable orators.)

Across the country, between two ocean shore lines,
where cities cling to rail and water routes,
there people and horses stop in their foot tracks,
cars and wagons stop in their wheel tracks—
faces at street crossings shine with a silence
of eggs laid in a row on a pantry shelf—
among the ways and paths of the flow of the Republic
faces come to a standstill, sixty clockticks count—
in the name of the Boy, in the name of the Republic.

   (A million faces a thousand miles from Pennsylvania
   Avenue stay frozen with a look, a clocktick, a
   moment—skeleton riders on skeleton horses—the
   nickering high horse laugh, the whinny and the
   howl up Pennsylvania Avenue: who? why? where?)

(So people far from the asphalt footing of Pennsyl-
vania Avenue look, wonder, mumble—the riding
white-jaw phantoms ride hi-eeee, hi-eeee, hi-yi, hi-yi,
hi-eeee—the proclamations of the honorable orators
mix with the top-sergeants whistling the roll call.)

If when the clockticks counted sixty,
when the heartbeats of the Republic
came to a stop for a minute,
if the Boy had happened to sit up,
happening to sit up as Lazarus sat up, in the story,
then the first shivering language to drip off his mouth
might have come as, " Thank God," or " Am I
    dreaming? "
or " What the hell " or " When do we eat? "
or " Kill 'em, kill 'em, the . . ."
or " Was that . . . a rat . . . ran over my face? "
or " For Christ's sake, gimme water, gimme water,"
or " Blub blub, bloo bloo. . . . . . ."
or any bubbles of shell shock gibberish
from the gashes of No Man's Land.

Maybe some buddy knows,
some sister, mother, sweetheart,
maybe some girl who sat with him once
when a two-horn silver moon
slid on the peak of a house-roof gable,
and promises lived in the air of the night,
when the air was filled with promises,
when any little slip-shoe lovey
could pick a promise out of the air.

" Feed it to 'em,
    they lap it up,
      bull . . . bull . . . bull,"
Said a movie news reel camera man,
Said a Washington newspaper correspondent,
Said a baggage handler lugging a trunk,
Said a two-a-day vaudeville juggler,
Said a hanky-pank selling jumping-jacks.
" Hokum—they lap it up," said the bunch.

And a tall scar-face ball player,
Played out as a ball player,
Made a speech of his own for the hero boy,
Sent an earful of his own to the dead buck private:
    " It's all safe now, buddy,
    Safe when you say yes,
    Safe for the yes-men."

He was a tall scar-face battler
With his face in a newspaper
Reading want ads, reading jokes,
Reading love, murder, politics,
Jumping from jokes back to the want ads,
Reading the want ads first and last,
The letters of the word JOB, " J-O-B,"
Burnt like a shot of bootleg booze
In the bones of his head—
In the wish of his scar-face eyes.

The honorable orators,
Always the honorable orators,
Buttoning the buttons on their prinz alberts,
Pronouncing the syllables " sac-ri-fice,"
Juggling those bitter salt-soaked syllables—
Do they ever gag with hot ashes in their mouths?
Do their tongues ever shrivel with a pain of fire
Across those simple syllables " sac-ri-fice " ?

(There was one orator people far off saw.
He had on a gunnysack shirt over his bones,
And he lifted an elbow socket over his head,
And he lifted a skinny signal finger.
And he had nothing to say, nothing easy—
He mentioned ten million men, mentioned them as having
    gone west, mentioned them as shoving up the daisies.
We could write it all on a postage stamp, what he said.
He said it and quit and faded away,
A gunnysack shirt on his bones.)

        Stars of the night sky,
        did you see that phantom fadeout,
        did you see those phantom riders,
        skeleton riders on skeleton horses,
        stems of roses in their teeth,
        rose leaves red on white-jaw slants,
        grinning along on Pennsylvania Avenue,
        the top-sergeants calling roll calls—
        did their horses nicker a horse laugh?
        did the ghosts of the boney battalions
        move out and on, up the Potomac, over on the Ohio,

and out to the Mississippi, the Missouri, the Red
    River,
and down to the Rio Grande, and on to the Yazoo,
over to the Chattahoochee and up to the Rappa-
    hannock?
did you see 'em, stars of the night sky?

And so to-day—they lay him away—
the boy nobody knows the name of—
they lay him away in granite and steel—
with music and roses—under a flag—
under a sky of promises.

BLACK HORIZONS

BLACK horizons, come up.
Black horizons, kiss me.
That is all; so many lies; killing ɛɔ cheap;
babies so cheap; blood, people, so cheap; and
land high, land dear; a speck of the earth
costs; a suck at the tit of Mother Dirt so
clean and strong, it costs; fences, papers,
sheriffs; fences, laws, guns; and so many
stars and so few hours to dream; such a big
song and so little a footing to stand and
sing; take a look; wars to come; red rivers
to cross.
Black horizons, come up.
Black horizons, kiss me.

SEA   SLANT

On up the sea slant,
On up the horizon,
This ship limps.

The bone of her nose fog-gray,
The heart of her sea-strong,
She came a long way,
She goes a long way.

On up the horizon,
On up the sea-slant,
She limps sea-strong, fog-gray.

She is a green-lit night gray.
She comes and goes in sea fog.
Up the horizon slant she limps.

UPSTREAM

THE strong men keep coming on.
They go down shot, hanged, sick,
    broken.
They live on fighting, singing,
    lucky as plungers.
The strong mothers pulling them
    on . .
The strong mothers pulling them
    from a dark sea, a great prairie,
    a long mountain.
Call hallelujah, call amen, call
    deep thanks.
The strong men keep coming on.

FOUR STEICHEN PRINTS

THE earth, the rock and the oil of the earth, the slippery frozen places of the earth, these are for homes of rainbow bubbles, curves of the circles of a bubble, curves of the arcs of the rainbow prisms—between sun and rock they lift to the sun their foam feather and go.

. .

Throw your neck back, throw it back till the neck muscles shine at the sun, till the falling hair at the scalp is a black cry, till limbs and knee bones form an altar, and a girl's torso over the fire-rock torso shouts hi yi, hi yee, hallelujah.

. .

Goat girl caught in the brambles, deerfoot or fox-head, ankles and hair of feeders of the wind, let all the covering burn, let all stopping a naked plunger from plunging naked, let it all burn in this wind fire, let the fire have it in a fast crunch and a flash.

. .

They threw you into a pot of thorns with a wreath in your hair and bunches of grapes over your head—your hard little buttocks in the thorns—then the black eyes, the white teeth, the nameless muscular flair of you, rippled and twisted in sliding rising scales of laughter, the earth never had a gladder friend; pigs, goats, deer, tawny tough-haired jaguars might understand you.

FINS

PLOW over bars of sea plowing,
the moon by moon work of the sea,
the plowing, sand and rock, must
be done.

Ride over, ride over bars of sea riding,
the sun and the blue riding of the sea—
sit in the saddles and say it, sea riders.

Slant up and go, silver breakers; mix
the high howls of your dancing; shoot
your laugh of rainbow foam tops.

Foam wings, fly; pick the comers, the fin pink,
the belly green, the blue rain sparks, the
white wave spit—fly, you foam wings.

The men of the sea are gone to work; the women
of the sea are off buying new hats, combs, clocks;
it is rust and gold on the roofs of the sea.

BEAT, OLD HEART

Beat, old heart, these are the old bars
All strugglers have beat against.
Beat on these bars like the old sea
Beats on the rocks and beaches.
Beat here like the old winter winds
Beat on the prairies and timbers.
Old grizzlies, eagles, buffalo,
Their paws and beaks register this.
Their hides and heads say it with scars.

MOON RIDERS

I

WHAT have I saved out of a morning?
The earliest of the morning came with moon-mist
And the travel of a moon-spilt purple;
    Bars, horseshoes, Texas longhorns,
    Linked in night silver,
    Linked under leaves in moonlit silver,
    Linked in rags and patches
    Out of the ice houses of the morning moon.
    Yes, this was the earliest—
    Before the cowpunchers on the eastern rims
    Began riding into the sun,
    Riding the roan mustangs of morning,
    Roping the mavericks after the latest stars.
    What have I saved out of a morning?
    Was there a child face I saw once
    Smiling up a stairway of the morning moon?

2

" It is time for work," said a man in the morning.
He opened the faces of the clocks, saw their works,
Saw the wheels oiled and fitted, running smooth.
" It is time to begin a day's work," he said again,
Watching a bull-finch hop on the rain-worn boards

Of a beaten fence counting its bitter winters.
The slinging feet of the bull-finch and the flash
Of its flying feathers as it flipped away
Took his eyes away from the clocks, his flying eyes.
He walked over, stood in front of the clocks again
And said, " I'm sorry; I apologize forty ways."

3

The morning paper lay bundled
Like a spear in a museum
Across the broken sleeping room
Of a moon-sheet spider.
The spinning work of the morning spider's feet
Left off where the morning paper's pages lay
In the shine of the web in the summer dew grass.
The man opened the morning paper, saw the first page,
The back page, the inside pages, the editorials,
Saw the world go by, eating, stealing, fighting,
Saw the headlines, date lines, funnies, ads,
The marching movies of the workmen going to work,
the workmen striking,
The workmen asking jobs—five million pairs of eyes look
for a boss and say, " Take *me*,"
People eating with too much to eat, people eating with
nothing in sight to eat to-morrow, eating as though
eating belongs where people belong.

" Hustle, you hustlers, while the hustling's good,"
Said the man, turning the morning paper's pages,
Turning among headlines, date lines, funnies, ads.

" Hustlers carrying the banner," said the man
Dropping the paper and beginning to hunt the city,
Hunting the alleys, boulevards, back-door by-ways,
Hunting till he found a blind horse dying alone,
Telling the horse, " Two legs or four legs—it's all the
    same with a work plug."

A hayfield mist of evening saw him
Watching moon riders lose the moon
For new shooting stars—he asked,
" Christ, what have I saved out of a morning? "
He called up a stairway of the morning moon
And he remembered a child face smiling up that same
    stairway.

AT THE GATES OF TOMBS

CIVILIZATIONS are set up and knocked down
the same as pins in a bowling alley.

Civilizations get into the garbage wagons
and are hauled away the same as potato
peelings or any pot scrapings.

Civilizations, all the work of the artists,
inventors, dreamers of work and genius,
go to the dumps one by one.

Be silent about it; since at the gates of tombs
silence is a gift, be silent; since at the epitaphs
written in the air, since at the swan songs hung in
the air, silence is a gift, be silent; forget it.

If any fool, babbler, gabby mouth, stand up and say:
Let us make a civilization where the sacred and
beautiful things of toil and genius shall last—

If any such noisy gazook stands up and makes himself
heard—put him out—tie a can on him—lock him up
in Leavenworth—shackle him in the Atlanta hoosegow
—let him eat from the tin dishes at Sing Sing—
slew him in as a lifer at San Quentin.

It is the law; as a civilization dies and goes down
to eat ashes along with all other dead civilizations
—it is the law all dirty wild dreamers die first—
gag 'em, lock 'em up, get 'em bumped off.

And since at the gates of tombs silence is a gift,
be silent about it, yes, be silent—forget it.

HAZARDOUS OCCUPATIONS

Jugglers keep six bottles in the air.
Club swingers toss up six and eight.
The knife throwers miss each other's
      ears by a hair and the steel quivers
      in the target wood.
The trapeze battlers do a back-and-forth
      high in the air with a girl's feet
      and ankles upside down.
So they earn a living—till they miss
      once, twice, even three times.
So they live on hate and love as gypsies
      live in satin skins and shiny eyes.
In their graves do the elbows jostle once
      in a blue moon—and wriggle to throw
      a kiss answering a dreamed-of applause?
Do the bones repeat: It's a *good* act—
      we got a *good* hand. . . . ?

PROPS

1

Roll open this rug; a minx is
in it; see her toe wiggling;
roll open the rug; she is a
runaway; or somebody is trying
to steal her; here she is;
here's your minx; how can we
have a play unless we have
this minx?

2

The child goes out in the storm
stage thunder; " erring daughter,
never darken this door-sill again ";
the tender parents speak their curse;
the child puts a few knick-knacks in
a handkerchief; and the child goes;
the door closes and the child goes;
she is out now, in the storm on the
stage, out forever; snow, you son-of-a-gun,
snow, turn on the snow.

GYPSY MOTHER

In a hole-in-a-wall on Halsted Street sits a gypsy
    woman,
In a garish gas-lit rendezvous, in a humpback higgling
    hole-in-a-wall.

The left hand is a tattler; stars and oaths and alphabets
Commit themselves and tell happenings gone, happenings
    to come, pathways of honest people, hypocrites.

" Long pointed fingers mean imagination; a star on the
    third finger says a black shadow walks near."
Cross the gypsy's hand with fifty cents and she takes
    your left hand and reads how you shall be happy in
    love, or not, and whether you die rich, or not.
Signs outside the hole-in-a-wall say so, misspell the
    promises, scrawl the superior gypsy mysteries.

A red shawl on her shoulders falls with a fringe hem to
    a green skirt;
Chains of yellow beads sweep from her neck to her tawny
    hands.
Fifty springtimes must have kissed her mouth holding a
    calabash pipe.
She pulls slow contemplative puffs of smoke; she is a
    shape for ghosts of contemplation to sit around and

ask why something cheap as happiness is here and
more besides, chapped lips, rough eyes, red shawl.
She is thinking about somebody and something the same
as Whistler's mother sat and thought about some-
body and something.

In a hole-in-a-wall on Halsted Street are stars, oaths,
alphabets.

GOLD MUD

(For R. F.)

THE pot of gold at the rainbow end
        is a pot of mud, gold mud,
        slippery shining mud.

Pour it on your hair and you will
        have a golden hair.
Pour it on your cat and you will
        have a golden cat.
Pour it on your clock and you will
        have a golden clock.

Pour it on a dead man's thumb and
        you will have a golden thumb
        to bring you bad dreams.
Pour it on a dead woman's ear and
        you will have a golden ear
        to tell hard luck stories to.
Pour it on a horse chestnut and you
        will have a golden buckeye
        changing your luck.

Gold Mud

Pour it in the shape of a holy cross,
    fasten it on my shirt for me to wear
    and I will have a keepsake.
I will touch it and say a prayer for you.

CROSSING THE PACES

THE Sioux sat around their wigwam fires
in winter with some papooses hung up
and some laid down.
And the Sioux had a saying, " Love grows
like hair on a black bear's skin."

The Arabians spill this: The first gray
hair is a challenge of death.
A Polish blacksmith: A good black-
smith is not afraid of smoke.
And a Scandinavian warns: The world was born
in fire and he who is fire himself will be
at home anywhere on earth.
So a stranger told his children: You are
strangers—and warned them:

Bob your hair; or let it grow long;
Be a company, a party, a picnic;
Be alone, a nut, a potato, an orange blossom,
    a keg of nails; if you get lost try a
    want ad; if night comes try a long sleep.

COUPLES

Six miasmic women in green
danced an absinthe dance
hissing oaths of laughter
at six men they cheated.

Six miasmic men did the same
for six women they cheated.

It was a stand-off
in oaths of laughter hissed;

The dirt is hard where they danced.
The pads of their feet made a floor.

The weeds wear moon mist mourning veils.
The weeds come high as six little crosses,
  One little cross for each couple.

CALIGARI

Mannikins, we command you.
Stand up with your white beautiful skulls.
Stand up with your moaning sockets.
Dance your stiff limping dances.
We handle you with spic and span gloves.
We tell you when and how
And how much.

FEATHER LIGHTS

MACABRE and golden the moon opened a slant of light.

A triangle for an oriole to stand and sing, " Take me home."

A layer of thin white gold feathers for a child queen of gypsies.

So the moon opened a slant of light and let it go.

So the lonesome dogs, the fog moon, the pearl mist, came back.

PEARL HORIZONS

UNDER a prairie fog moon
in a circle of pearl mist horizons,
a few lonesome dogs scraping thongs,
midnight is lonely; the fog moon midnight
takes up again its even smooth November.

Memories: you can flick me and sting me.
Memories, you can hold me even and smooth.

A circle of pearl mist horizons
is not a woman to be walked up to and kissed,
nor a child to be taken and held for a good-night,
nor any old coffee-drinking pal to be smiled at in
        the eyes and left with a grip and a handshake.

Pearl memories in the mist circling the horizon,
flick me, sting me, hold me even and smooth.

HOOF DUSK

THE dusk of this box wood
is leather gold, buckskin gold,
and the hoofs of a dusk goat
leave their heel marks on it.

The cover of this wooden box
is a last-of-the-sunset red,
a red with a sandman sand
fixed in evening siftings—
late evening sands are here.

The gold of old clocks,
forgotten in garrets,
hidden out between battles
of long wars and short wars,
the smoldering ember gold
of old clocks found again—
here is the small smoke fadeout
of their slow loitering.

Feel me with your fingers,
measure me in fire and wind:
maybe I am buckskin gold, old clock gold,
late evening sunset sand—
                    Let go
                    and loiter
                    in the smoke fadeout.

HARSK, HARSK

1

Harsk, harsk, the wind blows to-night.
What a night for a baby to come into the world!
What a night for a melodrama baby to come
    And the father wondering
    And the mother wondering
What the years will bring on their stork feet
Till a year when this very baby might be saying
On some storm night when a melodrama baby is born:
      " What a night
       for a baby
       to come into the world!! "
Harsk, harsk, the wind blows to-night.

2

It is five months off.
Knit, stitch, and hemstitch.
Sheets, bags, towels, these are the offerings.
When he is older—or she is a big girl—
There may be flowers or ribbons or money
For birthday offerings. Now, however,
We must remember it is a naked stranger
Coming to us, and the sheath of the arrival

Is so soft we must be ready, and soft too.
Knit, stitch, hemstitch, it is only five months.

3

It would be easy to pick a lucky star for this baby
If a choice of two stars lay before our eyes,
One a pearl gold star and one pearl silver,
And the offer of a chance to pick a lucky star.

4

When the high hour comes
Let there be a light flurry of snow,
A little zigzag of white spots
  Against the gray roofs.
The snow-born all understand this as a luck-wish.

BRANCUSI

BRANCUSI is a galoot; he saves tickets to take him no-where; a galoot with his baggage ready and no time table; ah yes, Brancusi is a galoot; he understands birds and skulls so well, he knows the hang of the hair of the coils and plaits on a woman's head, he knows them so far back he knows where they came from and where they are going; he is fathoming down for the secrets of the first and the oldest makers of shapes.

Let us speak with loose mouths to-day not at all about Brancusi because he has hardly started nor is hardly able to say the name of the place he wants to go when he has time and is ready to start; O Brancusi, keeping hardwood planks around your doorsteps in the sun waiting for the hardwood to be harder for your hard hands to handle, you Brancusi with your chisels and hammers, birds going to cones, skulls going to eggs—how the hope hugs your heart you will find one cone, one egg, so hard when the earth turns mist there among the last to go will be a cone, an egg.

Brancusi, you will not put a want ad in the papers telling God it will be to his advantage to come around and see you; you will not grow gabby and spill God earfuls of prayers; you will not get fresh and familiar as if God is a next-door neighbor and you have counted His shirts on a clothes line; you will go stammering, stuttering and mumbling or you will be silent as a mouse in a church garret when the pipe organ is pouring ocean waves on the sunlit rocks of ocean shores; if God is saving a corner for any battling bag of bones, there will be one for you, there will be one for you, Brancusi.

AMBASSADORS OF GRIEF

THERE was a little fliv of a woman loved one man and lost out. And she took up with another and it was a blank again. And she cried to God the whole layout was a fake and a frame-up. And when she took up with Number Three she found the fires burnt out, the love power, gone. And she wrote a letter to God and dropped it in a mail-box. The letter said:

O God, ain't there some way you can fix it up so the little flivs of women, ready to throw themselves in front of railroad trains for men they love, can have a chance? I guessed the wrong keys, I battered on the wrong panels, I picked the wrong roads. O God, ain't there no way to guess again and start all over back where I had the keys in my hands, back where the roads all came together and I had my pick?

And the letter went to Washington, D. C., dumped into a dump where all letters go addressed to God—and no house number.

WITHOUT THE CANE AND THE DERBY

(For C. C.)

THE woman had done him wrong.
Either that . . . or the woman was clean as a white rose
    in the morning gauze of dew.
It was either one or the other or it was the two things,
    right and wrong, woven together like two braids of
    a woman's head of hair hanging down woven together.

The room is dark. The door opens. It is Charlie playing
    for his friends after dinner, " the marvelous urchin,
    the little genius of the screen," (chatter it like a
    monkey's running laughter cry.)
No . . . it is not Charlie . . . it is somebody else. It
    is a man, gray shirt, bandana, dark face. A candle
    in his left hand throws a slant of light on the dark
    face. The door closes slow. The right hand leaves
    the door knob slow.

He looks at something. What is it? A white sheet on a
    table. He takes two long soft steps. He runs the
    candle light around a hump in the sheet. He lifts the
    sheet slow, sad like.
A woman's head of hair shows, a woman's white face. He
    takes the head between his hands and looks long at

it. His fingers trickle under the sheet, snap loose
something, bring out fingers full of a pearl necklace.
He covers the face and the head of hair with the white
sheet. He takes a step toward the door. The necklace
slips into his pocket off the fingers of his right hand.
His left hand lifts the candle for a good-by look.

Knock, knock, knock. A knocking the same as the time
of the human heartbeat.
Knock, knock, knock, first louder, then lower. Knock,
knock, knock, the same as the time of the human
heartbeat.
He sets the candle on the floor . . . leaps to the white
sheet . . . rips it back . . . has his fingers at the
neck, his thumbs at the throat, and does three slow
fierce motions of strangling.
The knocking stops. All is quiet. He covers the face and
the head of hair with the white sheet, steps back,
picks up the candle and listens.
Knock, knock, knock, a knocking the same as the time
of the human heartbeat.
Knock, knock, knock, first louder, then lower. Knock,
knock, knock, the same as the time of the human
heartbeat.
Again the candle to the floor, the leap, the slow fierce
motions of strangling, the cover-up of the face and
the head of hair, the step back, the listening.
And again the knock, knock, knock . . . louder . . .
lower . . . to the time of the human heartbeat.
Once more the motions of strangling . . .then . . .
nothing at all . . . nothing at all . . . no more

knocking . . . no knocking at all . . . no knocking
at all . . . in the time of the human heartbeat.

He stands at the door . . . peace, peace, peace every-
where only in the man's face so dark and his eyes
so lighted up with many lights, no peace at all, no
peace at all.

So he stands at the door, his right hand on the door knob,
the candle slants of light fall and flicker from his
face to the straight white sheet changing gray against
shadows.

So there is peace everywhere . . . no more knocking . . .
no knocking at all to the time of the human heart-
beat . . . so he stands at the door and his right hand
on the door knob.

And there is peace everywhere . . . only the man's face
is a red gray plaster of storm in the center of peace
. . . so he stands with a candle at the door . . . so
he stands with a red gray face.

After he steps out the door closes; the door, the door
knob, the table, the white sheet, there is nothing at
all; the owners are shadows; the owners are gone;
not even a knocking; not even a knock, knock,
knock . . . louder, lower, in the time of the human
heartbeat.

The lights are snapped on. Charlie, "the marvelous
urchin, the little genius of the screen" (chatter it
with a running monkey's laughter cry) Charlie is
laughing a laugh the whole world knows.

The room is full of cream yellow lights. Charlie is
   laughing . . . louder . . . lower . . .
And again the heartbeats laugh . . . the human heart-
   beats laugh. . . .

THE RAKEOFF AND THE GETAWAY

" SHALL we come back? " the gamblers asked.
" If you want to, if you feel that way," the answer.

And they must have wanted to,
they must have felt that way;
for they came back,
hats pulled down over their eyes
as though the rain or the policemen
or the shadows of a sneaking scar-face Nemesis
followed their tracks and hunted them down.

" What was the clean-up?   Let's see the rakeoff,"
somebody asked them, looking into their eyes
far under the pulled-down hat rims;
and their eyes had only the laugh of the rain in them,
lights of escape from a sneaking scar-face Nemesis
hunting their tracks, hunting them down.

Anvils, pincers, mosquitoes, anguish, raspberries,
steaks and gravy, remorse, ragtime, slang,
a woman's looking glass to be held in the hand
for looking at the face and the face make-up,
blackwing birds fitted onto slits
of the sunsets they were flying into,
bitter green waters, clear running waters,

standing pools ringing the changes
of all the triangles of the equinoxes of the sky,
  and a woman's slipper
  with a tarnished buckle,
  a tarnished Chinese silver buckle.

The gamblers snatched their hats off babbling,
" Some layout—take your pick, kid."

And their eyes had yet in them
the laugh of the rain
and the lights of their getaway
from a sneaking scar-face Nemesis.

TWO HUMPTIES

THEY tried to hand it to us on a platter,
Us hit in the eyes with marconigrams from moon
    dancers—
And the bubble busted, went flooey, on a thumb touch.

  So this time again, Humpty,
We cork our laughs behind solemn phizzogs,
Sweep the floor with the rim of our hats
And say good-a-by and good-a-by, just like that.

    To-morrow maybe they will be hit
    In the eyes with marconigrams
    From moon dancers.
Good-a-by, our hats and all of us say good-a-by.

IMPROVED FARM LAND

TALL timber stood here once, here on a corn belt farm
along the Monon.

Here the roots of a half mile of trees dug their runners
deep in the loam for a grip and a hold against wind
storms.

Then the axmen came and the chips flew to the zing of
steel and handle—the lank railsplitters cut the big
ones first, the beeches and the oaks, then the brush.

Dynamite, wagons and horses took the stumps—the
plows sunk their teeth in—now it is first class corn
land—improved property—and the hogs grunt over
the fodder crops.

It would come hard now for this half mile of improved
farm land along the Monon corn belt, on a piece of
Grand Prairie, to remember once it had a great
singing family of trees.

HELL ON THE WABASH

WHEN country fiddlers held a convention in Danville, the big money went to a barn dance artist who played Turkey in the Straw, with variations.

They asked him the name of the piece calling it a humdinger and he answered, " I call it ' Hell On The Wabash.' "

The two next best were The Speckled Hen, and Sweet Potatoes Grow in Sandy Land, with variations.

THIS—FOR THE MOON—YES?

THIS is a good book?   Yes?
Throw it at the moon.
Stand on the ball of your right foot
And come to the lunge of a center fielder
Straddling in a throw for the home plate,
Let her go—spang—this book for the moon
    —yes?
And then—other books, good books, even the
    best books—shoot 'em with a long twist
    at the moon—yes?

PRIMER LESSON

Look out how you use proud words.
When you let proud words go, it is
    not easy to call them back.
They wear long boots, hard boots; they
    walk off proud; they can't hear you
    calling—
Look out how you use proud words.

SLABS OF THE SUNBURNT WEST

1

INTO the night, into the blanket of night,
Into the night rain gods, the night luck gods,
Overland goes the overland passenger train.

   Stand up, sandstone slabs of red,
Tell the overland passengers who burnt you.

Tell 'em how the jacks and screws loosened you.
Tell 'em who shook you by the heels and stood you on
     your heads,
Who put the slow pink of sunset mist on your faces.

Panels of the cold gray open night,
Gates of the Great American Desert,
    Skies keeping the prayers of the wagon men,
    The riders with picks, shovels and guns,
On the old trail, the Santa Fe trail, the Raton pass
Panels, skies, gates, listen to-night while we send up our
     prayers on the Santa Fe trail.

     (A colossal bastard frog
     squats in stone.
     Once he squawked.
     Then he was frozen and
     shut up forever.)

Into the night the overland passenger train,
Slabs of sandstone red sink to the sunset red,
Blankets of night cover 'em up.
Night rain gods, night luck gods, are looking on.

March on, processions.
Tie your hat to the saddle and ride, O Rider.
Let your ponies drag their navels in the sand.
Go hungry; leave your bones in the desert sand.
When the desert takes you the wind is clean.
The winds say so on a noisy night.

> The fingerbone of a man
> lay next to the handle of a frying pan
> and the footbone of a horse.
" Clean, we are clean," the winds whimper on a noisy
night.

Into the night the overland passenger train,
And the engineer with an eye for signal lights,
And the porters making up berths for passengers,
And the boys in the diner locking the ice-box—
And six men with cigars in the buffet car mention
" civilization," " history," " God."

Into the blanket of night goes the overland train,
Into the black of the night the processions march,
> The ghost of a pony goes by,
> A hat tied to the saddle,
> The wagon tongue of a prairie schooner
> And the handle of a Forty-niner's pickax

Do a shiver dance in the desert dust,
In the coyote gray of the alkali dust.
And—six men with cigars in the buffet car mention
"civilization," "history," "God."

Sleep, O wonderful hungry people.
Take a shut-eye, take a long old snooze,
    and be good to yourselves;
Into the night the overland passenger train
And the sleepers cleared for a morning sun
    and the Grand Canyon of Arizona.

2

A bluejay blue
and a gray mouse gray
ran up the canyon walls.

A rider came to the rim
Of a slash and a gap of desert dirt—
A long-legged long-headed rider
On a blunt and a blurry jackass—
Riding and asking, "How come? How come?"

And the long-legged long-headed rider said:
"Between two ears of a blurry jackass
I see ten miles of auburn, gold and purple—
I see doors open over doorsills
And always another door and a doorsill.
Cheat my eyes, fill me with the float
Of your dream, you auburn, gold, and purple.

Cheat me, blow me off my pins onto footless floors.
Let me put footsteps in an airpath.
Cheat me with footprints on auburn, gold, purple
Out to the last violet shimmer of the float
Of the dream—and I will come straddling a jackass,
Singing a song and letting out hallelujahs
To the door sill of the last footprint."

And the man took a stub lead pencil
And made a long memo in shorthand
On the two blurry jackass ears:—

" God sits with long whiskers in the sky."
I said it when I was a boy.
I said it because long-whiskered men
Put it in my head to say it.
      They lied . . . about you . . . God . . .
      They lied. . . .

The other side of the five doors
and doorsills put in my house—
how many hinges, panels, doorknobs,
how many locks and lintels,
put on the doors and doorsills
winding and wild between
the first and the last doorsill of all?

" Out of the footprints on ten miles
of auburn, gold and purple—an old song comes:
These bones shall rise again,
Yes, children, these bones shall rise.

" Yonder past my five doors
are fifty million doors, maybe,
stars with knobs and locks and lintels,
stars with riders of rockets,
stars with swimmers of fire.

" Cheat my eyes—and I come again—
straddling a jackass—singing a song—
letting out hallelujahs.

" If God is a proud and a cunning Bricklayer,
Or if God is a King in a white gold Heaven,
Or if God is a Boss and a Watchman always watching,
I come riding the old ride of the humiliation,
Straddling a jackass, singing a song,
Letting out hallelujahs.

" Before a ten mile float
of auburn, gold, and purple,
footprints on a sunset airpath haze,
    I ask:
How can I taste with my tongue a tongueless God?
How can I touch with my fingers a fingerless God?
How can I hear with my ears an earless God?
Or smell of a God gone noseless long ago?
Or look on a God who never needs eyes for looking?

" My head is under your foot, God.
My head is a pan of alkali dust
your foot kicked loose—your foot of air
with its steps on the sunset airpath haze.

(A bluejay blue
and a gray mouse gray
ran up the canyon walls.)

" Sitting at the rim of the big gap
at the high lash of the frozen storm line,
I ask why I go on five crutches,
tongues, ears, nostrils—all cripples—
eyes and nose—both cripples—
I ask why these five cripples
limp and squint and gag with me,
why they say with the oldest frozen faces:
    Man is a poor stick and a sad squirt;
    if he is poor he can't dress up;
    if he dresses up he don't know any place to go.

" Away and away on some green moon
a blind blue horse eats white grass
    And the blind blue horse knows more than I do
    because he saw more than I have seen
    and remembered it after he went blind.

" And away and away on some other green moon
is a sea-kept child who lacks a nose I got
and fingers like mine and all I have.
And yet the sea-kept child knows more than
I do and sings secrets alien to me as light
to a nosing mole underground.
I understand this child as a yellow-belly
catfish in China understands peach pickers
at sunrise in September in a Michigan orchard.

" The power and lift of the sea
and the flame of the old earth fires under,
I sift their meanings of sand in my fingers.
I send out five sleepwalkers to find out who I am,
    my name and number, where I came from,
    and where I am going.
They go out, look, listen, wonder, and shoot a fire-white
    rocket across the night sky; the shot and the flare
    of the rocket dies to a whisper; and the night is the
    same as it always was.
They come back, my five sleepwalkers; they have an
    answer for me, they say; they tell me: *Wait*—the
    password all of them heard when the fire-white rocket
    shot across the sky and died to a whisper, the pass-
    word is: *Wait*.

" I sit with five binoculars, amplifiers, spectroscopes
I sit looking through five windows, listening, tasting,
    smelling, touching.
I sit counting five million smoke fogs.
Repeaters, repeaters, come back to my window sills.
Some are pigeons coming to coo and coo and clean their
    tail feathers and look wise at me.
Some are pigeons coming with broken wings to die with
    pain in their eyes on my window sills.

" I walk the high lash of the frozen storm line;
I sit down with my feet in a ten-mile gravel pit.
Here I ask why I am a bag of sea-water fastened
to a frame of bones put walking on land—here I
look at crawlers, crimson, spiders spotted with

purple spots on their heads, flinging silver nets,
two, four, six, against the sun.
Here I look two miles down to the ditch of the sea
and pick a winding ribbon, a river eater, a water
grinder; it is a runner sent to run by a stop-watch,
it is a wrecker on a rush job."

> (A bluejay blue
> and a gray mouse gray
> ran up the canyon walls.)

Battering rams, blind mules, mounted policemen,
trucks hauling caverns of granite, elephants
grappling gorillas in a death strangle, cathedrals,
arenas, platforms, somersaults of telescoped rail-
road train wrecks, exhausted egg heads, piles of
skulls, mountains of empty sockets, mummies of kings
and mobs, memories of work gangs and wrecking crews,
sobs of wind and water storms, all frozen and held
on paths leading on to spirals of new zigzags—

An arm-chair for a one-eyed giant;
two pine trees grow in the left arm of the chair;
a bluejay comes, sits, goes, comes again;
a bluejay shoots and twitters . . out and across . .
tumbled skyscrapers and wrecked battleships,
walls of crucifixions and wedding breakfasts;
ruin, ruin—a brute gnashed, dug, kept on—
kept on and quit: and this is It.

Falling away, the brute is working.
Sheets of white veils cross a woman's face.
An eye socket glooms and wonders.
The brute hangs his head and drags on to the job.
The mother of mist and light and air murmurs: Wait.

The weavers of light weave best in red,
    better in blue.
The weavers of shadows weave at sunset;
      the young black-eyed women run, run, run
      to the night star homes; the old women
      sit weaving for the night rain gods,
      the night luck gods.

Eighteen old giants throw a red gold shadow ball;
they pass it along; hands go up and stop it; they
bat up flies and practice; they begin the game, they
knock it for home runs and two-baggers; the pitcher
put it across in an out- and an in-shoot drop; the
Devil is the Umpire; God is the Umpire; the game
is called on account of darkness.

      A bluejay blue
      and a gray mouse gray
      ran up the canyon walls.

3

Good night; it is scribbled on the panels
of the cold grey open desert.

Good night; on the big sky blanket over the
Santa Fe trail it is woven in the oldest
Indian blanket songs.

Buffers of land, breakers of sea, say it and
say it, over and over, good night, good night.

  Tie your hat to the saddle
  and ride, ride, ride, O Rider.
  Lay your rails and wires
  and ride, ride, ride, O Rider.

  The worn tired stars say
  you shall die early and die dirty.
  The clean cold stars say
  you shall die late and die clean.

  The runaway stars say
  you shall never die at all,
  never at all.

GOOD MORNING,

AMERICA

TO

A. H.

TENTATIVE (FIRST MODEL)
DEFINITIONS OF POETRY

1 *Poetry is a projection across silence of cadences arranged to break that silence with definite intentions of echoes, syllables, wave lengths.*

2 *Poetry is an art practised with the terribly plastic material of human language.*

3 *Poetry is the report of a nuance between two moments, when people say, 'Listen!' and 'Did you see it?' 'Did you hear it? What was it?'*

4 *Poetry is the tracing of the trajectories of a finite sound to the infinite points of its echoes.*

5 *Poetry is a sequence of dots and dashes, spelling depths, crypts, cross-lights, and moon wisps.*

6 *Poetry is a puppet-show, where riders of skyrockets and divers of sea fathoms gossip about the sixth sense and the fourth dimension.*

7 *Poetry is a plan for a slit in the face of a bronze fountain goat and the path of fresh drinking water.*

8 *Poetry is a slipknot tightened around a time-beat of one thought, two thoughts, and a last interweaving thought there is not yet a number for.*

9 *Poetry is an echo asking a shadow dancer to be a partner.*

10 *Poetry is the journal of a sea animal living on land, wanting to fly the air.*

11 *Poetry is a series of explanations of life, fading off into horizons too swift for explanations.*

12 *Poetry is a fossil rock-print of a fin and a wing, with an illegible oath between.*

13 *Poetry is an exhibit of one pendulum connecting with other and unseen pendulums inside and outside the one seen.*

14 *Poetry is a sky dark with a wild-duck migration.*

15 *Poetry is a search for syllables to shoot at the barriers of the unknown and the unknowable.*

16 *Poetry is any page from a sketchbook of outlines of a doorknob with thumb-prints of dust, blood, dreams.*

17 *Poetry is a type-font design for an alphabet of fun, hate, love, death.*

18 *Poetry is the cipher key to the five mystic wishes packed in a hollow silver bullet fed to a flying fish.*

19 *Poetry is a theorem of a yellow-silk handkerchief knotted with riddles, sealed in a balloon tied to the tail of a kite flying in a white wind against a blue sky in spring.*

20 *Poetry is a dance music measuring buck-and-wing follies along with the gravest and stateliest dead-marches.*

21 *Poetry is a sliver of the moon lost in the belly of a golden frog.*

22 *Poetry is a mock of a cry at finding a million dollars and a mock of a laugh at losing it.*

23 *Poetry is the silence and speech between a wet struggling root of a flower and a sunlit blossom of that flower.*

24 *Poetry is the harnessing of the paradox of earth cradling life and then entombing it.*

25 *Poetry is the opening and closing of a door, leaving those who look through to guess about what is seen during a moment.*

26 *Poetry is a fresh morning spider-web telling a story of moonlit hours of weaving and waiting during a night.*

27 *Poetry is a statement of a series of equations, with numbers and symbols changing like the changes of mirrors, pools, skies, the only never-changing sign being the sign of infinity.*

28 *Poetry is a pack-sack of invisible keepsakes.*

29 *Poetry is a section of river-fog and moving boat-lights, delivered between bridges and whistles, so one says, 'Oh!' and another, 'How?'*

30 *Poetry is a kinetic arrangement of static syllables.*

31 *Poetry is the arithmetic of the easiest way and the primrose path, matched up with foam-flanked horses, bloody knuckles, and bones, on the hard ways to the stars.*

32 *Poetry is a shuffling of boxes of illusions buckled with a strap of facts.*

33 *Poetry is an enumeration of birds, bees, babies, butterflies, bugs, bambinos, babayagas, and bipeds, beating their way up bewildering bastions.*

34 *Poetry is a phantom script telling how rainbows are made and why they go away.*

35 *Poetry is the establishment of a metaphorical link between white butterfly-wings and the scraps of torn-up love-letters.*

36 *Poetry is the achievement of the synthesis of hyacinths and biscuits.*

37 *Poetry is a mystic, sensuous mathematics of fire, smoke-stacks, waffles, pansies, people, and purple sunsets.*

38 *Poetry is the capture of a picture, a song, or a flair, in a deliberate prism of words.*

CONTENTS

Tentative (First Model) Definitions of Poetry   PAGE VII

GOOD MORNING, AMERICA

Good Morning, America   3

SPRING GRASS

Spring Grass   31
Moist Moon People   32
Spring Cries   33
Frog Songs   35
Lumber Yard Pools at Sunset   36
Spring Carries Surprises   37
More Country People   38
Spring Wind   39
Crisscross   40
Baby Song of the Four Winds   41
Blossom Themes   42
Small Homes   44

CORN BELT

She Opens the Barn Door Every Morning   47
Milk White Moon, Put the Cows to Sleep   48
Slow Program   49
Field People   50
Sunsets   51
Grassroots   52
Canadians and Pottawattomies   53
Corn and Beans   54

Mockers Go to Kansas in Spring   55
Bird Talk   56
Kansas Lessons   58
Cricket March   59
Summer Grass   60
Nocturn Cabbage   61
Crabapples   62
Poplar and Elm   63
Brown Gold   64
Ripe Corn   65
Auburn   66
Redhaw Rain   68
Without Notice Beforehand   70
Corn Prattlings   72
Haze Gold   73
Winter Gold   74
Maroon with Silver Frost   75
Cornfield Ridge and Stream   76
On a Railroad Right of Way   77
So to Speak   78

VALLEY MIST

Silver Point   81
Mist Marches Across the Valley   82
Methusaleh Saw Many Repeaters   83
Sketch of a Poet   84
Whiffs of the Ohio River at Cincinnati   86
Suburban Sicilian Sketches   88
Flat Waters of the West in Kansas   90
Three Slants at New York   92
Landscape Including Three States of the Union   93
Crossing Ohio When Poppies Bloom in Ashtabula   94

March of the Hungry Mountains   96
Dialogue   97
Smoke Blue   98
Again   100
Even Numbers   102
Chillicothe   103
Splinter   108
Santa Fe Sketches   109

LITTLE ALBUM

New Hampshire Again   119
A Couple   121
Chicago Boy Baby   122
Joke Gold   123
The Old Flagman   124
Iglits and His Wife   125
Medley   126
Implications   128
To the Ghost of John Milton   129
Heavy and Light   130
Early Hours   131
Hungry and Laughing Men   132
Fate   133
Cheap Blue   134
Lavender Lilies   135
Half Way   136
Between Worlds   137
M'Liss and Louie   138

BITTER SUMMER THOUGHTS

Phizzog   143
Bitter Summer Thoughts   144

Bitter Summer Thoughts—No. 3   146
Bitter Summer Thoughts—No. XXII   147
Bars   148
They Ask: Is God, Too, Lonely?   149
Two Nocturns   150
Wanting the Impossible   151
Money, Politics, Love and Glory   152
The Way of the World   153
Useless Words   154
Early Lynching   155
Plunger   156

RAIN WINDS

Rain Winds Blow Doors Open   159
Wind Horses   160
River Moon   161
They Met Young   162
Yellow Evening Star   164
Face   165
Head   166
Explanations of Love   167
Seven Eleven   168
Spray   169
Broken Hearted Soprano   170
Epistle   171
Monkey of Stars   172

GREAT ROOMS

Sea Chest   175
We Have Gone Through Great Rooms Together   176
Love in Labrador   177
Sleep Impression   178
Bug Spots   179

Understandings in Blue   180
Maybe   181
Let Them Ask Your Pardon   182
Striped Cats, Old Men and Proud Stockings   183
Moon Hammock   185
Thimble Islands   186
Clefs   188
The Great Proud Wagon Wheels Go On   189
Tall Timber   190
Proud Torsos   191
To Know Silence Perfectly   192

SKY PIECES

Sky Pieces   195
Lovable Babblers   196
Oomba   197
Seventeen Months   198
Sarah's Letter to Peter   199
Destroyers   200
Two Women and Their Fathers   202
Very Very Important   203
Foolish About Windows   204
Love Letter to Hans Christian Andersen   205
Mysterious Biography   206
Rat Riddles   207
Winter Weather   208
The Dinosaur Bones   209
Unintentional Paint   210
People of the Eaves, I Wish You Good Morning   211
Wedding Postponed   212
Two Women   214
Snatch of Sliphorn Jazz   215

Landscape   216
Different Kinds of Good-by   217
Three Hills Look Different in the Moonshine   218
Proud of Their Rags   219
Broken Sky   220
Hells and Heavens   221
Three Fragments for Fishers of Destiny   222

TIMBER MOON

Timber Moon   225
Flowers Tell Months   226
Landscape   227
Counting   228
Oak Arms   229
Moon-Path   230
There Are Different Gardens   231
Windflower Leaf   232
Little Sketch   233
Butter Colors   234
Webs   235
Peace, Night, Sleep   236
Bundles   237
Man and Dog on an Early Winter Morning   238
Precious Moments   239
October Paint   240
Many Hats   242

GOOD MORNING, AMERICA

GOOD MORNING, AMERICA

1

In the evening there is a sunset sonata comes to the cities.
There is a march of little armies to the dwindling of drums.
The skyscrapers throw their tall lengths of walls into black
      bastions on the red west.
The skyscrapers fasten their perpendicular alphabets far
      across the changing silver triangles of stars and
      streets.

And who made 'em? Who made the skyscrapers?
Man made 'em, the little two-legged joker, Man.
Out of his head, out of his dreaming, scheming skypiece,
Out of proud little diagrams that danced softly in his head—
      Man made the skyscrapers.
With his two hands, with shovels, hammers, wheelbarrows,
      with engines, conveyors, signal whistles, with girders,
      molds, steel, concrete—
Climbing on scaffolds and falsework with blueprints, riding
      the beams and dangling in mid-air to call, Come on,
      boys—
                    Man made the skyscrapers.

When one tall skyscraper is torn down
To make room for a taller one to go up,
Who takes down and puts up those two skyscrapers?
Man . . . the little two-legged joker . . . Man.

2

"There's gold in them hills,"
Said old timers on their wagon seats.
And on the wagons was a scribble:
    Pike's Peak or Bust.

The Rocky Mountains are stacked tall on the skyline.
Sunrise and dawns wash on the skyline every morning.
Sunset feathers of foam float red and fade pink.

    And so,
    Quite so,
Facts are facts, nailed down, fastened to stay.
And facts are feathers, foam, flying phantoms.
Niagara is a fact or a little bluebird cheeping in a flight
    over the Falls—
Chirping to itself: What have we here?
                And how come?

The stone humps of old mountains
Sag and lift in a line to the sky.
The sunsets come with long shadowprints.
The six-cylinder go-getters ask:
    What time is it?
    Who were the Aztecs and the
        Zunis anyhow?
    What do I care about Cahokia?
    Where do we go from here?
    What are the facts?

3

Facts stay fastened; facts are phantom.
An old one-horse plow is a fact.
A new farm tractor is a fact.
Facts stay fastened; facts fly with bird wings.
Blood and sweat are facts, and
The commands of imagination, the looks back and ahead,
The spirals, pivots, landing places, fadeaways,
The signal lights and dark stars of civilizations.

Now the head of a man, his eyes, are facts.
He sees in his head, as in looking glasses,
A cathedral, ship, bridge, railroad—a skyscraper—
And the plans are drawn, the blueprints fixed,
The design and the line, the shape written clear.
So fact moves from fact to fact, weaves, intersects.
Then come more, then come blood and sweat.
Then come pain and death, lifting and groaning,
And a crying out loud, between paydays.
Then the last ghost on the job walks.
The job stands up, the joined stresses of facts,
The cathedral, ship, bridge, railroad—the skyscraper—
Speaks a living hello to the open sky,
Stretches forth as an acknowledgement:
    "The big job is done.
      By God, we made it."
Facts stay fastened; facts fly with phantom bird wings.

4

I have looked over the earth and seen the swarming of dif-
ferent people to a different God—

White men with prayers to a white God, black men with
prayers to a black God, yellow-faces before altars to
a yellow-face God—

Amid burning fires they have pictured God with a naked
skin; amid frozen rocks they have pictured God clothed
and shaggy as a polar bear—

I have met stubs of men broken in the pain and mutilation
of war saying God is forgetful and too far off, too far
away—

I have met people saying they talk with God face to face;
they tell God, hello God and how are you God; they get
familiar with God and hold intimate conversations—

Yet I have met other people saying they are afraid to see
God face to face for they would ask questions even as
God might ask them questions.

I have seen these facts of God and man and anxious earth-
worms hunting for a home.

I have seen the facts of humble bees and scarlet butterflies,
orioles and flickers, goldwing moths and pink lady-
bugs—

I have seen the spotted sunset sky filled with flights and
wings—and I have heard high in the twilight blue the
propellers of man and the evening air mail droning
from Omaha to Chicago, droning across Iowa and
Illinois—

I have said: The prints of many new wings, many fresh flights, many clean propellers, shall be on the sky before we understand God and the work of wings and air.

5

I have seen the figures of heroes set up as memorials, testimonies of fact—

Leif Ericson in a hard, deep-purple bronze, stands as a frozen shadow, lean, with searching eyes, on a hill in Wisconsin overlooking Lake Michigan—

Columbus in bronze is the center of a turmoil of traffic from world ends gathered on Manhattan Island—

Washington stands in marble shaped from life, in the old Romanesque temple on Capitol Hill, in Richmond, Virginia, with an arrogant laughter heard from circling skyscrapers—

Andrew Jackson in bronze on a bronze horse, a rocking horse on its hind legs with forepaws in the air, the tail brandishing, as the General lifts a cockade from his head in salutation to the citizens and soldiers of the Republic—

Ulysses S. Grant, somber and sober, is on a pony high in bronze listening to the endless white horses of Lake Michigan talking to Illinois—

Robert E. Lee, recumbent in white stone, sleeps a bivouac sleep in peace among loved ones of the southern Shenandoah Valley—

Lincoln's memory is kept in a living, arterial highway
      moving across state lines from coast to coast to the
      murmur, Be good to each other, sisters; don't fight,
      brothers.

6

And may we ask—is a flower a fact?
Shall a thin perishable blossom
Mount out of homeland soil
And give the breath of its leaves
For a memorial printed a few days,
For a symbol kept by the bees and the wind?
Shall each state pick its favorite flower
And say, This is Me, Us, this comes from the dirt of the
      earth, the loam, the mulch, this is a home greeting to
      our eyes, these leaves touch our footloose feet, our
      children and our children's children.
The blue cornflower along the railroad tracks in Illinois—
The pink moccasin hiding in the big woods of Minnesota—
The wild prairie rose scrambling along Iowa roads—
Golden poppy of California, giant cactus of Arizona—
Apple blossom of Michigan, Kentucky's trumpet vine—
The rhododendrons of Washington and West Virginia—
The Indian paintbrush of Wyoming, Montana's bitter
      root—
Vital and endless goldenrod crossing Nebraska—
Mariposa lily of Utah, pasque flower of South Dakota—
Ox-eyed daisy of North Carolina, Florida's orange
      blossom—

The magnolia of Louisiana, the Delaware peach blossom—
The silent laughing salutations of the Kansas sunflower—
The old buffalo clover, the marching Texas bluebonnet—
The pine cone and tassel of the lonesome State of Maine—
    Shall these be among our phantom facts?

7

Facts are phantom; facts begin
With a bud, a seed, an egg.

A hero, a hoodlum, a little of both,
A toiling two-faced driven destiny,
Sleeps in the secret traceries of eggs.
If one egg could speak and answer the question,
    Egg, who are you, what are you, where did you
        come from and where are you going?
If one egg could break through the barriers, pass
    all interference and tell that much, then we
    could tell how the earth came—
            how we came with hair, lungs, noses
            to sit on the earth and eat our breakfasts,
            to sleep with our mates
            and to salute the moon between sleeps,
            to meditate on worms in the dust
            and how they fail to divulge the designs
            of the dark autocracies of their fates.
Let one egg tell and we would understand a billion eggs.

The newborn child, dried behind the ears,
Swaddled in soft cloths and groping for nipples,
Comes from a payday of love so old,
So involved, so traced with circles of the moon,
So cunning with secrets of the salts of blood,
It must be older than the moon, older than the salt sea.
And do nations go back to the secret traceries of eggs?
To beginnings that fail to divulge the designs?
Can we say to the unborn, Egg, who are you? Egg, divulge
  your design.

Nations begin young the same as babies.
They suckle and struggle; they grow up;
They toil, fight, laugh, suffer, die.
They obey the traced circles of the moon.
They follow the ordained times of night, morning, after-
  noon, evening, and night again.
They stand up and have their day on the pavilion of the
  Four Winds.
The night sky of stars watches them begin, wear out, and
  fade away before newcomers, before silence, before
  empty pavilions.
They leave flags, slogans, alphabets, numbers, tools, tales
  of flaming performances; they leave moths, manu-
  scripts, memories.

And so, to the pavilion of the four winds
Came the little one they called America,
One that suckled, struggled, toiled, laughed, grew.
America began young the same as a baby.
The little new republic had its swaddling cloths,

Its child shirt, its tussle to knit long bone joints.
> And who can read the circle of its moons now?
> And who shall tell beforehand the secrets of its
> salts and blood?

8

Turn back and look at those men riding horses, sitting in
saddles, smelling of leather, going to Boston, to Rich-
mond, in velvet knickerbockers, in silk stockings, in
slippers with silver buckles, white-powdered wigs on
their heads, speaking of "the honor of a gentleman,"
singing "God rest ye, merry gentlemen," meeting car-
penters who built staircases and gables with their
hands, the work-day was sunup till sundown; they
drove handwrought nails; the smoothing of their own
hands was on their woodwork.

Look back; they are pinching their fingers in silver and
gold snuff boxes, lifting tankards of ale, discussing
titles to many miles of land, counties and townships of
land; a gentleman rides all day to round his bounda-
ries; and the jail doors cling to their brass locks hold-
ing the dregs, the convicts of debt.

Look back,
And that was long ago.
America was new born.
The republic was a baby, a child,

Fresh wiped behind the ears,
Blinking, tussling to knit the long
    new bone joints.

Look back; there is an interlude; men in covered wagons,
    in buckskin, with plows, rifles, six-shooters, sweep
    west; the Havana cigar, the long pantaloons, the
    Mississippi steamboat, the talking wires, the iron
    horse.

    Yes, there was an interlude.
    Something happened, always something happens.
History is a living horse laughing at a wooden horse.
History is a wind blowing where it listeth.
History is no sure thing to bet on.
History is a box of tricks with a lost key.
History is a labyrinth of doors with sliding panels, a book
    of ciphers with the code in a cave of the Sargossa sea.
History says, if it pleases, Excuse me, I beg your pardon, it
    will never happen again if I can help it.

Yes, there was an interlude,
And phantoms washed their white shirts
Over and over again in buckets of blood—
And the saddest phantom of all stood up at Gettysburg
And tried to tell right from wrong and left the most
    of it unsaid, in the air.

The years go by with their numbers, names,
    So many born, so many gone.
Again the Four Horsemen take their laughter.
Men walk on air and tumble from the sky.

Men grapple undersea and soak their bones along rust-
    brown, rust-flaked turbines on the sea bottom.
Men bite the dust from bullets, bombs, bayonets, gas,
Till ten million go west without time for a good-by,
Till double ten million are cripples for life,
Blind, shocked, broken storm children.
Boys singing Hinky Dinky Parley Voo
Come back from the oversea vortex,
From the barrages of No Man's Land,
Saying with gleams deep in their eyes,
"There is nothing to say, ask me no questions."

9

Steel, coal, oil, the test tube arise as facts, dominions,
Standing establishments with world ambassadors.
Between two seashores comes a swift interweaving of blood
    and bones, nerves and arteries, rail and motor paths,
    airways and airports, tunnels, wires, broadcasts on
    high and low frequencies to the receiving sets.
The train callers call All Aboard for transcontinental
    flyers; it is seaboard to seaboard; and the tincan
    tourists buy gas and follow the bird migrations.

The concrete highways crack under the incessant tires of
    two-ton, ten-ton trucks—and the concrete mixers
    come with laughing bellies filled with gravel for the
    repair jobs.
The talk runs—of the boll-weevil in the cotton, the doodle
    bug in the oil fields, the corn borer—of the lame duck

in Congress, the farm bloc, the Ku Klux, a new sucker
born every minute, sales canvass and selling spiels—
The talk runs—of crime waves, boy murderers, two women
and a man, two men and a woman, bootleggers, the
beer racket and the highjackers, gang fights, cloud-
bursts, tornadoes, floods, the Lakes-to-Gulf waterway,
Boulder Dam—
The latest songs go from Broadway west across the country
—the latest movies go from Hollywood east across the
country—in a million homes they set their dials and
listen to jazz numbers, the classics, the speech of the
President in Washington, the heavyweight champion-
ship fight, the symphonies of the music masters.

10

Voices—telling mankind to look itself in the face—who are
you? what are you? we'll tell you—here is the latest—
this is what Man has done today on the pavilion of the
four winds, on the arcs of the globe—

As the dusty red sun settles in the dayend the sport sheets
blaze forth telling the box scores, the touchdowns, the
scandals—pictures of dying champions, of new claim-
ants, fresh aspirants calling challenges—of over-sea
flyers, winners and losers—of new and old darlings of
destiny—

Fate's crapshooters fading each other, big Dick or snake
eyes, midnights and deuces, chicken one day and

feathers the next, the true story of how an ashcan
became a verandah and vice versa.

11

A code arrives ; language ; lingo ; slang ;
behold the proverbs of a people, a nation :
Give 'em the works. Fix it, there's always
a way. Be hard boiled. The good die young.

Be a square shooter. Be good ; if you can't
be good be careful. When they put you in
that six foot bungalow, that wooden kimono,
you're through and that's that.

Sell 'em, sell 'em. Make 'em eat it. What
if we gyp 'em ? It'll be good for 'em. Get their
names on the dotted line and give 'em the haha.

The higher they go the farther they drop.
The fewer the sooner. Tell 'em. Tell 'em.
Make 'em listen. They got to listen when
they know who you are. Don't let 'em know
what you got on your hip. Hit 'em where
they ain't. It's good for whatever ails
you and if nothing ails you it's good for
that. Where was you raised—in a barn ?

They're a lot of muckers, tin horns ; show
those slobs where they get off at. Tell 'em

you're going to open a keg of nails. Beat 'em
to a fare-thee-well. Hand 'em the razz-berries.
Clean 'em and then give 'em car-fare home.
Maybe all you'll get from 'em you can put in
your ear, anyhow.

They got a fat nerve to try to tie a can
on you. Send 'em to the cleaners. Put the
kibosh on 'em so they'll never come back.
You don't seem to know four out of five
have pyorrhea in Peoria.

Your head ain't screwed on wrong, I trust.
Use your noodle, your nut, your think tank,
your skypiece. God meant for you to use it.
If they offer to let you in on the ground
floor take the elevator.

Put up a sign: Don't worry; it won't last;
nothing does. Put up a sign: In God we
trust, all others pay cash. Put up a sign:
Be brief, we have our living to make. Put
up a sign: Keep off the grass.

Aye, behold the proverbs of a people:
The big word is Service.
Service—first, last and always.
Business is business.
What you don't know won't hurt you.
Courtesy pays.
Fair enough.
The voice with a smile.

Say it with flowers.

Let one hand wash the other.

The customer is always right.

Who's your boy friend?

Who's your girl friend?

O very well.

God reigns and the government at Washington lives.

Let it go at that.

There are lies, dam lies and statistics.

Figures don't lie but liars can figure.

There's more truth than poetry in that.

You don't know the half of it, dearie.

It's the roving bee that gathers the honey.[1]

A big man is a big man whether he's a president or a prizefighter.[2]

Name your poison.

Take a little interest.

Look the part.

It pays to look well.

Be yourself.

Speak softly and carry a big stick.[3]

War is hell.

Honesty is the best policy.

It's all in the way you look at it.

Get the money—honestly if you can.

It's hell to be poor.

Well, money isn't everything.

[1] On hearing from his father "A rolling stone gathers no moss," John L. Sullivan won one of his important early fights and telegraphed this reply.

[2] John L. Sullivan's greeting spoken to President Theodore Roosevelt in the White House.

[3] A Spanish proverb first Americanized by Theodore Roosevelt.

Well, life is what you make it.

Speed and curves—what more do you want?

I'd rather fly than eat.[4]

There must be pioneers and some of them get killed.[4]

The grass is longer in the backyard.[5]

Give me enough Swedes and snuff and I'll build a railroad
    to hell.[6]

How much did he leave? All of it.[7]

Can you unscramble eggs?[8]

Early to bed and early to rise and you never meet any
    prominent people.[9]

Let's go. Watch our smoke. Excuse our dust.

Keep your shirt on.

12

First come the pioneers, lean, hungry, fierce, dirty.

They wrangle and battle with the elements.

They gamble on crops, chills, ague, rheumatism.

They fight wars and put a nation on the map.

They battle with blizzards, lice, wolves.

[4] Charles A. Lindbergh.

[5] Based on a Republican campaign story in 1892 alleging that a man on all fours eating grass on the White House lawn told President Grover Cleveland, "I'm hungry" and was advised, "The grass is longer in the backyard."

[6] A saying that took rise from James J. (Jim) Hill.

[7] A folk tale in Chicago chronicles two ditch diggers on the morning after Marshall Field I died, leaving an estate of $150,000,000, as having this dialogue.

[8] J. Pierpont Morgan's query as to court decrees dissolving an inevitable industrial combination.

[9] George Ade.

They go on a fighting trail
To break sod for unnumbered millions to come.

Then the fat years arrive when the fat drips.
Then come the rich men baffled by their riches,
Bewildered by the silence of their tall possessions.
Then come the criers of the ancient desperate taunt:
    Stuff your guts
    and strut your stuff,
    strut it high and handsome;
    when you die you're dead
    and there's no come-back
    and not even the winds
    will say your name—
    feed, oh pigs, feed, oh swine.

Old timer, dust of the earth so kindly,
Old timer, dirt of our feet and days.
Old time gravel and gumbo of the earth,
Take them back kindly,
These pigs, these swine.
The bones of them and their brothers blanch to the same
    yellow of the years.

13

Since we sell the earth with a fence around it,
Since one man sells the ocean to another and guarantees a
    new roof and all modern conveniences,
Since we sell everything but the blue sky and only the Blue
    Sky Laws stop us selling that,

Since we sell justice, since we sell pardons for crimes,

Since we sell land titles, oil claims, ninety-nine year options, all day suckers and two minute eggs—

Since we have coined a slogan, Never give the sucker an even break and the Old Army Game goes—

Since the selling game is the big game and unless you know how to sell you're a bum and that ain't all—

Since the city hicks and the hicks from the sticks go to the latest Broadway hit hoping to fix their glims on a birdie with her last feather off in a bathtub of booze—

Let the dance go on—let the stalking stuffed cadavers of old men run the earth and call up the Four Horsemen. . . .

14

Now it's Uncle Sam sitting on top of the world.

Not so long ago it was John Bull and, earlier yet, Napoleon and the eagles of France told the world where to get off at.

Spain, Rome, Greece, Persia, their blunderbuss guns, their spears, catapults, ships, took their turn at leading the civilizations of the earth—

One by one they were bumped off, moved over, left behind, taken for a ride; they died or they lost the wallop they used to pack, not so good, not so good.

One by one they no longer sat on top of the world—now the Young Stranger is Uncle Sam, is America and the song goes, "The stars and stripes forever!" even though "forever" is a long time.

Even though the oldest kings had their singers and clowns
  calling, "Oh king, you shall live forever."

15

In God we trust; it is so written.
The writing goes onto every silver dollar.
The fact: God is the great One who made us all.
We is you and me and all of us in the United States of
  America.
And trusting God means we give ourselves, all of ourselves,
  the whole United States of America, to God, the great
  One.
Yes . . . perhaps . . . is that so?

16

The silent litany of the workmen goes on—
Speed, speed, we are the makers of speed.
We make the flying, crying motors,
Clutches, brakes, and axles,
Gears, ignitions, accelerators,
Spokes and springs and shock absorbers.
The silent litany of the workmen goes on—
Speed, speed, we are the makers of speed;
Axles, clutches, levers, shovels,
We make the signals and lay the way—
    Speed, speed.

The trees come down to our tools.
We carve the wood to the wanted shape.
The whining propeller's song in the sky,
The steady drone of the overland truck,
Comes from our hands; us; the makers of speed.

Speed; the turbines crossing the Big Pond,
Every nut and bolt, every bar and screw,
Every fitted and whirling shaft,
They came from us, the makers,
Us, who know how,
Us, the high designers and the automatic feeders,
Us, with heads,
Us, with hands,
Us, on the long haul, the short flight,
We are the makers; lay the blame on us—
The makers of speed.

17

There is a Sleepwalker
goes walking and talking—
I promise you nothing, there are too many promises.
I bring you a package so little, so thin, you can hide it
anywhere, in your shoes, in your ear, in a corner of
your heart.
I bring you a handkerchief, so filmy a gauze of silk, so
foamy a fabric, you pick it up and put it away as you
put away a bubble, a morning cobweb in the sun, a
patch of moon dropped from two lilacs.

I bring you gold, beaten so thin with so many little ham-
mers it is thinner than the morning laughter of hum-
mingbirds flitting among diamond dewdrops yet hard
as an anvil wearing out the strongest hammers.

There is a Sleepwalker
goes walking and talking—

Go alone and away from all books, go with your own heart
into the storm of human hearts and see if somewhere
in that storm there are bleeding hearts, sacred hearts
taking a bitter wages of doom, red-soaked and crim-
son-plunged hearts of the Redeemer of Man.
Walk by yourself and find the silence where a whisper of
your lips is the same as a pounding and a shouting at
the knobs and panels of great doors.
Walk again where the mass human shadows foregather,
where the silhouettes and pantomimes of the great
human procession wind with a crying out loud, and
rotten laughters mix with raging tumults—
And between the being born and the being dead of the gen-
erations they march, march, march, to the drums,
drums, drums, of the three facts of arriving, living,
departing—
Go where the shadows string from winding pilgrim cohorts,
where the line of the march twists and reels, and a
hundred years is nothing much and a thousand or a
million years nothing much, as they march, march,
march, to the drums, drums, drums, of the three facts.
Go there and let your heart be soft, fading as rainbows on
slants of rain in the sun: let your heart be full of
riddles as white steel and its blue shadows.

There is a Sleepwalker
goes walking and talking—

> We are afraid. What are we afraid of?
> We are afraid of what we are afraid of.
> We are afraid of this, that, these, those, them.

We are afraid the earth will blow up and bomb the human
family out of its sleep, its slumber, its sleepwalking,
its pass and repass of shadows.

We are afraid the sky will come apart and fall on us and in
a rain of stars we will wash out into the Great Alone,
the Deep Dark, saying, "Good-bye old Mother Earth,
we always were afraid of you."

We are afraid; what are we afraid of? We are afraid of
nothing much, nothing at all, nothing in the shape of
god, man or beast, we can eat any ashes offered us, we
can step out before the fact of the Fact of Death and
look it in the eye and laugh, "You are the begining or
the end of something, I'll gamble with you, I'll take a
chance."

18

And we, us, the people,
We who of course are no sleepwalkers,
Perhaps we may murmur—
Perhaps as the airmen slip into their leather coats,
Gambling for the time tables as against the skull and cross-
bones,

Riding with mail sacks across orange blossoms, the desert
    cactus, the Rockies, the Great Plains, the Mississippi,
    the corn belt, the Appalachians,
Riding with mail sacks, with a clutch on the steering wheels
    in storms and stars, with a passing cry, "Good luck
    and God bless you,"
Perhaps while they ride and gamble on the new transcon-
    tinental sky paths, perhaps we may ask and murmur—
        Good morning, America.
        Good morning, Mr. Who, Which, What.
        Good morning, let's all of us tell our
            real names.
        Good morning, Mr. Somebody, Nobody, Any-
            body-who-is-Anybody-at-all.
        Good morning, Worms in the Dust, Eagles
            in the Air, Climbers to the Top of
            the Sky.

19

You have kissed good-by to one century, one little priceless
    album.
You will yet kiss good-by to ten, twenty centuries. Ah! you
    shall have such albums!
Your mothers, America, have labored and carried harvests
    of generations—
Across the spillways come further harvests, new tumultu-
    ous populations, young strangers, crying, "We are
    here! We belong! look at us!"

Good morning, America!
Morning goes as morning-glories go!
High noon goes, afternoon goes!
Twilight, sundown, gloaming—
The hour of writing: Good night, America!
Good night, sleep, peace, and sweet dreams!

20

The prints of many new ships shall be on the sky.
The Four Horsemen shall ride again in a bitter dust,
The granaries of great nations shall be the food of fat rats,
And the shooting stars shall write new alphabets on the sky
     Before we come home,
     Before we understand.

Off in our western sky,
Off in a burning maroon,
Shall come in a wintrish haze,
Shall come in points and crystals—
A shovel of stars.

Let us wigwag the moon.
Let us make new propellers,
Go past old spent stars
And find blue moons on a new star path.

Let us make pioneer prayers.
Let working clothes be sacred.

Let us look on
And listen in
On God's great workshop
Of stars . . . and eggs . . .

There shall be—
Many many girls in a wild windy moonlight,
Many many mothers carrying babies.

21

Sea sunsets, give us keepsakes.
Prairie gloamings, pay us for prayers.
Mountain clouds on bronze skies—
    Give us great memories.
Let us have summer roses.
Let us have tawny harvest haze in pumpkin time.
Let us have springtime faces to toil for and play for.
Let us have the fun of booming winds on long waters.
Give us dreamy blue twilights—of winter evenings—to
    wrap us in a coat of dreaminess.
Moonlight, come down—shine down, moonlight—meet
    every bird cry and every song calling to a hard old
    earth, a sweet young earth.

SPRING GRASS

SPRING GRASS

Spring grass, there is a dance to be danced
    for you.
Come up, spring grass, if only for young feet.
Come up, spring grass, young feet ask you.

Smell of the young spring grass,
You're a mascot riding on the wind horses.
You came to my nose and spiffed me. This is
    your lucky year.

Young spring grass just after the winter,
Shoots of the big green whisper of the year,
Come up, if only for young feet.
Come up, young feet ask you.

MOIST MOON PEOPLE

The moon is able to command the valley tonight.
The green mist shall go a-roaming, the white river shall
     go a-roaming.
Yet the moon shall be commanding, the moon shall take a
     high stand on the sky.

When the cats crept up the gullies,
And the goats fed at the rim a-laughing,
When the spiders swept their rooms in the burr oaks,
And the katydids first searched for this year's accordions,
And the crickets began a-looking for last year's concer-
     tinas—

I was there, I saw that hour, I know God had grand
     intentions about it.
If not, why did the moon command the valley, the green
     mist and white river go a-roaming, and the moon by
     itself take so high a stand on the sky?
If God and I alone saw it, the show was worth putting on,
Yet I remember others were there, Amos and Priscilla,
     Axel and Hulda, Hank and Jo, Big Charley and
     Little Morningstar,
They were all there; the clock ticks spoke with castanet
     clicks.

SPRING CRIES

1

Call us back, call us with your sliding silver,
Frogs of the early spring, frogs of the later days
When spring crosses over, when spring spills over
And spills the last of its sliding silvers
Into the running wind, the running water, of summer.
Call us back then, call over, call under—only call—
Frogs of the early spring, frogs of the later days.

2

Birds we have seen and known and counted,
Birds we have never learned the names of,
Call us back, you too, call us back.
Out of the forks and angles of branches,
High out of the blacksmith arms of oak and ash,
Sweet out of the Lombardy poplar's arrow head,
Soft out of the swinging, swaying,
The bending and almost broken branch
Of the bush of the home of the wild gooseberry—
Yellow feather, white throat, gray neck, red wing,
Scarlet head, blue shoulder, copper silver body line—
All you birds—call us back—call us under, over—
Birds we know, birds we never can know,
Birds spilling your one-two-three
Of a slur and a cry and a trill—
Call us back, you too call us.

3

Warble us easy and old ones.
Open your gates up the sunset in the evening.
Lift up your windows of song in the morning lights.
Wind on your spiral and zigzag ways.
Birds, we have heard baskets of you, bushes of you.
In a tree of a hundred windows ten of you sat
On the song sills of every window.
Warble us easy and old ones now.
Call us back, spill your one-two-three
Of a slur and a cry and a trill.

FROG SONGS

The silver burbles of the frogs wind and swirl.
The lines of their prongs swing up in a spray.
They cut the air with bird line curves.
The eye sees nothing, the ear is filled, the head remembers
The beat of the swirl of frog throat silver prongs
In the early springtime when eggs open, when feet learn,
When the crying of the water begins a new year.

LUMBER YARD POOLS AT SUNSET

The rain pools in the old lumber yard
change as the sky changes.

No sooner do lightfoot sunset maroons
cross the west than they cross the rain
pools too.

So now every blue has a brother
and every singing silver a sister.

SPRING CARRIES SURPRISES

Be gay now.
Shadows go fast these days
Unlocking the locks of blossoms.

The lilacs never know how,
The oleanders along the old walls,
The peach trees over the hills—
Out of the lock-ups they go,
Out and crying with leaves.
They never know how.
Be gay—this is the time.

The little keys of the climbing runners,
The opening of the doors again,
The letting loose of the shut-ins—
Here is the time—be gay now.

Ask spring why.
Ask in your heart why.
Go around gay and foolish asking why.
God be easy on your fool heart
If you don't go around asking spring
In your heart, "Why, why, why,"
      Three times like that, or else
      One long, "Why?"

Be gay now.

MORE COUNTRY PEOPLE

The six pigs at the breast of their mother
Equal six spots of young brown against a big spot of old
        brown.
The bleating of the sheep was an arithmetic
Of the long wool coats thick after winter.

The collar of white hair hung on the neck of the black hog,
The roosters of the Buff Cochin people strutted.

Cherry branches stuck their blossoms against the sky.
Elbows joined elbows of white blossoms.
Zigzags blent into a mass.
"Look once at us—today is the day we call today."

SPRING WIND

Be flip with us if you want to, spring wind.
Be gay and make us sniff at your slow secrets.
    Be easy with us, spring wind.
Be lovely and yet be lovely not too fast with us.

If a child came crying out of a snowstorm
And sat down with secrets of new playthings,
Crying because lovelier things than ever came that year—

If a child came crying out of sheet ice,
A white carving of a lithe running torso,
Holding in its hands new baffling playthings—

If a child came crying so,
Wet and smiling, smelling of promises
Of yellow roses blowing in the river backwashes,
Potato blossoms across the prairie flat lands,
And even so much as one new honest song to sing—

If a child came so,
We would say, 'Come and sit on our back porch;
Listen with us and tell us more, tell us all you know;
Tell us the secrets of the spring wind;
Tell us if this is a lucky year;
Be lovely and yet be lovely not too fast with us.'

CRISSCROSS

Spring crosses over into summer.
This is as it always was.

Buds on the redhaw, beetles in the loam,
And the interference of the green leaves
At the blue roofs of the spring sky
Crossing over into summer—
These are ways, this is out and on.
This always was.

The tumble out and the push up,
The breaking of the little doors,
The look again at the mother sun,
The feel of the blue roofs over—
This is summer? This always was?

The whispering sprigs of buds stay put.
The spiders are after the beetles.
The farmer is driving a tractor turning furrows.
The hired man drives a manure spreader.
The oven bird hops in dry leaves.
The woodpecker beats his tattoo.
Is this it? Is spring crossing over?
Is it summer? And this always was?
The whispering pinks, the buds on the redhaw,
The blue roofs of the sky . . . stay put.

BABY SONG OF THE FOUR WINDS

Let me be your baby, south wind.
Rock me, let me rock, rock me now.
Rock me low, rock me warm.
Let me be your baby.

Comb my hair, west wind.
Comb me with a cow lick.
Or let me go with a pompadour.
Come on, west wind, make me your baby.

North wind, shake me where I'm foolish.
Shake me loose and change my ways.
Cool my ears with a blue sea wind.
I'm your baby, make me behave.

And you, east wind, what can I ask?
A fog comfort? A fog to tuck me in?
Fix me so and let me sleep.
I'm your baby—and I always was.

BLOSSOM THEMES

1

Late in the winter came one day
When there was a whiff on the wind,
a suspicion, a cry not to be heard
    of perhaps blossoms, perhaps green
    grass and clean hills lifting roll-
    ing shoulders.
Does the nose get the cry of spring
    first of all? is the nose thankful
    and thrilled first of all?

2

If the blossoms come down
so they must fall on snow
because spring comes this year
before winter is gone,
then both snow and blossoms look sad;
peaches, cherries, the red summer apples,
all say it is a hard year.
The wind has its own way of picking off
the smell of peach blossoms and then
carrying that smell miles and miles.
    Women washing dishes in lonely farmhouses
    stand at the door and say, "Something is
    happening."

A little foam of the summer sea
    of blossoms,
    a foam finger of white leaves,
    shut these away—
    high into the summer wind runners.
Let the wind be white too.

SMALL HOMES

The green bug sleeps in the white lily ear.
The red bug sleeps in the white magnolia.
Shiny wings, you are choosers of color.
You have taken your summer bungalows wisely.

CORN BELT

SHE OPENS THE BARN DOOR EVERY MORNING

Open the barn door, farm woman,
It is time for the cows to be milked.
Their udders are full from the sleep night.
Open the door with your right hand shuttling a cleat,
Your left hand pulling a handle.
The smell of the barn is let out to the pastures.
Dawn lets itself in at the open door.
A cow left out in the barnyard all the night
Looks on as though you do this every morning.
Open the barn door, farm woman, you do it
As you have done it five hundred times.
As a sleep woman heavy with the earth,
Clean as a milk pail washed in the sun,
You open the barn door a half mile away
And a cow almost turns its head and looks on.

MILK WHITE MOON, PUT THE COWS TO SLEEP

Milk-white moon, put the cows to sleep.
Since five o'clock in the morning,
Since they stood up out of the grass,
Where they slept on their knees and hocks,
They have eaten grass and given their milk
And eaten grass again and given milk,
And kept their heads and teeth at the earth's face.
     Now they are looking at you, milk-white moon.
     Carelessly as they look at the level landscapes,
     Carelessly as they look at a pail of new white milk,
     They are looking at you, wondering not at all, at all,
     If the moon is the skim face top of a pail of milk,
     Wondering not at all, carelessly looking.
     Put the cows to sleep, milk-white moon,
     Put the cows to sleep.

SLOW PROGRAM

The iron rails run into the sun.
The setting of the sun chooses an hour.
The red rail ribbons run into the red ball sun.
The ribbons and the ball change like red water lights.
The picture floats with a slow program of red haze lights.

FIELD PEOPLE

In the morning eyes of the brown-eyed Susans,
in the toadflax sheaves smiling butter-and-eggs,
in the white mushrooms sprung from air into air
since yesterday morning, since yesterday evening,
in the corn row corridor walls of cornstalks—
the same southwest wind comes again, knowing—

How the field people go away,
the corn row people, the toadflax, mushroom,
        thistlebloom people,
how they rise, sing songs they learn, and then go away,
leaving in the air no last will and testament at all,
leaving no last whisper at all on how this sister,
that brother, those friends, such and such a sweetheart
is remembered with a gold leaf, a cup rainbow home,
a cricket's hut for counting its summer heartbeats,
a caught shimmer of one haunted moonray to be passed on—
        the running southwest wind knows them all.

SUNSETS

There are sunsets who whisper a good-by.
It is a short dusk and a way for stars.
Prairie and sea rim they go level and even
And the sleep is easy.

There are sunsets who dance good-by.
They fling scarves half to the arc,
To the arc then and over the arc.
Ribbons at the ears, sashes at the hips,
Dancing, dancing good-by. And here sleep
Tosses a little with dreams.

GRASSROOTS

Grass clutches at the dark dirt with finger holds.
Let it be blue grass, barley, rye or wheat,
Let it be button weed or butter-and-eggs,
Let it be Johnny-jump-ups springing clean blue streaks.
Grassroots down under put fingers into dark dirt.

CANADIANS AND POTTAWATTOMIES

I have seen a loneliness sit
in the dark and nothing lit up.
I have seen a loneliness sit
in the dark lit up like a Christ-
mas tree, a Hallowe'en pumpkin.

If two Canadians understand snow
they are then both Canadians.
If one Canadian understands snow
and another doesn't understand
snow at all, then one is a Canadian
and the other is no Canadian at all.

The Pottawattomie Indians sang something
like this in their early winter songs.
They sang it digging holes in the ice to
let down fish-hooks, they chattered it in
the wigwams when blizzards shook the wigwams.

CORN AND BEANS

Having looked long at two garden rows
And seen how the rain and dirt have used them
I have decided the corn and beans shall have names.

And one is to be known as the Thwarted Corn of a Short
    Year
While the other shall be called the Triumphant Beans of
    Plenty Rain.

If I change these names next Sunday I shall let you know
    about it.

MOCKERS GO TO KANSAS IN SPRING

Riding from Topeka, Kansas, to Manhattan, Kansas,
Marco saw and heard three mockingbirds.
He mentioned it to the Kansas Authors' Club.
Two mockers were heard that night in Manhattan.
A man from Chicago sleeping in the Gillett House
Heard one of the mockers before breakfast the morning
    after.
This is evidence, testimony, offered in behalf of those who do
    not understand how mockers roam north from Texas
    and Arkansas, sometimes as far north as Manhattan,
    Kansas.

BIRD TALK

And now when the branches were beginning to be heavy,
It was the time when they once had said, "This is the
   beginning of summer."
The shrilling of the frogs was not so shrill as in the
   first weeks after the broken winter;
The birds took their hops and zigzags a little more
   anxious; a home is a home; worms are worms.
The yellow spreads of the dandelions and buttercups
   reached across the green pastures.
Tee whee and *tee whee* came on the breezes, and the grackles
   chuzzled their syllables.
And it was the leaves with a strong soft wind over them
   that talked most of all and said more than any others
   though speaking the fewest words.
It was the green leaves trickling out the gaunt nowhere
   of winter, out on the gray hungry branches—
It was the leaves on the branches, beginning to be heavy,
   who said as they said one time before, "This is the be-
   ginning of summer."

We shall never blame the birds who come
   where the river and the road make the Grand Crossing
   and talk there, sitting in circles talking bird talk.
If they ask in their circles as to who is here
   and as to who is not here and who used to be here,
Or if instead of counting up last year as against
   this year, they count up this year as against next

year, and have their bird chatter about who is here
this year who won't be here next year,
We shall never blame the birds.

If I have put your face among leaf faces, child,
Or if I have put your voice among bird voices,
Blame me no more than the bluejays.

KANSAS LESSONS

Often the mockingbird is only a mocker
singing the songs of other birds,
pouring their trills over the bushes.
  And sometimes the mocker is all alone
    the child playing all-aloney all—aloney.
And sometimes the mocker calls, calls, calls,
the fables, texts and cries of all heartbreaks,
all the wild nights a blood gold moon can buy.

CRICKET MARCH

As the corn becomes higher
The one shrill of a summer cricket
Becomes two and ten
With a shrilling surer than last month.

As the banners of the corn
Come to their highest flying in the wind,
The summer crickets come to a marching army.

SUMMER GRASS

Summer grass aches and whispers.

It wants something; it calls and sings; it pours
out wishes to the overhead stars.

The rain hears; the rain answers; the rain is slow
coming; the rain wets the face of the grass.

NOCTURN CABBAGE

Cabbages catch at the moon.
It is late summer, no rain, the pack of the soil
    cracks open, it is a hard summer.
In the night the cabbages catch at the moon, the
    leaves drip silver, the rows of cabbages are
    series of little silver waterfalls in the moon.

CRABAPPLES

Sweeten these bitter wild crabapples, Illinois
October sun. The roots here came from the
wilderness, came before man came here. They
are bitter as the wild is bitter.

Give these crabapples your softening gold,
October sun, go through to the white wet
seeds inside and soften them black. Make
these bitter apples sweet. They want you, sun.

The drop and the fall, the drop and the fall,
the apples leaving the branches for the black
earth under, they know you from last year,
the year before last year, October sun.

POPLAR AND ELM

Silver leaves of the last of summer,
Poplar and elm silver leaves,
Leaves not least of all of the Lombardy poplar,
Standing before the autumn moon and the autumn wind
      as a woman waits in a doorway for some one who
      must be coming,
All you silver leaf people, you I have seen and heard
      in a hundred summer winds,
It is October, it is a week, two weeks, till the rain and frost
      break on us and the leaves are washed off, washed
      down.
In January when the trees fork gray against a clear winter
      blue in the spare sun silver of winter or the lengthened
      frost silver of the long nights—
I shall remember then the loans of the sun to you in June,
      I shall remember the hundred winds who kissed you.

BROWN GOLD

The time of the brown gold comes softly.
Oat shocks are alive in brown gold belts,
 the short and the shambling oat shocks
 sit on the stubble and straw.
The timothy hay, the fodder corn, the cabbage
 and the potatoes, across their leaves are
 footsteps.
There is a bold green up over the cracks in
 the corn rows where the crickets go criss-
 cross errands, where the bugs carry pack-
 ages.
Flutter and whirr, you birdies, you newcomers
 in lines and sashes, tellers of harvest
 weather on the way, belts of brown gold
 coming softly.
It is very well the old time streamers take
 up the old time gold haze against the west-
 ern timber line.
It is the old time again when months and birds
 tell each other, "Oh, very well," and repeat it
 where the fields and the timber lines meet
 in belts of brown gold hazes, "Oh, very
 well, Oh, very well."

RIPE CORN

The wind blows. The corn leans. The corn leaves go rustling. The march time and the windbeat is on October drums. The stalks of fodder bend all one way, the way the last windstorm passed.

"Put on my winter clothes; get me an ulster; a yellow ulster to lay down in January and shut my eyes and cover my ears in snow drifts."

The wind blows. The corn leans. The fodder is russet. October says to the leaves, "Rustle now to the last lap, to the last leg of the year."

AUBURN

Auburn autumn leaves, will you come back?
Auburn autumn oaks, foxprints burning soft,
 burning the oaken autumn coats, burning
 the auburn autumn fire—
How can you burn so, how can you go on with
 all this burning, and bring back more to
 burn next year?
Ask and let go, lift this burning of this year
 so much like last year's burning; let next
 year's burning come; ask; let go.
The burnings of the auburn autumn leaves, the
 slow burnt foxprints of the oaken auburns,
 house of leaves and branches, house of leaves
 to burn and branches to be here in the
 white howling, the white quiet of winter—
Going so, going so, auburn house-roof of eaves and
 leaves, the child and the old man, the child and
 the old woman shoot a good-by to you.

The tall old man with clean bones, clean-shape toes
 counting ten against the bed footboard—
This is the tall old man telling a son with clean
 bones a passover auburn and oaken secret—
There are fall leaves, foxprint burnings, this year,
 last year, next year, in all houses, and
Most of all in the house of the tall old man with
 clean bones, clean-shape toes counting ten against
 the bed footboard.

In all houses are leaves burnt and burning, in all hous-
es branches to be here in the white howling, the patched
black quiet of winter.

REDHAW RAIN

The red rain spatter under the redhaw
tree, the hut roof branches of the red-
haw tree, the floor level loam under the
redhaw tree, the meeting place of the
fall red rain and the loam of the first
fall frost—the Pottawattamies took this
into their understanding of why October
so seldom fails, why October so often
brings the red rain spatter under the red-
haw tree.

The slow rain soaks. The farmers fix
wagon axles, patch the barn roof shin-
gles, peek in the thatch of the empty
swallow homes. The farm wives keep to
the kitchens cleaning pans. The slow
rain soaks.

The head at the end of a horse's neck
holds its bone and meat, teeth and eye-
balls, tongue and ears, to the west, to
the east, to the browse of the last of
the sweetgrass range this year. Snow
comes soon, out of the north, to the south
and south. The tongue of the head in
the sweetgrass knows.

The grey west opens for a spear of blue
longer than fifty, a hundred and fifty,
prairie miles.

The grey west opens a triangle silver,
an arch of bar clouds over the prairie.

And the sun washes the spear, the arch,
the triangle, over and over.

WITHOUT NOTICE BEFOREHAND

The frozen rain of the first November days
came down without notice beforehand
the same as the wind and the frost
loosening the leaves of the buckeye tree,
dropping a yellow rain of flat swirling leaves,
all without notice beforehand, came down,
the same as the far hiding out of lady bugs,
woggle bugs spotted black polka dots
on box car red, on banana yellow,
the same as this going away of the bug families
all went on without notice beforehand.

Under the hedgethorn tree the bugs got together,
families from many directions; they dappled
the dark soil and made a red weather
of the Indian summer afternoon among thorns;
if a man should live a day for every bug
with a paint of box car red, a lamp shade red
on his back, a man would live many years
counting a day for a bug under the Indian summer
hedgethorn afternoon; the farmers husked their
corn in old fashioned Studebaker wagons;
the cream and gold corn ears sent a shine
between the green wagon boards, over the tops
of the green wagon boards; so the bug families
held a pow wow, making a red weather
among thorns in sun patches of Indian summer;
it seemed to be all in a bug family lifetime

coming as it did with no warnings ahead,
no shadow line to tell how soon or late
the frozen rain of the first November days,
coming without notice beforehand.

The buckeye built itself a house of gold and black,
the green leaf roof, the green leaf walls of summer
belted their eaves with bucklers of gold,
changed their arches and let the rich glooms
of the black inside rafters play out;
the shine was loam crossing its heart with gold,
the running out of russet and cream yellow
on the loam black of the forks of the branches
was a sign of summer people leaving
the house the buckeye built itself; and this too
came with no warnings ahead, no shadow line
of the frozen rain of the first November days
coming without notice beforehand.

CORN PRATTLINGS

The wind came across the corn laughing.
It was late in summer, the limit of summer,
The deadline of early fall time,
And the wind in the laughing corn,
The wind came across.

The wind ran on the tops of the corntossels,
And the pointed long leaves hung over,
Hands obedient to the wind.
And the wind ran once and again for each leaf,
Each pointed long leaf, the wind sang running
Across the corntossels and leaves of corn.

There is a floor the corn grows on,
The roots of the corn go under and twist and hold.
The trunk of the corn stands over the floor,
The leaf and the corntossel signal our winds
And take notice of the path of the sun.

The ears laugh in the husks now.
The big job of the year is done.
It's all over again till next year.
Out of maroon silk and fading greens,
Up over the wandering pumpkin stems,
The yellow and gold kernels laugh.
The big job is over and the laugh of the yellow ears
And the laugh of the running wind go together.
They come across together now late, late, in summer
Early in the fall time of the corntossels.

HAZE GOLD

Sun, you may send your haze gold
Filling the fall afternoon
With a flimmer of many gold feathers.
Leaves, you may linger in the fall sunset
Like late lingering butterflies before frost.
Treetops, you may sift the sunset cross-lights
Spreading a loose checkerwork of gold and shadow.
Winter comes soon—shall we save this, lay it by,
Keep all we can of these haze gold yellows?

WINTER GOLD

The same gold of summer was on the winter hills,
the oat straw gold, the gold of slow sun change.

The stubble was chilly and lonesome,
The stub feet clomb up the hills and stood.

The flat cry of one wheeling crow faded and came,
ran on the stub gold flats and faded and came.

Fade-me, find-me, slow lights rang their changes
on the flats of oat straw gold on winter hills.

MAROON WITH SILVER FROST

Whispers of maroon came on the little river.
The slashed hill took up the sunset,
Took up the evening star.
The brambles crackled in a fire call
To the beginnings of frost.
"It is almost night," the maroon whispered
    in widening blood rings on the little river.
"It is night," the sunset, the evening star
    said later over the hump of the slashed hill.
"What if it is?" the brambles crackled across
    the sure silver beginnings of frost.

CORNFIELD RIDGE AND STREAM

The top of the ridge is a cornfield.
It rests all winter under snow.
It feeds the broken snowdrifts in spring
To a clear stream cutting down hill to the river.
Late in summer the stream dries; rabbits run and
      birds hop along the dry mud bottom.
Fall time comes and it fills with leaves; oaks and
      shagbark hickories drop their summer hats,
      ribbons, handkerchiefs.
"This is how I keep warm all winter," the stream
      murmurs, waiting till the snowdrifts melt and
      the ice loosens and the clear singing babble
      of spring comes back.

ON A RAILROAD RIGHT OF WAY

Stream, go hide yourself.
In the tall grass, in the cat tails,
In the browns of autumn, the last purple
    asters, the yellow whispers.
On the moss rock levels leave the marks
    of your wave-lengths.
Sing in your gravel, in your clean gully.
Let the moaning railroad trains go by.
Till they stop you, go on with your song.

The minnies spin in the water gravel,
In the spears of the early autumn sun.
There must be winter fish.
Babies, you will be jumping fish
In the first snow month.

SO TO SPEAK

Dreams, graves, pools, growing
flowers, cornfields—these are
silent, so to speak.

Northwest blizzards, sea rocks
apounding in high wind, southeast
sleet after a thaw—these are heard,
so to speak.

VALLEY MIST

SILVER POINT

The silver point of an evening star
dropping toward the hammock of new moon
over Lake Okoboji, over prairie waters in Iowa,—
it was framed in the lights just after twilight.

MIST MARCHES ACROSS THE VALLEY

Mist marches across the valley.
Down a long slope the mist marches
And then up a long slope the mist marches
And kingdoms, armies, guns, magic of bookmen, axmen,
The mist marches through them all, gathers them all
And goes to the next valley, goes to the next night,
Goes to the next lookers-on, gathers them all,
Gathers valleys, nights, lookers-on.

Come on down the valley: come on, oh mist.
Whiten us with some of your white.
Show us your gift, your great gift, your white gift
Of gathering all, gathering kingdoms, armies, guns,
Magic of bookmen, axmen, gathering valleys, nights,
            lookers-on.
Whiten us, oh mist, whiten us with some of this strong soft
            white of yours.

METHUSALEH SAW MANY REPEATERS

Methusaleh was a witness to many cabbages and kings,
Many widows of the sod and many grass widows,
Many a mother-in-law, many a triangle of one woman and
    two men or one man and two women,
Many who died hungry and crying for their babies, many
    who died hungry and no babies at all to cry for.

Methusaleh must have lived eight hundred years or a
    thousand or two hundred years.
Methusaleh was an old man when he died and you if you see
    what Methusaleh saw,
You will be an old man or an old woman when you die.

Repeat it: Methusaleh saw many cabbages and kings, he
    was a witness, a looker-on like me, like you.
Repeat it: Methusaleh was an old man, he saw much before
    he was through, and you or I, if we see what Methu-
    saleh saw, if we see it all before we are through,
You and I will be old, old as Methusaleh, old with our look-
    ing on at cabbages and kings, widows of the sod and
    the grass, triangles, and people with babies to cry for
    and no babies at all to cry for.
Repeat it: Methusaleh was a witness of repeating figures,
    sea patterns in the sea sand, land patterns of the land
    wind, Methusaleh was a witness, a looker-on like me,
    like you.

SKETCH OF A POET

He wastes time walking and telling the air, "I am superior even to the wind."

On several proud days he has addressed the wide circumambient atmosphere, "I am the wind myself."

He has poet's license 4-11-44; he got it even before writing of those "silver bugs that come on the sky without warning every evening."

He stops for the buzzing of bumblebees on bright Tuesdays in any summer month; he performs with a pencil all alone among dun cat-tails, amid climbing juniper bushes, notations rivaling the foot tracks of anxious spiders; he finds mice homes under beach logs in the sand and pursues inquiries on how the mice have one room for bed-room, dining-room, sitting-room and how they have no front porch where they sit publicly and watch passers-by.

He asks himself, "Who else is the emperor of such elegant english? Who else has slipped so often on perilous banana peels and yet lived to put praise of banana peels on sonorous pages?"

One minute he accuses God of having started the world on a shoestring; the next minute he executes a simple twist of the wrist and a slight motion of the hand and insinuates these bones shall rise again.

Yet he wastes time walking and telling the air, "I am superior to the wind," or on proud days, "I am the wind myself."

WHIFFS OF THE OHIO RIVER AT CINCINNATI

1

A young thing in spring green slippers, stockings,
    silk vivid as lilac-time grass,
And a red line of a flaunt of fresh silk again up under
    her chin—
She slipped along the street at half-past six in the evening,
    came out of the stairway where her street address is,
    where she has a telephone number—
Just a couple of blocks from the street next to the
    Ohio river, where men sit in chairs tipped back,
    watching the evening lights on the water of the
    Ohio river—
She started out for the evening, dark brown calf eyes,
    roaming and hunted eyes,
And her young wild ways were not so young any more,
    nor so wild.

Another evening primrose stood in a stairway, with a
    white knit sweater fitting her shoulders and ribs close.
She asked a young ballplayer passing for a few kind words
    and a pleasant look—and he slouched up to her like an
    umpire calling a runner out at the home plate—he
    gave her a few words and passed on.
She had bells on, she was jingling, and yet—her young
    wild ways were not so young any more, nor so wild.

2

When I asked for fish in the restaurant facing the Ohio river, with fish signs and fish pictures all over the wooden, crooked frame of the fish shack, the young man said, "Come around next Friday—the fish is all gone today."

So, I took eggs, fried, straight up, one side, and he murmured, humming, looking out at the shining breast of the Ohio river, "And the next is something else; and the next is something else."

The customer next was a hoarse roustabout, handling nail kegs on a steamboat all day, asking for three eggs, sunny side up, three, nothing less, shake us a mean pan of eggs.

And while we sat eating eggs, looking at the shining breast of the Ohio river in the evening lights, he had his thoughts and I had mine thinking how the French who found the Ohio river named it La Belle Riviere meaning a woman easy to look at.

SUBURBAN SICILIAN SKETCHES

1

The cockleburs came on the burdocks,
a little of thistle, a little of flower,
a light red purple tip on raw green bur.

The burdocks came like hoodlums come ;
they came with neither permits nor requests ;
they took what they wanted. "If anybody
asks you, this is us, and we are here because
we decided to come to the party—we invited
ourselves and we are welcome."

Listen in the summer when the roots dig in,
the hoodlum roots of the burdock gangs ;
what each one sings is much like—
"I'm gonna live anyhow until I die."

In the time of the turning leaves
the light red purple tip and the raw green bur
pass and turn to a brown, to a drab and dirty brown.

2

In Mel-a-rose among the sons of Sicily
I saw a sheep, a dirty undersized sheep,
In the front yard cabbage patch of a son of Sicily,

And the wool of the sheep had never been combed,
The wool of the sheep was snarled and knotted.
And the burdock gang was there,
Burs in the wool with a drab and hoodlum mutter,
'This is us, we invited ourselves and we're welcome.'

3

The sober-faced goat crops grass next to the sidewalk.
A clinking chain connects the collar of the goat with a steel
      pin driven in the ground.
Next to the sidewalk the goat crops November grass,
Pauses seldom, halts not at all, incessantly goes after grass.

4

The playhouse of the Sicilian children
thatched with maple branches their father
threw over for a roof in summer,
the playhouse roof is dry;
It sags and crackles in the west wind.

5

The Sicilian father is tying cornstalks
for a winter vest at the roots of the young apple tree.
This, and the red peppers drying on the cellar door,
this is one of the signs of November.

FLAT WATERS OF THE WEST IN KANSAS

After the sunset in the mountains
there are shadows and shoulders
standing to the stars.
After the sunset on the prairie
there are only the stars,
the stars standing alone.

The flat waters of the west in Kansas
take up the sunset lights
one by one and all—
the bars, the barriers, the slow-down,
the loose lasso handy on the saddle,
the big hats, the slip-knot handkerchiefs,
the cattle horns, the hocks and haunches
ready for the kneel-down, the sleep
of the humps and heads in the grass,
the pony with a rump to the wind
or curving a neck to a front foot—
if a baby moon comes after the sunset
it is a witness of many homes,
many home-makers under the night sky-shed—
and the flat waters of the west in Kansas
take up the baby moon, the witness,
take it and let it ride,
take it and let it have a home.

The great plains
gave the buffalo grass.

The great plains
gave the buffalo grass.

THREE SLANTS AT NEW YORK

New York is a city of many cats.
Some say New York is Babylon.
There is a rose and gold mist New York.

New York is a city of many cats; they eat the swill of the poor and the swell swill; they rub their backs against fire escapes and weep to each other from alley barrels; they are born to the cat life of New York.

Some say New York is Babylon; here are Babylonian dancers stripped to the flash of the navel, while the waiters murmur, "Yes," in undertones to regular customers calling for the same whiskey as last time; and having seen a thing of much preparation, toil and genius, having spoken to each other of how marvelous it is, they eat and drink till it is forgotten; and the topics are easy topics, such as which bootleggers take the biggest risks, and what light risks superior bootleggers travel under.

There is a rose and gold New York of evening lights and sunsets; there is a mist New York seen from steamboats, a massed and spotted hovering ghost, a shape the fists of men have lifted out of dirt and work and daylight and early morning oaths after sleep nights.

New York is a city of many cats.
Some say New York is Babylon.
There is a rose and gold mist New York.

LANDSCAPE INCLUDING THREE STATES OF THE UNION

The mountains stand up around the main street in Harper's
Ferry.

Shadows stand around the town, and mist creeps up the
flanks of tall rocks.

A terrible push of waters sometime made a cloven way for
their flood here.

On the main street the houses huddle; the walls crouch for
cover.

And yet—up at Hilltop House, or up on Jefferson's Rock,
there are lookouts;

There are the long curves of the meeting of the Potomac
and the Shenandoah;

There is the running water home of living fish and silver of
the sun.

The lazy flat rocks spread out browns for green and blue
silver to run over.

Mascots of silver circles move around Harper's Ferry.

No wonder John Brown came here to fight and be hanged.

No wonder Thomas Jefferson came here to sit with his
proud red head writing notes on the great State of
Virginia.

Borders hem the town, borders of Virginia, West Virginia,
Maryland;

Be absent minded a minute or two and you guess at what
state you are in.

Harper's Ferry is a meeting place of winds and waters,
rocks and ranges.

CROSSING OHIO WHEN POPPIES
BLOOM IN ASHTABULA

1

Go away. Leave the high winds of May
blowing over the fields of grape vines
near the northwest corner of Pennsylvania.
    Leave the doorstep peonies
    pushing high bosoms at passers-by
    in northern Ohio towns in May.

Leave the boys flying light blue kites
on a deep blue sky; and the yellow, the
yellow spilling over the drinking rims
of the buttercups, piling their yellows
into foam blown sea rims of yellow;
    Go away; go to New York,
    Broadway, Fifth Avenue, glass
    lights and leaves, glass faces,
    fingers; go . . .

2

    Pick me poppies in Ohio,
    mother.
    Pick me poppies in a back yard
    in Ashtabula.

May going, poppies coming, summer humming:
make it a poppy summer, mother; the leaves
sing in the silk, the leaves sing a tawny
red gold; seven sunsets saved themselves
to be here now.

Pick me poppies, mother; go, May; wash me,
summer; shoot up this back yard in Ashta-
bula, shoot it up, give us a daylight fire-
works in Ohio, burn it up with tawny red
gold.

MARCH OF THE HUNGRY MOUNTAINS

Across Nevada and Utah
Look for the march of the hungry mountains.

They are cold and white,
They are taking a rest,
They washed their faces in awful fires,
They lifted their heads for heavy snows.

White, O white, are the vapors,
And the wind in the early morning,
White are the hungry mountains.

The tireless gray desert,
The tireless salt sea,
The tireless mountains,
They are thinking over something.
They are wondering, "What next?"
They are thankful, thinking it over,
Waiting, sleeping, drying their faces from awful fires,
Lifting their heads into higher snow,
White in the early morning wind.

"Come and listen to us,"
Said the marching, hungry mountains.
"You will hear nothing at all,
And you will learn only a little,
And, yet listening, your ears may grow longer and softer;
You may yet have long, clear, listening ears.
Come and listen," said the mocking, hungry mountains.

DIALOGUE

LAKE MICHIGAN : We have been here quite a while.

ILLINOIS PRAIRIE : Maybe.

LAKE : We have seen ten cities.

PRAIRIE : Eleven.

LAKE : Eleven with Chicago.

SMOKE BLUE

The mountains stood on their bottom ends;
the smoky mountains stood around in blue;
the blue mountains stood around in smoke;

The higher the line of the burnt timber climbed,
the lower the line of the green timber crept;
the creep of the burnt and the green
was a couple of shadows moving through each other.

The farms and the fences came,
And the farmers fixing fences.
The snake rail fences measured the farms;
Hog tight, horse high, they held for the owners
The hogs for hams and the horses for hauls.

The farms came to the valley,
And the mountains stood on their bottom ends;
The mountains stood in a smoke and a blue.

The cities came, the lumber wagons,
The lumber carpenters, the lathers, the plasterers;
The bricklayers came in their overalls,
And the hod-carriers up and down the ladders with mortar
And the bricklayers calling down to the hod-carriers,
        "Mort!"
And the concrete mixers came with their endless bellies
For sand and crushed stone and gravel and cement;
The cities came, stood up, and swore, "This is us, by God."

The cities, the families, the tall two-fisted men, swearing,
   "This is us, by God, this is God's country."

   The boomers boomed the boosters,
   The boosters boosted the boomers.

And the mountains stood on their bottom ends.
The mountains stood in a smoke and a blue.

AGAIN?

Old Man Woolworth put up a building.
There it was; his dream; all true;
The biggest building in the world.
Babel, the Nineveh Hanging Gardens,
Karnak, all old, outclassed.
And now, here at last, what of it?
What about it? Well, every morning
We'll walk around it and look up.
And every morning we'll ask what
It means and where it's going.
It's a dream; all true; going somewhere,
That's a cinch; women buying mousetraps,
Wire cloth dishrags, ten cent sheet music,
They paid for it; the electric tower
Might yell an electric sign to the inbound
Ocean liners, 'Look what the washerwomen
Of America can do with their nickels,' or
'See what a nickel and a dime can do,'
And that wouldn't clear Old Man Woolworth's
Head; it was a mystery, a dream, the biggest
Building in the world; Babel, the Nineveh
Hanging Gardens, Karnak, all old,
Outclassed. So the old man cashes in,
The will of the old man is dug out,
And the widow gets thirty million dollars,
Enough to put up another building,
Another bigger than any in the world,
Bigger than Babel, the Nineveh Hanging Gardens,

Karnak, another mystery, another dream
To stand and look up at
And ask what it means.

EVEN NUMBERS

1

A house like a man all lean and coughing,
a man with his two hands in the air at a cry,
"Hands up."

A house like a woman shrunken and stoop-shouldered,
shrunken and done with dishes and dances.

These two houses I saw going uphill in Cincinnati.

2

Two houses leaning against each other like drunken
brothers at a funeral,

Two houses facing each other like two blind wrestlers
hunting a hold on each other,

These four scrawny houses I saw on a dead level
cinder patch in Scranton, Pennsylvania.

3

And by the light of a white moon in Waukesha, Wisconsin,
I saw a lattice work in lilac time . . . white-mist lavender
. . . a sweet moonlit lavender . . .

CHILLICOTHE

There was a man walked out
Of a house in Chillicothe, Ohio,—
Or the house was in Chillicothe, Illinois,
Or again in Chillicothe, Missouri,—

And the man said to himself,
Speaking as men speak their thoughts
To themselves after a funeral or a wedding,
After seeing a baby born with raw, red toes
And the toe-nails pink as the leaves of fresh flowers,
Or after seeing a kinsman try to hold on
To the fading door-frames of life
And then languish, let go, and sleep,—

Speaking his own thoughts,
Or what he believed in so far as he knew
To be thoughts peculiar to himself alone,
At that hour of time, under the clocks and suns,
He said, and to himself:

"I have never seen myself live a day.
I have told myself I get up in the morning,
I wash my face, I reach for a towel, I find a razor,
I shave off a day or a two-day growth of whiskers.
I look in the looking-glass and say,
'Birdie, whither away to-day?' or I say,
'You old hound dog, are you on to yourself?' or
'What's in the wind for this evening?' or,

'Who put the fish in efficiency?' or,
'What packages will be handed us this morning?'

"Yes, I stand in front of the looking-glass,
And while I am shaving I sometimes ask questions
Exactly as though the house I am shaving in
Is a wagon crossing Oklahoma looking for a home,
Or a steamboat on the tossing salt, two days from Sandy
        Hook,
Or a Pullman sleeper crossing the divide in Colorado—
This must be why I say to the looking-glass,
'You are the same when I am shaving, always,
Whether we are in Oklahoma, off Sandy Hook,
Or hitting the high spot of the Colorado divide;
Your business as a looking-glass is to say 'Me, too,'
'Here it is,' 'Here you are,' 'I don't want to tell you no lie.
If I tell a lie, I lose out as a looking-glass.'

"There are hinged elbows of arms, sockets in shoulder-
        bones.
And out beyond the elbows are finger-bones, finger-ends.
And after a while the command runs out to the finger-ends
To wipe off the lather, throw a hot towel, witch hazel,
Then dry smooth the face, talcum, and call it a once over.
This action finished, I can testify all day, 'I shaved this
        morning'
Or if there is a murder or a robbery, and I am called as a
        witness
In the matter of an identity or an alibi or *corpus delicti*,
I can solemnly swear at this hour I shaved my face, at this
        hour

I commanded the members and parts of my body in these
　　　　performances.
I shaved this morning.

"Yet all this is only a whiff, a little comic beginning.
Ever since I have owned more than one shirt
I have had to decide which shirt to wear to-day.
There was a year when I had only one shirt,
And even then I had to decide whether I would wear that
　　　　one shirt
Or whether I would get along with no shirt at all.
Now, having six shirts, I must pick one and let five others
　　　　go.
If there are buttons off the shirt, I decide
How many new buttons go on.

"Decisions—see? It is early in the day, it is not a half-hour
Since I was in the sheets of unremembering slumber.
Yet the day's decisions have mounted steadily as the climb
　　　　of the sun
Up and on across the elements of the sky.

"Yes? Quite so. And sure, Mike.
These things count for nothing much.
There is no special destiny about them.
They are different from falling in love
Or calling up a doctor to tie an artery
Or writing a lawyer about a bastardy case,
Or telling a panhandler you are broke yourself,
And do your shopping by looking in the show-windows.

"Yes, they are all different.
Yet they all connect up with civilization
Or tombs and ramparts earlier than civilization.
So God help your soul when you get tired of them and say:
'I want something new. I want two and two to be five. I want
    a miracle to happen, miracles now and henceforth. I
    want the light that never was on land or sea."

And all the time it is the same man speaking,
The same man who walked out of his house
In Chillicothe, Ohio, Chillicothe, Illinois, or Chillicothe,
    Missouri;
It is the same man speaking his own thoughts,
As if thoughts come to him and belong to him alone,
And as though it is useless to pass them on—
It is the same man speaking.

"I have never seen myself live a day.
I have pulled up a chair to the breakfast-table
And watched children tuck napkins under their chin,
Spill the yellow of eggs down their bibs,
Clean their plates, lick their spoons, call for more to eat,
While they banged their spoons and bowls on the table
And went on yammering for more to eat.
I have seen them use their tongues as cats and dogs
Employ their tongues, as utensils, conveniences,
With laughters shining in their eyes.
And when they began talking, they lied to each other,
They lied with an importance of falsifying large.
They broke out with impossible propositions.
They acted as though they live in a republic of separate
    laws,

Under a government whose laws go deeper than the speech
Of people expert and renowned for their ways of speech.
Their laughter ran as the water of waterfalls runs.

"They were so proud, so sure, in all their ways, I said:
'What goes? What drops off? What is the sheath they lose
When they grow up and get big and leave behind them
Their republic of separate laws,
Their government of laws deeper than speech,
Their civilization of impossible propositions?
Why shall they seem no longer so proud, so sure,
With laughter running as the water of waterfalls runs?'

"I ask myself just that question.
I asked it far inside of myself.
And it was such a far-off question, if I had whispered it
They would have known it was not to be answered."

And this was only one morning
Among the many mornings of that man
Speaking to himself what he considered his own thoughts
Going out of the door of his house in Chillicothe.

And these are only a few of the thoughts of that one
morning.
For, when he reached the gate and stepped to the sidewalk,
He said again to himself:

"I have never seen myself live a day."

SPLINTER

The voice of the last cricket
across the first frost
is one kind of good-by.
It is so thin a splinter of singing.

SANTA FE SKETCHES

1

The valley was swept with a blue broom to the west.

And to the west, on the fringes of a mesa sunset,
there are blue broom leavings, hangover blue wisps—
bluer than the blue floor the broom touched
before and after it caught the blue sweepings.

The valley was swept with a blue broom to the west.

2

When a city picks a valley—and a valley picks a city—
it is a marriage—and there are children.

Since the bluebirds come by twenties
and the blackbirds come by forties
in March, when the snow skirls in a sunshine wind;
since they come up the valley to the city, heading north,
it is taken as a testimony of witnesses.

When the bluebird barriers drop,
when the redwing bars go down,
the flurries of sun flash now on the tail feathers—
it is up the valley—up and on—
by twenties and forties—
and the tail feathers flashing.

In the cuts of the red dirt arroyos,
at the change of the mist of the mountain waterfalls,
in cedars and pinons, at the scars and gashes,
at the patches where new corn will be planted,
at the Little Canyon of the Beans,
they stop and count how far they have come,
the twenties and forties stop and count.

Whoever expected them to remember,
to carry little pencils between their toes,
notebooks under their wings?
By twenties, by forties—it is enough;
"When wings come, and sun, and a new wind
out of the Southwest whispering—
and especially wings—we forget—
we forget."

They saw Navajos ride with spears and arrows,
Spaniards ride with blunderbusses,
cowboys ride with Colts and Winchesters—
they saw the changing shooting irons—
and now the touring-car and flivver
creep up the red dirt valley, among the rabbit bushes,
passing the clean-piled clean-cut woodpiles
on the backs of mountain-born burros.

3

The valley sits with its thoughts.

"Have I not had my thoughts by myself
four hundred years?" she asks.

"Have I not seen the guns of Spain, Mexico
and America go up and down the valley?

"Is not holy faith and the name of a saint
in my name?

"Was I not called La Villa de Sante Fe de
San Francisco de Assisi?

"Do they not name a railroad from Chicago
to Los Angeles after me?

"Did they not give a two-thousand-mile wagon
trail of the first gold diggers, the forty-niners,
my name, the short pet name, Santa Fe?

"Do you wonder I sit here, like an easy woman,
not young, not old—
Do you wonder I sit here, shrewd, faded, asking:
What next? who next?
And answering my own questions: I don't care—
let the years worry."

4

By twenties and forties,
the bluebirds and the redwings,
out of the bars, the barriers,
in a flash of tail feathers
on and up the valley—

"When wings come
and the Southwest whispering,
we forget."

5

The valley city sits among its brooding facts,
"Six years ago—only ponies, bridles, saddles circled
around the public square, the plaza, the place of the
Summer band concerts—
And now—the varnished motor-cars stand with funeral
faces filling the old pony hitching places.

"I have seen candles keep the night watch till the coal
oil came and then the live wires—
Thirty miles away the mountain villages see two strings
of lights hung like Summer flies—the penitentiary night
lights of Santa Fe.

"The fast travelers with extra tires come in a hurry
and solve me and pass on to say all their lives,
'Santa Fe? oh yes, Santa Fe, I have seen Santa Fe.'
'Hurry up,' is their first and last word on my zigzag
streets, my lazy 'dobe corners.
'Hurry up, we must see the Old Church, the Old Bell, the
Oldest House in the United States, touch the doors,
and then go on—hurry up!'

"They are afraid grass will grow under their feet—they
say so as a proverb—
And I am afraid they will knock loose some cool green
whisper of moss in a chink of a wall."

6

In April the little farmers go out in the foothills,
up the mountain patches.
They go to gamble against the weather, the rain.

"If the rain comes like last year, we shall have a fat
winter,
If the rain comes like year before last, it is a lean
Christmas for us."

They put in their beans, the magic frijole, the chile,
they stretch open hands to the sky,
and tell the rain to come,
to come, come, come.

With a willing rain the gamblers win.
If the rain says, "Not this year," they lose.

So the little farmers go out in the foothills,
up the mountain patches in April,
telling every bean in the sack
to send up a wish to God
for water to come . . . out of the sky.

7

A loose and changeable sky
looks on a loose and changeable land.

The rain rips the wagon road ruts
too deep for wheels—the wagons make a new road,
the rain makes a new little arroyo.

Pack burros tussling under bundled woodpiles go by
    with eyes murmuring, "Everything is the same as it
    always was."
The tough little tussling foot of a burro, the wag of
    a left ear to a right ear, are they joking, "Every-
    thing is the same as it always was?"

8

Proud and lazy Spaniards with your pearl swords
    of conquest, your blunderbuss guns of flags and
    victory—

Who did you conquer and fasten down as your vassals?

The blood is dry and mixed in a mixing-bowl.
The passion kiss and the sunlit blaze of the Indian woman's
    eye—the faces and the hair of Spain and the Aztecs,
    Moors and the Navajos—are mixed in a mixing bowl
    —and a passer-by writes:

"In Mexico nobody knows how to sing
and everybody sings."

Come back and pick up your pearl-handled swords,
your blunderbuss guns.
Sniff with the tourists in the Santa Fe Museum—
See them look at their stop-watches—
"A little gas now—and we're on our way—come on
kid—on your way."

9

The valley was swept with a blue broom to the west,
there are blue broom leavings on the sky,
hangover blue wisps.
The valley city sits with its thoughts.
"Have I not had my thoughts by myself
four hundred years?" she asks.
"Do you wonder I sit here, shrewd, faded,
asking: What next? who next?
And answering: I don't care—let the
years worry."

10

By twenties and forties,
the bluebirds and the redwings,
out of the bars, the barriers,
in a flash of tail feathers
on and up the valley—
"When wings come
and the Southwest whispering,
we forget."

LITTLE ALBUM

NEW HAMPSHIRE AGAIN

I remember black winter waters,
I remember thin white birches,
I remember sleepy twilight hills,
I remember riding across New
Hampshire lengthways.
I remember a station named
"Halcyon," a brakeman call-
ing to passengers "Halcyon!!
Halcyon!!"
I remember having heard the
gold diggers dig out only
enough for wedding rings.
I remember a stately child tell-
ing me her father gets letters
addressed "Robert Frost, New
Hampshire."
I remember an old Irish saying,
"His face is like a fiddle and
every one who sees him must
love him."
I have one remember, two re-
members, ten remembers; I
have a little handkerchief
bundle of remembers.

One early evening star just over
a cradle moon,

One dark river with a spatter of
later stars caught,
One funnel of a motorcar head-
light up a hill,
One team of horses hauling a
bob sled load of wood,
One boy on skis picking himself
up after a tumble—
I remember one and a one and a
one riding across New Hamp-
shire lengthways: I have a lit-
tle handkerchief bundle of re-
members.

A COUPLE

He was in Cincinnati, she in Burlington.
He was in a gang of Postal Telegraph linemen.
She was a pot rassler in a boarding house.
"The crying is lonely," she wrote him.
"The same here," he answered.
The winter went by and he came back and they married
And he went away again where rainstorms knocked down
      telegraph poles and wires dropped with frozen sleet.
And again she wrote him, "The crying is lonely."
And again he answered, "The same here."
Their five children are in the public schools.
He votes the Republican ticket and is a taxpayer.
They are known among those who know them
As honest American citizens living honest lives.
Many things that bother other people never bother them.
They have their five children and they are a couple,
A pair of birds that call to each other and satisfy.
As sure as he goes away she writes him, "The crying is
        lonely"
And he flashes back the old answer, "The same here."
It is a long time since he was a gang lineman at Cincinnati
And she was a pot rassler in a Burlington boarding house;
Yet they never get tired of each other; they are a couple.

CHICAGO BOY BABY

The baby picked from an ash barrel by the night police
came to the hospital of the Franciscan brothers
in a diaper and a white sheet.

It was a windy night in October, leaves and geese scurrying
across the north sky, and the curb pigeons more ravenous
than ever for city corn in the cracks of the street stones.

The two policemen who picked the baby from the ash barrel
are grayheads; they talk about going on the pension list
soon; they talk about whether the baby, surely a big man
now, votes this year for Smith or Hoover.

JOKE GOLD

It arose with him as a joke,
His saying so often with a mystical gesture
Known to all as a joke,
"There's gold in them hills, Jack."
All of us laughed and he laughed most
At the comic illusion of gold hunters
Picking hills to gamble in, with
Hopes and shovels, burros and frying pans,
The yellow shine of the high lure
Overlying life's high points.
It was all there in his sudden interjection,
"There's gold in them hills, Jack."
His wife, his other women, his new jobs
One after the other, his swaggering neckties,
Sport shirts, and allusions to men with fat
Checkbooks he lunched with chummily,
It all tied in with his always saying
Gold lay in hills beyond, joke gold
In joke hills to be made into real gold
In real hills for wishing, for only enough
Wishing—it was all in his voice when he
Went away and was never heard from again,
Stepping on the outbound train west
Saying, "Gold in them hills, Jack."

THE OLD FLAGMAN

The old flagman has great-grand-children.
Ruddy as a hard nut, hair in his ears, clear sea lights
    in his eyes,
He goes out of his shanty and lifts a sign: Stop.

"Y'see where the sign is dented?.
I hit a fellah over the head with it,
The only way to stop him gettin' run over.
They want to get killed; I have to stop 'em.
That's my job."

He was twenty years a policeman in Chicago.
"I carry a bullet in my guts an I got an abscess in
    my gall bladder—I picked this shanty for a rest.
"I go slow and careful; I got a leak in the heart; if
I laugh too hard my heart stops—and I fall down;
I have to watch myself."

A third rail car hoots up the line.
He goes out with a warning in his hand: Stop.
"These damn fools, they want to get under the wheels.
I have to stop 'em."

Ruddy as a hard nut, hair in his ears, clear sea lights
    in his eyes.

IGLITS AND HIS WIFE

Iglit's wife spoke of her own novel, of a Norwegian's novel and came finally to speak of Whimsley and Whimsley's wife and egg spots on the wallpaper and fly specks on the new white kalsomining of the sleeping room of Whimsley and Whimsley's wife.

Iglit's wife went on patching a picture together in clean polite language, hearsay and circumstance. The cool abstraction of the scientist, the mocking sleight-of-hand passes of the artist, the galloping babble of the gossip who mixes names and dates for the sake of the story and only asks a laugh or a giggle before going on to another laugh—

These were lost in the list of witnesses ready to testify to the egg spots on the wallpaper, the fly specks on the new white kalsomining of the sleeping room of Whimsley and Whimsley's wife.

Iglits mentions the weather to the housemaid serving washed apricots for breakfast, mentions letters and filing devices to the stenographer in the downtown office.

Iglits buys whiskey from two booze runners; a bottle is in his desk always; Iglits says he wants to be lit up a little every day.

MEDLEY

Ignorance came in stones of gold;
The ignorant slept while the hangmen
Hanged the keepers of the lights
Of sweet stars: such were the apothegms,
Offhand offerings of mule-drivers
Eating sandwiches of rye bread,
Salami and onions.

"Too Many Books," we always called him;
A landscape of masterpieces and old favorites
Fished with their titles for his eyes
In the upstairs and downstairs rooms
Of his house. Whenever he passed
The old-time bar-room where Pete Morehouse
Shot the chief of police, where
The sponge squads shot two bootleggers,
He always remembered the verse story,
The Face on the Bar-room Floor—
The tramp on a winter night,
Saddened and warmed with whiskey,
Telling of a woman he wanted
And a woman who wanted him,
How whiskey wrecked it all;
Taking a piece of chalk,
Picturing her face on the bar-room floor,
Fixing the lines of her face
While he told the story,

Then gasping and falling with finished heartbeats,
Dead.

And whenever he passed over the bridge at night
And took the look up the river to smaller bridges,
Barge lights, and looming shores,
He always thought of Edgar Allan Poe,
With a load of hootch in him,
Going to a party of respectable people
Who called for a speech,
Who listened to Poe recite the Lord's Prayer,
Correctly, word for word, yet with lush, unmistakable
Intonations, so haunting the dinner-party people
All excused themselves to each other.

Whenever Too Many Books
Passed over the town bridge in the gloaming,
He thought of Poe breaking up that party
Of respectable people. Such was Too Many Books—
We called him that.

IMPLICATIONS

When the charge of election bribery was brought against an Illinois senator, he replied, "I read the Bible and believe it from cover to cover."

When his accusers specified five hundred dollars of corruption money was paid in a St. Louis hotel bath room, his friends answered, "He is faithful to his wife and always kind to his children."

When he was ousted from the national senate and the doors of his bank were closed by government receivers and a grand jury indicted him, he took the vows of an old established church.

When a jury acquitted him of guilt as a bank wrecker, following the testimony of prominent citizens that he was an honest man, he issued a statement to the public for the newspapers, proclaiming he knew beforehand no jury would darken the future of an honest man with an unjust verdict.

TO THE GHOST OF JOHN MILTON

If I should pamphleteer twenty years against royalists,
With rewards offered for my capture dead or alive,
And jails and scaffolds always near,

And then my wife should die and three ignorant daughters
Should talk about their father as a joke, and steal the
Earnings of books, and the poorhouse always reaching for
      me,

If I then lost my eyes and the world was all dark and I
Sat with only memories and talk—

I would write "Paradise Lost," I would marry a second wife
And on her dying I would marry a third pair of eyes to
Serve my blind eyes, I would write "Paradise Regained," I
Would write wild, foggy, smoky, wordy books—

I would sit by the fire and dream of hell and heaven,
Idiots and kings, women my eyes could never look on **again,**
And God Himself and the rebels God threw into hell.

HEAVY AND LIGHT

And you, old woman, are carrying scrub buckets to-night.
Just like last year, just like the year before,
Every Saturday night you come gripping the handles,
Throwing the suds, cleaning this room's floor.
They call you "Mrs. Swanson," your hair is thin and gray,
It is a lean little wiry frame you move in.
In your eyes you are ready for whatever comes next.
Your sons have scrubbed ship decks, an uncle somewhere
Stood at a wheel in a Baltic storm—why must there be
Some rag of romance, some slant of a scarlet star
Over and around your scrub buckets?

.   .   .

Fritters used to say, "There is poetry in neckties."
He picked neckties with a theory of color and design.
He knew haberdashers the way book bugs know where
        second hand book stores are.
For a picnic he wore pink, for a fall fog day a grey blue,
And a four-in-hand, a bow, a bat-eye, each of its separate
        individual in silk, plain or striped or spotted,
Each had its message, its poem, its reminders, for Fritters.
"I know how to pick 'em," he used to say, "I know the right
        scarf for either a wedding or a funeral or a poker
        party, there is poetry in neckties."

EARLY HOURS

(To A. W. F.)

Since you packed your rubber bottom boots
And took the night train for northern Wisconsin
To hunt deer in the ten days allowed by law,
I have remembered your saying the hunters
Get up out of bed and dress for shooting,
For reading snow tracks, circling, waiting, firing,
At the hour of half past four in the morning;
Now this has been in my mind sometimes
When after a long day's work and more than half a night
I opened the east window before going to bed
At half past three o'clock in the morning
And there were deer feet and horns of stars on the sky.
I listened to the chiming of a watch and said,
"A couple of hours and Jim'll kill a deer, maybe."
There are different kinds of early hours.

HUNGRY AND LAUGHING MEN

Love to keep? There is no love to keep.
There is memory to keep of running water,
    running horses, running weather, running days.

When I see the rain-glad eaves filling and the
    beat of the running spills on the ferns,
Or if I come to a pony heel mark, a half loop on
    a smooth Kentucky blue grass,
Or stand in a Dutch landscape of running threats
    in changing lights of interchangeable running
    sun and rain-cloud—
I shall take old note-books of Hokusai and Hiroshige,
    memoirs of the wonderful hungry laughing men, and in
    an off corner, write my code:
        Love to keep? There is no love to keep.
        There is memory of runners, foot-glad flingers,
        heel marks in the blue grass, running
        threats of interchangeable sun and rain-cloud.

FATE

Fate comes with pennies or dollars.
An Indian head or the Goddess of Liberty:
    it is all the same to Fate.
One day copper, one day silver, and these
    are samples:
        The cry held back
        the kiss kept under
        the song choked down
        the wish never spoken.
They are pennies and dollars these.
The girl at the sink washing dishes knows them.
The girl who has breakfast in bed knows them.

CHEAP BLUE

Hill blue among the leaves in summer,
Hill blue among the branches in winter—
Light sea blue at the sand beaches in winter,
Deep sea blue in the deep deep waters—
Prairie blue, mountain blue—
    Who can pick a pocketful of these blues,
        a handkerchief of these blues,
    And go walking, talking, walking as though
    God gave them a lot of loose change
    For spending money, to throw at the birds,
    To flip into the tin cups of blind men?

LAVENDER LILIES

The lavender lilies in Garfield Park lay lazy in the morning
    sun.
A cool summer wind flicked at our eyebrows and the pansies
    fixed their yellow drops and circles for a day's show.
The statue of Lincoln, an ax in his hand, a bronze ax, was
    a chum of five bluejays crazy and calling, "Another
    lovely morning, another lovely morning."
And the headline of my newspaper said, "Thirty dead in
    race riots."
And Lincoln with the ax, and all the lavender lilies and the
    cool summer wind and the pansies, the living lips of
    bronze and leaves, the living tongues of bluejays, all
    they could say was,
    "Another lovely morning, another lovely morning."

HALF WAY

At the half-way house the pony died.
The road stretched ahead, the sunny hills,
    people in the fields, running waters,
     towns with new names, windmills pointing
    circles in the air at holy cross roads.
It was here we stopped at the half-way house,
    here where the pony died.
Here the keeper of the house said, "It is strange
    how many ponies die here."

BETWEEN WORLDS

And he said to himself
in a sunken morning moon
between two pines,
between lost gold and lingering green:

I believe I will count up my worlds.
There seem to me to be three.
There is a world I came from which is Number One.
There is a world I am in now, which is Number Two.
There is a world I go to next, which is Number Three.

There was the seed pouch, the place I lay dark in, nursed
and shaped in a warm, red, wet cuddling place; if I
tugged at a latchstring or doubled a dimpled fist or
twitched a leg or a foot, only the Mother knew.

There is the place I am in now, where I look back and
look ahead, and dream and wonder.

There is the next place—

And he took a look out of a window
at a sunken morning moon
between two pines,
between lost gold and lingering green.

M'LISS AND LOUIE

When M'Liss went away from the old home
with its purple lilacs in front and white
fence pickets and green grass—

Where the slow black covers of evening and
night came dropping softly before the gold
moon came on the yellow roses—

Louie, the lonesome, spoke his thoughts to himself,
sitting in that same moonlight coming on the lilacs,
the roses:—

> Let her win her own thoughts; let her be
> M'Liss always; let her sit alone after
> whatever happens and see some of the outs
> and ins of it;
>
> Let her know the feel of the bones of
> one of her hands resting on the other;
>
> Let her lose love, gold,
> names, promises, savings;
>
> Let her know hot lips, crazy love letters,
> cool heels, good wings, birds crossing big
> windows of blue skies, time, oh God, time to
> think things over; let her be M'Liss;

Let her be easy with all meanings of quiet
new sunsets, quiet fresh mornings, and long
sleeps in the old still moonlight;

Let her be M'Liss always.

Well . . . well . . . it was growing late in the evening of
that day when M'Liss went away, late, late into the night,
as Louie, the lonesome, sat sleepy in the gold of that same
moon coming on the fence pickets and the green grass, the
purple lilacs, the yellow roses.

He was sleepy. Yet he could not sleep.

BITTER SUMMER THOUGHTS

PHIZZOG

This face you got,
This here phizzog you carry around,
You never picked it out for yourself,
    at all, at all—did you?
This here phizzog—somebody handed it
    to you—am I right?
Somebody said, "Here's yours, now go see
    what you can do with it."
Somebody slipped it to you and it was like
    a package marked:
"No goods exchanged after being taken away"—
This face you got.

BITTER SUMMER THOUGHTS

The riders of the wind
Weave their shadows,
Trample their time-beats,
Take their time-bars,
Shake out scrolls,
And run over the oats, the barley,
Over the summer wheat-fields.

The farmer and the horse,
The steel and the wagon
Come and clean the fields
And leave us stubble.
The time-bars of the wind are gone;
The shadows, time-beats, scrolls,
They are woven away, put past,
Into the hands of threshers,
Into chaff, into dust,
Into rust and buff of straw stacks,
Into sliding, shoveling oats and wheat.
Over the wheat-fields,
Over the oats,
Summer weaves, is woven away, put past,
Into dust, into rust and buff.

Indian runners ran along this river-road.
They cleaned the wind they clutched in ribs and lungs,
Up over the clean ankles, the clean elbows.

The Frenchmen came with lessons and prayers.
The Scotchmen came with horses and rifles.
Cities, war, railroads came.

In the rain-storms, in the blizzards,
This river-road is clean.

BITTER SUMMER THOUGHTS—No. 3

Firecrackers came from China.
Watermelons came from Egypt.
The horses of the sun hoist their heads and nicker at the
    fence where the first old evening stars fish for faces.
And the light of the eyes of a child at a morning window
    calling to an early morning snow, this too is a stranger
    among strangers.

The splendors of old books may be counted.
The spears of brass lights, shining in the dawn of the tug-
    boats and warehouses, throw other splendors.
Yet a corn wind is in my ears, a rushing of corn leaves
    swept by summer, it is in my ears, the corn wind.

BITTER SUMMER THOUGHTS—No. XXII

QUICKER AND EASIER

The billboards and the street car signs told the people,
"Say it with flowers" and those who could buy flowers
And who knew no other way of saying found themselves
In the habit of saying it with flowers.
Men whose personal fragrance had no special whiff
Of fresh air, clean dirt, and growing things,
Found it easier to telephone the florist
And say it with flowers—quicker and easier.

YES, SAY IT WITH FLOWERS!

Women rather wear flowers than no flowers.
Gift flowers never tell where they came from.
A woman's flowers ought to whisper she has
    secrets worth hearing told.
If a woman tells a man, "Send me no flowers,"
    that is the end.
All women try to guess who would send an armful
    of roses for the coffin if one dies, if one has
    a funeral, if all one's friends know there is a
    funeral.
Each woman knows what one flower she would wear if
    called on to wear a flower at a wedding to-morrow.

BARS

Beat at the bars.
Cry out your cry of want.
Let yourself out if you can.
Find the sea, find the moon,
    if you can.
Shut the windows, open the doors.
There are no windows, are no doors?
There is no sea, is no moon?
Cry your cry, let yourself out if you can.

THEY ASK: IS GOD, TOO, LONELY?

When God scooped up a handful of dust,
And spit on it, and molded the shape of man,
And blew a breath into it and told it to walk—
That was a great day.

And did God do this because He was lonely?
Did God say to Himself he must have company
And therefore He would make man to walk the earth
And set apart churches for speech and song with God?

These are questions.
They are scrawled in old caves.
They are painted in tall cathedrals.
There are men and women so lonely they believe
      God, too, is lonely.

TWO NOCTURNS

1

The sea speaks a language polite people never repeat.
It is a colossal scavenger slang and has no respect.
Is it a terrible thing to be lonely?

2

The prairie tells nothing unless the rain is willing.
It is a woman with thoughts of her own.
Is it a terrible thing to love much?

WANTING THE IMPOSSIBLE

Suppose he wishes balloon routes
      to five new moons, one woman,
      and a two-acre bean farm with
      bean poles and waltzing scare-
      crows wearing clown hats:
Ah-hah, ah-hah, this to God,
      this to me, this is something.

MONEY, POLITICS, LOVE AND GLORY

Who put up that cage?
Who hung it up with bars, doors?
Why do those on the inside want to get out?
Why do those outside want to get in?
What is this crying inside and out all the time?
What is this endless, useless beating of baffled
    wings at these bars, doors, this cage?

THE WAY OF THE WORLD

(After Gustave Fröding in the Swedish)

The sea roars, the storm whistles,
Waves roll ashen gray;
"Man overboard, captain!"
    Is that so?

"You can save his life yet, captain!"
The sea roars, the storm whistles.
"Throw a rope to him, you can reach him."
    Is that so?

Waves roll ashen gray.
"He's gone down, you can't see him
    any more, captain!"
    Is that so?
The sea roars, the storm whistles.

USELESS WORDS

So long as we speak the same language and never under-
    stand each other,
So long as the spirals of our words snarl and interlock
And clutch each other with the irreckonable gutturals,
Well . . .

EARLY LYNCHING

Two Christs were at Golgotha.
One took the vinegar, another looked on.
One was on the cross, another in the mob.
One had the nails in his hands, another the stiff
     fingers holding a hammer driving nails.
There were many more Christs at Golgotha, many more
     thief pals, many many more in the mob howling the
     Judean equivalent of, "Kill Him! kill Him!"
The Christ they killed, the Christ they didn't kill,
     those were the two at Golgotha.

Pity, pity, the bones of these broken ankles.
Pity, pity, the slimp of these broken wrists
The mother's arms are strong to the last.
She holds him and counts the heart drips.

The smell of the slums was on him.
Wrongs of the slums lit his eyes.
Songs of the slums wove in his voice
The haters of the slums hated his slum heart.

The leaves of a mountain tree,
Leaves with a spinning star shook in them,
Rocks with a song of water, water, over them,
Hawks with an eye for death any time, any time,
The smell and the sway of these were on his sleeves,
     were in his nostrils, his words.

The slum man they killed, the mountain man lives on.

PLUNGER

Empty the last drop.
Pour out the final clinging heartbeat.
Great losers look on and smile.
Great winners look on and smile.

Plunger:
Take a long breath and let yourself go.

RAIN WINDS

RAIN WINDS BLOW DOORS OPEN

Dreaming of grips at her heart
She asked in a sleep and between sleeps,
"What is mercy and why am I asking mercy?"

The doors in her dreams opened
And a rain wind blew in the doorway
And treetops moaned under footsteps over.

Dreaming of a road running off
Into the roads gone crossways on the sky,
She shook in a dream and cried between sleeps,
"How many miles, how many days, how many years?"

The strips of the sun
Spelled a name on the floor in the morning.
She tried to spell out the name, the letters.
"A rain wind blows in the doorway," she said,
"And a road goes crossways on the sky," she said,
"And the night lets nobody know how many miles,
     how many days, how many years."

WIND HORSES

Roots, go deep: wrap your coils; fasten your knots:
Fix a loop far under, a four-in-hand far under:
The wind drives wild horses, gnashers, plungers:
    Go deep, roots.
Hold your four-in-hand knots against all wild horses.

RIVER MOON

The moon in the river, mother, is a red, red moon to-night.
I am going away on the wild, wild moon, the moon so red on
the river to-night, mother.

A man with a wild dream on his tongue, a flying wild dream
in his head and his heart,
A man is here with a runaway drum in his ribs, and shots of
the sun in the runners of his blood.

I am going away on the red, wild runaway moon.
The moon on the river, mother, is red to-night.

The mist on the river is white and the moon on the mist
is white.
I remember, mother, I remember he came when the moon was
red, with a runaway drum in his ribs.
I remember, mother, the shots of the sun in the runners of
his blood, the flying wild dream on his tongue.
To-night I remember, to-night with the mist on the river
white and the moon on the mist white.

Something is gone—is it him that's gone or is it the red,
wild runaway moon that's gone?

THEY MET YOUNG

1

"I could cry for roses, thinking of you,
Thinking of your lips, so like roses,
Thinking of the meetings of lips
And the crying of eyes meeting."

"I could love you in shadows, drinking
Of you, drinking till a morning sun.
I could touch the young heart of you
And learn all your red songs."

"I could answer the metronomes of blood,
The timebeats of your sweet kisses.
I could sing a star song or a sun song
In the crying of eyes meeting."

2

"Give me your lips.
Let Egypt come or Egypt go.
Open a window of stars.
Let a bag of shooting stars fall.
Wind us with a winding silk.
Pick us a slouching, foolish moon.
Take us to a silver blue morning.
It is too much—let your lips go.

The hammers call, the laws of the
     hammers knock on gongs, beat and
     beat on gongs.
It is too much—give me your lips
     —let your lips go."

YELLOW EVENING STAR

The flush pink runner of the sun
Ran out with a ribbon leap
In the line of a yellow evening star.

Was there a murmur?
"Whither thou goest thither will I go?"
Was there a run and a jump—
Then old sea cliffs, clean high bastions?

FACE

I would beat out your face in brass.
The side of your head I would beat out in brass.
The nose, the mouth, the hang of the hair thick over
  your head, the cool straight-looking forehead,
I would take a hammer and a sheet of brass and beat
   them out till your face would be set against rain,
   frost, storm, sea-water and sea-salt, against hoofs,
   wheels, nails, against tidewater, rust, verdigris.
I would set your face at a blue crossways of sea beaches,
   a dream of blue and brass.

HEAD

Here is a head with a blur of horizons.
She sits where a sweep of leaves is on.
When the wind swept in the spring leaves,
When the wind swept out the autumn leaves,
She sat here with her head a blur of horizons.
She sat here and a worker in brass asked her.
And no answer came and the winds swept on
And the leaves swept on and her head took form
Against the blur of horizons.

EXPLANATIONS OF LOVE

There is a place where love begins and a place
where love ends.

There is a touch of two hands that foils all
dictionaries.

There is a look of eyes fierce as a big Bethlehem open hearth
furnace or a little green-fire acetylene torch.

There are single careless bywords portentous as a
big bend in the Mississippi River.

Hands, eyes, bywords—out of these love makes
battlegrounds and workshops.

There is a pair of shoes love wears and the coming
is a mystery.

There is a warning love sends and the cost of it
is never written till long afterward.

There are explanations of love in all languages
and not one found wiser than this:

There is a place where love begins and a place
where love ends—and love asks nothing.

SEVEN ELEVEN

Among the grackles in a half circle on the grass
Two walked side by side on two legs apiece.

Treetops bent in the wind and bird nests shuddered.
This was why and only why the grackles sat in a half circle.

Seven grackles came at first and sat in the half circle.
Then there were eleven came with two legs apiece and sat in.

They might have been crapshooters full of hope and hot
      breaths.
They might have been believers in luck, come seven, come
      eleven.

SPRAY

I wonder what they called
Across the beaten spray,
Across the night's forehead.

"The long kiss lasts," he told her.
"I'm crazy about you," she answered.

So they called
  to the beaten spray,
  to the night's forehead.

BROKEN HEARTED SOPRANO

When the soprano sang,
"Ask the stars, O beloved,"
There was a wind piling a cover,
Over the sky a cover of black.

And the soprano was feeling
With a left hand over her heart
Trying to feel the deep hurt places,
Trying to measure the tired depths.

There is a wind piles covers.
The sky knows that wind out of old times.
The stars know that wind out of old times.

．　．　．

Have you pointed a finger
And beckoned a loose hand
Up at one star and found no answer?

EPISTLE

Jesus loved the sunsets on Galilee.
Jesus loved the fishing boats forming silhouettes
    against the sunsets on Galilee.
Jesus loved the fishermen on the fishing boats forming
    silhouettes against the sunsets on Galilee.
When Jesus said: Good-by, good-by, I will come again:
    Jesus meant that good-by for the sunsets, the fishing
    boats, the fishermen, the silhouettes all and any
    against the sunsets on Galilee: the good-by and the
    promise meant all or nothing.

MONKEY OF STARS

There was a tree of stars sprang up on a vertical panel of
the south.
And a monkey of stars climbed up and down in this tree of
stars.
And a monkey picked stars and put them in his mouth, tall
up in a tree of stars shining in a south sky panel.
I saw this and I saw what it meant and what it means was
five, six, seven, that's all, five, six, seven.
Oh hoh, yah yah, loo loo, the meaning was five, six, seven,
five, six, seven.

Panels of changing stars, sashes of vapor, silver tails of
meteor streams, washes and rockets of fire—
It was only a dream, oh hoh, yah yah, loo loo, only a dream,
five, six, seven, five, six, seven.

GREAT ROOMS

SEA CHEST

There was a woman loved a man
as the man loved the sea.
Her thoughts of him were the same
as his thoughts of the sea.
They made an old sea-chest for their belongings
together.

WE HAVE GONE THROUGH GREAT ROOMS TOGETHER

And when on the dark steel came the roads
Of a milky mist, and a spray of stars,
Bunches and squares and a spatter of stars,
We counted stars, one by one, a million and a million.
And we remembered those stars as fishermen remember fish,
As bees remember blossoms, as crops remember rains.
And these were rooms too ; we can so reckon.
We can always say we have gone through great rooms to-
gether.

LOVE IN LABRADOR

One arch of the sky
Took on a spray of jewels.

The crystals gleamed on the windows
Weaving their wintrish alphabets
Of spears and ovals fixed in frost
Fastened to a glass design
With a word: This must be.

There are shooters of the moon far north.
There are dying eyes holding diadems.
There are deaths sweet as laughing waters.
There are gold heelprints on the fading
      staircases of the stars.

SLEEP IMPRESSION

The dark blue wind of early autumn
ran on the early autumn sky
in the fields of yellow moon harvest.
    I slept, I almost slept,
    I said listening:
Trees you have leaves rustling like rain
When there is no rain.

BUG SPOTS

This bug carries spots on his back.
Last summer he carried these spots.
Now it is spring and he is back here again
With a domino design over his wings.
All winter he has been in a bedroom,
In a hole, in a hammock, hung up, stuck away,
Stashed while the snow blew over
The wind and the dripping icicles,
The tunnels of the frost.
Now he has errands again in a rotten stump.

UNDERSTANDINGS IN BLUE

The bird sat on a red handle
Counting five star flowers,
Five clover leafs.

The bird was a pigeon
Wearing a quiet understanding
Of how to wear blue.

There is pigeon blue
Picked out of baskets of big sky
When the springtime is blue.

This was the blue fadeout fire
Resting on the pigeon wings
In a quiet understanding.

The red handle, the star flowers,
The green clover leaves,
Wove into the weaves of blue.

The big sky stood back of it all
With a basket of springtime blue
And an understanding all alone.

MAYBE

Maybe he believes me, maybe not.
Maybe I can marry him, maybe not.
Maybe the wind on the prairie,
The wind on the sea, maybe,
Somebody somewhere, maybe, can tell.
I will lay my head on his shoulder
And when he asks me I will say yes,
Maybe.

LET THEM ASK YOUR PARDON

Child, what can those old men bring you?
If they can bring you a new handful
Absolutely warm and soft as summer rain,
Let them ask your pardon and do it soon.
Otherwise, why are they old?
Otherwise, why should they look at you
And carry assumptions in their old eyes
And speak such words as "ig-no-rance"
And "wisdom"—let them ask your pardon
Showing you how summer rain is an old pal
Of the wriggle of the angleworm,
The flip of the muskalonge,
And the step of the walking rain
Across the prairie. If the old men, child,
Tell you no stories about rockets,
Shooting stars, horses of high ranges,
Let them ask your pardon, excuse themselves,
And go away.

STRIPED CATS, OLD MEN AND
PROUD STOCKINGS

1

Ride a black horse with tan feet.
Let him have splashes of white,
Peninsulas of milk white.
Tell him, "Giddap, paint horse."
Ride him then with a bridle in your left hand
    and a hawk sitting on your right wrist.
Wear a yellow dress and an orange bandanna
    tied over your forehead.
So should a proud woman ride a proud horse.
So should a woman ride to a horse show, a bird show,
To a public procession, to a secret wedding,
To a crying menagerie of proud striped cats.

2

The old men who sit cross-legged in Hindustan
Naming the wedding days, the hungry days, the work days,
Handling their whiskers softly where the cascades
Come down numbering the years and the facts—
The old men look better close to the earth, cross-legged,
Pegged near the dirt, the home of the roots,
The home of years, facts.

3

They have chosen stockings to cover their legs
By a feeling for choices fine as air.
The appeal of stripes came to this one,
And spots, diamonds, clocks, anchors, to others,
The feeling for these choices was airy, fine,
Born of the deliberation of childbirths,
Thrust out with decision on the ends of their tongues.
If a black horse wishes white sox
Or a white horse calls for tan footwear
Or an ankle covering of pigeon blue gray—
It is a balance born of deliberations, childbirths.

MOON HAMMOCK

When the moon was a hammock of gold,
And the gold of the moon hammock kept changing
Till there was a blood hammock of a moon—
And the slow slipping down of it in the west,
The idle easy slipping down of it
Left a bridge of stars
And marchers among the stars—
That was an evening, a calendar date,
A curve of lines in an almanac.
People said it was an hour in September or April.
The astronomers stood at the mirror angles
Putting down another movement of the moon
The same as so many other movements of the moon
Put down in the big books of the regular watchers
Of the moon. This is the way things go by.
The gold hammock of a moon changes to blood,
Slips down, leaves a bridge of stars, marchers, almanacs.

THIMBLE ISLANDS

The sky and the sea put on a show.
Every day they put on a show.
There are dawn dress rehearsals.
There are sweet monotonous evening monologues.
The acrobatic lights of sunsets dwindle and darken.
The stars step out one by one with a bimbo, bimbo.

The red ball of the sun hung a balloon in the west,
And there was half a balloon, then no balloon at all,
And ten stars marched out and ten thousand more,
And the fathoms of the sky far over met the fathoms
     of the sea far under, among the thimble islands.

In the clear green water of dawn came a float of silver fila-
     ments, feelers circling a pink polyp's mouth;
The feelers ran out, opened and closed, opened and closed,
     hungry and searching, soft and incessant, floating the
     salt sea inlets sucking the green sea water as land roses
     suck the land air.

Frozen rock humps, smooth fire-rock humps—
Thimbles on the thumbs of the wives of prostrate sunken
        giants—
     God only knows how many sleep in the slack of the
     seven seas.

There in those places
under the sun balloons,
and fathoms, filaments, feelers—

The wind and the rain
sew the years
stitching one year into another.

Heavy hammers and high blowouts
take their pay, fill their contracts—
And there are dawn dress rehearsals, sweet
    monotonous evening monologues.

CLEFS

The little moon rode up a high corner.
The woman in a little room sat alone.
A violin the woman had sang for her.
The gut strings and the bow bent
A series of clefs climbing for memories.
"For remembering," she said, "A little moon
Up a high corner and climbing violin clefs."

THE GREAT PROUD WAGON WHEELS GO ON

The great proud wagon wheels
go on. Out of night and night's
nothings a steel shaft, a white
fire, a new star.

The great proud wagon wheels
go on. Out of night and night's
nothings a proud head, a skull
shape, a thing looking, a face
and eyes.

The great proud wagon wheels
go on. Night again and night's
nothings again and the star and
the skull and face gone.

I wait. I know. Look! The great
proud wagon wheels go on. Now
what? Now who? . . . coming . . .
out of night and night's nothings
. . . coming . . . you? . . . and you? . . .

TALL TIMBER

Night calls many witnesses
to supply evidence, to report honestly,
the meaning of dying, loving, being born.

Night has no better witnesses
than tall timber, rich in a moon, roaming in mist,
swearing a corroboration of relevant circumstances.

Call others to the court-houses of earth;
let them have counsel and all benefits of doubt;
let them report all they have seen and heard.

Then let Night come into court.
The tall timber testifies, the moon, the mist, testify.
Let us hear the oaths of these unimpeachable witnesses.

PROUD TORSOS

Just before the high time of autumn
Comes with the crush of its touch,
And the leaves fall, the leaves one by one,
The leaves by a full darkening sky fall,
The trees look proud, the horse chestnut
Stands with a gathered pride, the ivies
Are gathered around the stumps,
The ivies are woven thick with a green coat
Covering the stumps. Yes, the trees
Look proud now, it is the big time.
Have they not all had summer?
Didn't they all flimmer with faint
Lines of green in the spring,
A thin green mist as if it might
Be air or it might be new green leaves?
So, the first weeks of September are on
And each tree stands with a murmur,
"I stand here with a count of one more year,
One more number, one more ring in my torso."
Two weeks, five, six weeks, and the trees
Will be standing . . . stripped . . . gaunt . . .
The leaves gone . . . the coat of green gone . . .
And they will be proud but no longer
With the gathered pride of the days
In the high time.

TO KNOW SILENCE PERFECTLY

There is a music for lonely hearts nearly always.
If the music dies down there is a silence
Almost the same as the movement of music.
To know silence perfectly is to know music.

SKY PIECES

SKY PIECES

Proudly the fedoras march on the heads of the somewhat
    careless men.
Proudly the slouches march on the heads of the still more
    careless men.
Proudly the panamas perch on the noggins of dapper
    debonair men.
Comically somber the derbies gloom on the earnest solemn
    noodles.
And the sombrero, most proud, most careless, most dapper
    and debonair of all, somberly the sombrero marches on
    the heads of important men who know what they want.
Hats are sky-pieces; hats have a destiny; wish your hat
    slowly; your hat is you.

LOVABLE BABBLERS

What did that old philosopher say?
"The deadest deaths are the best."
For he was the same who said to a friend:
When you cry I cry, when you shake hands with
     me and ease my luck telling me it's too
     bad and the world's all wrong, it melts
     something inside of me and I break down.
So there are babblers we love for what they are.

OOMBA

Oomba went along years
Lugging a head
On a pikestaff of human neck.
"It is mine," said Oomba,
"If it is not mine who does it
Belong to?" he asked,
Oomba putting a straight quiz
To Oomba himself.

"Here it is," he muttered,
"Here on my neck, here on
My pikestaff of human neck;
And what is it for and how did I get it
And why do I say it is mine
And because it is mine it belongs to me?"
So Oomba went on talking to Oomba
Asking the simplest, oldest questions
Of himself.

SEVENTEEN MONTHS

This girl child speaks five words.
No for no and no for yes, "no" for either
    no or yes.
"Teewee" for wheat or oats or corn or barley
    or any food taken with a spoon.
"Go way" as an edict to keep your distance
    and let her determinations operate.

"Spoon" for spoon or cup or anything to be handled,
    all instruments, tools, paraphernalia of utility
    and convenience are SPOONS.
Mama is her only epithet and synonym for God and the
    Government and the one force of majesty and in-
    telligence obeying the call of pity, hunger, pain,
    cold, dark—MAMA, MAMA, MAMA.

SARAH'S LETTER TO PETER

When Sarah wrote Peter how she slept
among silver leaf poplars, waking to see
a light wind moving the under-side of the leaves—

She told him how to the north and east
there came a bath of light, a slow flush,
and the larks shot out into the air,
curved up and sang to meet the rose-red dawn.

But it wasn't dawn.
Four dark hours crept on till dawn arrived.
And the larks crept back to their nests
And later met the dawn that came and stayed,
Met it only with silence, with sore, dumb hearts.

Does every love have a false dawn?

She wrote her lover:
Others are but the showers of April, whilst
      thou art the seven seas.
Making a rendezvous and then not keeping it is wrong.
Do not be a false dawn; I want thee forever.

And this was one of the chapters.

DESTROYERS

Grandfather and grandfather's uncle stand looking at the harbor. "Look there," says grandfather, "and you see a torpedo boat. Next to it is a torpedo boat destroyer. And next to the torpedo boat destroyer is a destroyer of torpedo boat destroyers."

And grandfather's uncle says, "I heard my grandfather's uncle say every echo has a destroyer and for every echo destroyer there is a destroyer of echo destroyers."

And grandfather's uncle says, "I remember hearing my grandfather's uncle say every destroyer carries a pocket of eggs and the eggs wait and when they are ready they go blooey and the works of the destroyer blows up."

So they stand looking at the harbor, grandfather a grand old grey whiskered monochromic sea-dog and grandfather's uncle a grand old grey-whiskered monochromic landlubber.

"Columbus," says grandfather, "Columbus was only a little dago, a ginny, a wop, and he changed the shape of the earth; before Columbus came the shape of the earth in the heads of men was square and flat and he made it round and round in the heads of men."

"Yes," said grandfather's uncle, "He was bugs, he was loony, he saw things in a pig's eye, he had rats in his garret, bats in his belfry, there was a screw loose somewhere in him, he had a kink and he was a crank, he was nuts and belonged in a booby hatch."

And the two grand old grey-whiskered monochromic men, one a sea-dog, the other a landlubber, laughed, laughed, laughed in each other's sea-green, land-grey eyes.

TWO WOMEN AND THEIR FATHERS

1

Her father was a policeman who went fishing summer Sundays and caught a carp once with an old Spanish coin in its belly. As for her she picks up a good living high in the air in pink tights on a trapeze working for Ringling's circus.

2

Her father wore hip rubber boots and stood in yellow clay digging a tunnel for street cars to dip under the Chicago river. As for her she goes by a Hawaiian name and is known for a dance wherein she takes off one garment after another till there is a semblance of no garments at all.

VERY VERY IMPORTANT

I have no doubt that it is very important and so are you.
Put in two more of the word 'very' as a prefix to the
word 'important' if you like.
Make it read: I have no doubt it is very very very im-
portant and so are you.
Thus there are three of the word 'very' standing in a row
as prefixes to 'importance.'
If you wish more of the word 'very' go to the same place
these came from.

FOOLISH ABOUT WINDOWS

I was foolish about windows.
The house was an old one and the windows
    were small.
I asked a carpenter to come and open the
    walls and put in bigger windows.
"The bigger the window the more it costs,"
    he said.
"The bigger the cheaper," I said.
So he tore off siding and plaster and laths
And put in a big window and bigger windows.
I was hungry for windows.

One neighbor said, "If you keep on you'll be
    able to see everything there is."
I answered, "That'll be all right, that'll be
    classy enough for me."
Another neighbor said, "Pretty soon your house
    will be all windows."
And I said, "Who would the joke be on then?"
And still another, "Those who live in glass
    houses gather no moss."
And I said, "Birds of a feather should not throw
    stones and a soft answer turneth away rats."

LOVE LETTER TO HANS CHRISTIAN ANDERSEN

The kitchen chair speaks to the bread knife,
"Why have you no legs?"
The bread knife answers, "And you no teeth?"
It was a quarrel on a summer day.
It ran on till winter
And on to another winter and another.
In the cellar ultimately
The kitchen chair said,
"Your teeth are gone,"
And the bread knife,
"I see you have no legs."
It was quiet in the cellar, they found,
No yammering of people, no soup nor nuts,
A pile of coal, old mops, and broken tools,
These they could talk with . . . and mostly
None of them talked at all.

MYSTERIOUS BIOGRAPHY

Christofo Colombo was a hungry man,
hunted himself half way round the world;
he began poor, panhandled, ended in jail,
Christofo so hungry, Christofo so poor,
Christofo in the chilly, steel bracelets,
honorable distinguished Christofo Colombo.

RAT RIDDLES

There was a gray rat looked at me
with green eyes out of a rathole.

"Hello, rat," I said,
"Is there any chance for me
to get on to the language of the rats?"

And the green eyes blinked at me,
blinked from a gray rat's rathole.

"Come again," I said,
"Slip me a couple of riddles;
there must be riddles among the rats."

And the green eyes blinked at me
and a whisper came from the gray rathole:
"Who do you think you are and why is a rat?
Where did you sleep last night and why do
    you sneeze on Tuesdays? And why is the
    grave of a rat no deeper than the grave
    of a man?"

And the tail of a green-eyed rat
Whipped and was gone at a gray rathole.

WINTER WEATHER

It is cold.
The bitter of the winter
whines a story.
It is the colder weather when the truck
drivers sing it would freeze the whiskers
off a brass monkey.
It is the bitterest whining of the winter
now.

Well, we might sit down now, have a cup of coffee
apiece, and talk about the weather.
We might look back on things that happened long
ago, times when the weather was different.
Or we might talk about things ahead of us, funny
things in the days, days, days to come, days when
the weather will be different again.

Yes, a cup of coffee apiece.
Even if this winter weather is bitter,
The truck drivers are laughing:
It would freeze the whiskers off a brass monkey.

THE DINOSAUR BONES

The dinosaur bones are dusted every day.
The cards tell how old we guess the dinosaur
      bones are.
Here a head was seven feet long, horns with a
      hell of a ram,
Humping the humps of the Montana mountains.
               The respectable school children
Chatter at the heels of their teacher who ex-
      plains.
The tourists and wonder hunters come with
      their parasols
And catalogues and arrangements to do the
      museum
In an hour or two hours.
               The dinosaur bones
               are dusted
               every day.

UNINTENTIONAL PAINT

The flat gray banana store front
is visited by a union painter with no intentions
and a bucket of high maroon paint
and a pot of high yellow.

The high maroon banana store front
sings its contralto with two stripes
of yellow soprano on the door.

The union painter meant nothing
and we can not attribute intentions
to a bucket of maroon nor a pot of yellow.

The door and the lintels sing.
Two banjos strum on the threshold.
Two people hum a snatch of song
They know well from singing together often.
    I must come this way often
    and not only for bananas.

PEOPLE OF THE EAVES, I WISH YOU
GOOD MORNING

The wrens have troubles like us. The house of a wren will not run itself any more than the house of a man.

They chatter the same as two people in a flat where the laundry came back with the shirts of another man and the shimmy of another woman.

The shirt of a man wren and the shimmy of a woman wren are a trouble in the wren house. It is this or something else back of this chatter a spring morning.

Trouble goes so quick in the wren house. Now they are hopping wren jigs beaten off in a high wren staccato time.

People of the eaves, I wish you good-morning, I wish you a thousand thanks.

WEDDING POSTPONED

The arrangements are changed.
We were going to marry at six o'clock.
Now we shall not marry at all.

The bridegroom was all ready.
And the best man of the bridegroom was ready.

The bride fixed out in orchids and a long veil,
The bride and six bridesmaids were all ready.

Then the arrangements changed.
The date was changed not from six o'clock till later.
The date was changed to no time at all, to never.

Why the arrangements were changed is a long story.
Tell half of it and it is better than nothing at all.
Tell it with a hint and a whisper and it is told wrong.

We know why it was put off,
Why the arrangements shifted,
Why the organist was told to go,
Why the minister ready for the ring ceremony
Was told to drive away and be quick about it, please.
We know this in all its results and circumstances.

The disappointment of the best man,
The sorry look on the faces of the bridesmaids,
We, who chose them out of many, we could understand.

And we told them only what is told here:
The arrangements are changed, there will be no wedding,
We shall not marry at all, not to-day, not to-morrow, no
       time.

TWO WOMEN

They told me in an old book
about the wine-dark sea.

I saw the sea foam-lit and
green, sunset-red and changing.

I saw the sea wine-dark only
when I thought of you and your eyes.

         . . .

The fabrics shift in her eyes.
Persian cat fur is soft,
A Navajo blanket beautifully woven,
And is there anything more restful
      than a Japanese sea-mist silk?
The fabrics shift in her voice.

SNATCH OF SLIPHORN JAZZ

Are you happy? It's the only
way to be, kid.
Yes, be happy, it's a good nice
way to be.
But not happy-happy, kid, don't
be too doubled-up doggone happy.
It's the doubled-up doggone happy-
happy people . . . bust hard . . . they
do bust hard . . . when they bust.
Be happy, kid, go to it, but not too
doggone happy.

LANDSCAPE

On a mountain-side the real estate agents
Put up signs marking the city lots to be sold there.
A man whose father and mother were Irish
Ran a goat farm half-way down the mountain;
He drove a covered wagon years ago,
Understood how to handle a rifle,
Shot grouse, buffalo, Indians, in a single year,
And now was raising goats around a shanty.
Down at the foot of the mountain
Two Japanese families had flower farms.
A man and woman were in rows of sweet peas
Picking the pink and white flowers
To put in baskets and take to the Los Angeles market.
They were clean as what they handled
There in morning sun, the big people and baby-faces.
Across the road high on another mountain
Stood a house saying, "I am it," a commanding house.
There was the home of a motion picture director
Famous for lavish doll house interiors,
Clothes ransacked from the latest designs for women
In the combats of "male against female."
The mountain, the scenery, the layout of the landscape,
And the peace of the morning sun as it happened,
The miles of houses pocketed in the valley beyond—
It was all worth looking at, worth wondering about,
How long it might last, how young it might be.

Hollywood, 1923.

DIFFERENT KINDS OF GOOD-BY

Good-by is a loose word, a yellow ribbon
    fluttering in the wind.
Good-by is a stiff word, a steel slide rule—
    a fixed automatic phone number.
A thousand people? And you must say good-by
    to all? One at a time?—yes, I guess you
    need a thousand different good-bys.
There is a good-by for the Johnsons and another
    for the Smiths and another for the Poindexters
    and the Van Rensselaers.
And there is the big grand good-by to the thousand
    all at once, the whole works.

THREE HILLS LOOK DIFFERENT IN THE MOONSHINE

The hill of the white skull in the summer moon
shines; the hill of the red heart is a neighbor
in the summer moonshine; the hill of the climbing
clumsy shadows is another.

PROUD OF THEIR RAGS

They come down from the mountains, proud of their rags.
"What do you know about loons, panthers, hawks?
Wings, winds, slides—what do you know?
Hunger and hope, and how do you know who tore my rags?"
They come down from the mountains, proud of their rags,
    five or six out of sixty; they come down with proud
    heads.

BROKEN SKY

The sky of gray is eaten in six places,
Rag holes stand out.
It is an army blanket and the sleeper
    slept too near the fire.

HELLS AND HEAVENS

Each man pictures his hell or heaven different.
Some have snug home-like heavens, suburban, well-kept.
Some have a wild, storm-swept heaven; their happiness has
    been in storms, heaven must have storms mixed with
    fair weather.
And hell for some is a jail, for others a factory, for others
    a kitchen, for others a place of many polite liars full
    of blah, all gah gah.

THREE FRAGMENTS FOR FISHERS OF DESTINY

Methusaleh was a witness to many cabbages and kings.
They marched in procession for him like the marching
　　harvests of onions lift their green spears in Maytime
　　and go down the wind in thistledown fluff with the
　　leaves of October.

The same wind blew its crescendo and diminuendo in the
　　long beards of clear-eyed prophets and again in the
　　whiskers of the muddleheads who only called them-
　　selves prophets.

Methusaleh saw the old muddleheads sniff at the sun
And proclaim their wisdom as beyond the sun.

TIMBER MOON

TIMBER MOON

There is a way the moon looks into the timber at night
And tells the walnut trees secrets of silver sand—
There is a way the moon makes a lattice work
Under the leaves of the hazel bushes—
There is a way the moon understands the hoot owl
Sitting on an arm of a sugar maple throwing its
One long lonesome cry up the ladders of the moon—
There is a way the moon finds company early in the fall
      time.

FLOWERS TELL MONTHS

Gold buttons in the garden today—
Among the brown-eyed susans the golden spiders are
    gambling
The blue sisters of the white asters speak to each other.

> After the travel of the snows—
> Buttercups come in a yellow rain,
> Johnny-jump-ups in a blue mist—
> Wild azaleas with a low spring cry.

LANDSCAPE

See the trees lean to the wind's way of learning.
See the dirt of the hills shape to the water's
    way of learning.
See the lift of it all go the way the biggest
    wind and the strongest water want it.

COUNTING

Sweet lips, there are songs about kisses now.
Looking backward are kisses of remembrance
Looking ahead are kisses to be wished-for.
So time is counted, so far back, so far ahead, in
    measurements of sweet kisses.

OAK ARMS

The broken arm of the black oak
blisters in the list of numbers:
    "The sky hissed; I stand and remember."

And the gold of the gloaming flushes, floods by,
And the haze gold is cut across with the cricket's
    wisp of silver.

MOON-PATH

Creep up, moon, on the south sky.
Mark the moon path of this evening.
The day must be counted.
The new moon is a law.
The little say-so of the moon must be listened to.

THERE ARE DIFFERENT GARDENS

Flowers can be cousins of the stars.
The closing and speaking lips of the lily
And the warning of the fire and the dust—
They are in the gardens and the sky of stars.
Beyond the shots of the light of this sun
Are the little sprinkles, the little twinklers
Of suns to whose lips this lily never sent
A whisper from its closing and speaking lips.

WINDFLOWER LEAF

This flower is repeated
out of old winds, out of
old times.

The wind repeats these, it
must have these, over and
over again.

New windflowers so fresh,
oh beautiful leaves, here
now again.

    The domes over
    fall to pieces.
    The stones under
    fall to pieces.
    Rain and ice
    wreck the works.
The wind keeps, the windflowers
    keep, the leaves last,
The wind young and strong lets
    these last longer than stones.

LITTLE SKETCH

There are forked branches of trees
Where the leaves shudder obediently,
Where the hangover leaves
Flow in a curve downward;
And between the forks and leaves,
In patches and angles, in square handfuls,
The orange lights of the done sunset
Come and filter and pour.

BUTTER COLORS

The light of the yellow flowers
leaps to the light of the pool.

Butter under the chin of this slip
slides to the level water mirror.

Fan yellow films of light play fast
slipping all day on, on, to the water home.

Home, come home, water calls to light.
Fan yellow films leap and slide.

WEBS

Every man spins a web of light circles
And hangs this web in the sky
Or finds it hanging, already hung for him,
Written as a path for him to travel.
The white spiders know how this geography goes.
Their feet tell them when to spin,
How to weave in a criss-cross
Among elms and maples, among radishes and button weeds,
Among cellar timbers and old shanty doors.
Not only the white spiders, also the yellow and blue,
Also the black and purple spiders
Listen when their feet tell them to spin one.
And while every spider spins a web of light circles
Or finds one already hung for him,
So does every man born under the sky.

PEACE, NIGHT, SLEEP

"You shall have peace with night and sleep.
It was written in the creep of the mist,
In the open doors of night horizons.
Peace, night, sleep, all go together.
In the forgetting of the frogs and the sun,
In the losing of the grackle's off cry
And the call of the bird whose name is gone—
You shall have peace; the mist creeps, the doors open.
Let night, let sleep, have their way."

BUNDLES

I have thought of beaches, fields,
Tears, laughter.

I have thought of homes put up—
And blown away.

I have thought of meetings and for
Every meeting a good-by.

I have thought of stars going alone,
Orioles in pairs, sunsets in blundering
Wistful deaths.

I have wanted to let go and cross over
To a next star, a last star.

I have asked to be left a few tears
And some laughter.

MAN AND DOG ON AN EARLY WINTER MORNING

There was a tall slough grass
Too tough for the farmers to feed the cattle,
And the wind was sifting through, shaking the grass;
Each spear of grass interfered a little with the wind
And the interference sent up a soft hiss,
A mysterious little fiddler's and whistler's hiss;
And it happened all the spears together
Made a soft music in the slough grass
Too tough for the farmers to cut for fodder.
    "This is a proud place to come to
    On a winter morning, early in winter,"
    Said a hungry man, speaking to his dog,
Speaking to himself and the passing wind,
"This is a proud place to come to."

PRECIOUS MOMENTS

Bright vocabularies are transient as rainbows.
Speech requires blood and air to make it.
Before the word comes off the end of the tongue,
While the diaphragms of flesh negotiate the word,
In the moment of doom when the word forms
It is born, alive, registering an imprint—
Afterward it is a mummy, a dry fact, done and gone.
The warning holds yet: Speak now or forever hold
  your peace.
Ecce homo had meanings: Behold the Man! Look at
  him! Dying he lives and speaks!

OCTOBER PAINT

Flame blue wisps in the west,
Wrap yourselves in these leaves
And speak to winter about us.
Tell winter the whole story.

Red leaves up the oaken slabs,
You came, little and green spats
Four months ago; your climbers
Put scroll after scroll around
The oaken slabs. "Red, come red,"
Some one with an October paint
Pot said. And here you are,
Fifty red arrowheads of leaf paint
Or fifty mystic fox footprints
Or fifty pointed thumbprints.
Hold on, the winds are to come
Blowing, blowing, the gray slabs
Will lose you, the winds will
Flick you away in a whiff
One by one, two by two . . . Yet
I have heard a rumor whispered;
Tattlers tell it to each other
Like a secret everybody knows . . .
Next year you will come again.
Up the oaken slabs you will put
Your pointed fox footprints
Green in the early summer
And you will be red arrowheads

In the falltime . . . Tattlers
Slip this into each others' ears
Like a secret everybody knows.
. . . If I see some one with an
October paint pot I shall be
Full of respect and say,
"I saw your thumbprints everywhere;
How do you do it?"

MANY HATS

1

When the scrapers of the
deep winds were done, and
the haulers of the tall
waters had finished, this
was the accomplishment.

The drums of the sun never
get tired, and first off
every morning, the drums of
the sun perform an intro-
duction of the dawn here.

The moon goes down here
as a dark bellringer doing
once more what he has done
over and over already in
his young life.

Up on a long blue platform
comes a line of starprints.

If the wind has a song, it
is moaning; Good Lawd, I
done done what you told me
to do.

2

Whose three-ring circus is this? Who stipulated in a contract for this to be drunken, death-defying, colossal, mammoth, cyclopean, mystic as the light that never was on land or sea, bland, composed, and imperturbable as a cool phalanx of sphinxes? Why did one woman cry, The silence is terrible? Why did another smile, There is a sweet gravity here? Why do they come and go here and look as in a looking glass?

The Grand Canyon of Arizona, said one, this is it, hacked out by the broadax of a big left-handed God and left forgotten, fixed over and embellished by a remembering right-handed God who always comes back.

If you ask me, said an old railroader, I'll never tell you who took the excavation contract for this blowout—it took a lot of shovels and a lot of dynamite—several large kegs, I would guess—and maybe they had a case or two of T N T.

Yes, he went on, the Grand Canyon, the daddy of 'em all— the undisputed champeen—that range rider sure was righto—the elements had a hell of a rassle here.

The Grand Canyon—a long ride from where Brigham Young stands in bronze gazing on the city he bade rise out of salt and alkali—a weary walk from Santa Fe and the Mountains of the Blood of Christ—a bitter hike from where the Sonora dove at Tucson mourns, No hope, no hope—a sweet distance from where Balboa stripped for his first swim in the Pacific—a mean cross-country journey to where Roy Bean told the muchacho, By the white light of a moon on the walls of an arroyo last Tuesday you killed a woman and next Tuesday we're going to hang you—a traveler's route of many days and sleeps to reach the place of the declaration, God reigns and the government at Washington lives.

Shovel into this cut of earth all past and present possessions, creations, belongings of man; shovel furioso, appasionata, pizzicata; shovel cities, wagons, ships, tools, jewels; the bottom isn't covered; the wild burros and the trail mules go haw-hee, haw-hee, haw-hee.

Turn it into a Hall of Fame, said a rambler, let it be a series of memorials to the Four Horsemen, to Napoleon, Carl the Twelfth, Caesar, Alexander the Great, Hannibal and Hasdrubal, and all who have rode in blood up to the bridles of the horses, calling, Hurrah for the next who goes—let each have his name on a truncated cyclops of rock—let passers-by say, He was pretty good but he didn't last long.

Now I wonder, I wonder, said another, can they all find room here? Elijah fed by the ravens, Jonah in the belly of the whale, Daniel in the lion's den, Lot's wife transmogrified into salt, Elijah riding up into the sky in a chariot of fire—can they all find room? Are the broken pieces of the Tower of Babel and the Walls of Jericho here? Should I look for the ram's horn Joshua blew?

3

A phantom runner runs on the rim. "I saw a moon man throw hats in, hats of kings, emperors, senators, presidents, plumed hats of knights, red hats of cardinals, five gallon hats of cowboys, tasselled hats of Bavarian yodelers, mandarin hats, derbies, fedoras, chapeaus, straws, lady picture hats out of Gainsborough portraits—

"Hats many proud people handed over, dying and saying, Take this one too—hats furioso, appasionata, pizzicata— hats for remembrance, good-by, three strikes and out, fade me, there's no place to go but home—hats for man alone, God alone, the sky alone."

4

Think of the little birds, said another, the wee birdies—before God took a hunk of mud and made Man they were here, the birds, the robins, juncoes, nuthatches, bats, eagles, cedar birds, chickadees, bluejays, I saw a blackbird gleaming in satin, floating in the scrolls of his glamorous wings, stopping on an airpath and standing still with nothing under his feet, looking at the gray Mojave desert level interrupted by the Grand Canyon—the birds belong, don't they?

5

Comes along a hombre saying, Let it be dedicated to Time; this is what is left of the Big Procession when Time gets

through with it; the sun loves its stubs; we will give a name
to any torso broken and tumbled by Time; we will leave the
vanished torsos with no names.

Comes along a hombre accidentally remarking, Let it be
dedicated to Law and Order—the law of the Strong fight-
ing the Strong, the Cunning outwitting the Less Cunning—
and the Weak Ones ordered to their places by the Strong
and Cunning—aye—and ai-ee—Law and Order.

Comes along another hombre giving his slant at it, Now
this sure was the Gyarden of Eden, smooth, rich, nice,
watered, fixed, no work till to-morrow, Adam and Eve satis-
fied and sitting pretty till the day of the Snake Dance and
the First Sin; and God was disgusted and wrecked the
works; he ordered club-foot angels with broken wings to
shoot the job; now look at it.

Comes another hombre all wised up, This was the Devil's
Brickyard; here were the kilns to make the Kitchens of
Hell; after bricks enough were made to last Hell a million
years, the Devil said, "Shut 'er down"; they had a big pay-
day night and left it busted from hell to breakfast; the
Hopis looked it over and decided to live eighty miles away
where there was water; then came Powell, Hance, the Santa
Fe, the boys shooting the rapids, and Fred Harvey with El
Tovar.

6

Now Hance had his points; they asked him how he come to
find the Canyon and he told 'em, I was ridin' old Whitey

and the Mojaves after me when we comes to this gap miles across; I told Whitey, It's you now for the longest jump you ever took; Whitey jumped and was half way across when I pulled on the bridle, turned him around, and we come back to the same place on the Canyon rim we started from.

Yes, Hance told 'em, if they asked, how he come to dig the Canyon. "But where did you put all the dirt?" "Took it away in wheelbarrows and made San Francisco Peaks."

Hance sleeping near a big rock, woke up and saw seven rattlesnakes circle seven times around the rock, each with the tail of the snake ahead in his mouth, and all of them swallowing, till after a while there wasn't a snake left. Hance's wife got her leg caught between two rocks; couldn't get her loose, said Hance, so I had to shoot her to save her from starving to death; look down there between those two rocks and you can see her bones, said Hance.

This is where we find the original knuckle snake; he breaks to pieces if you try to pick him up; and when you go away he knuckles himself together again; yes, and down here, is the original echo canyon; we holler, "Has Smith been here?" and the echo promulgates back, "Which Smith?"

7

Down at the darkest depths, miles down, the Colorado River grinds, toils, driving the channel deeper—is it free or convict?—tell me—will it end like a great writer crying, I die with my best books unwritten?

Smooth as glass run the streaming waters—then a break into rapids, into tumblers, into spray, into voices, roars, growls, into commanding monotones that hunt far corners and jumping-off places.

And how should a beautiful, ignorant stream of water know it heads for an early release—out across the desert, running toward the Gulf, below sea level, to murmur its lullaby, and see the Imperial Valley rise out of burning sand with cotton blossoms, wheat, watermelons, roses, how should it know?

8

The hombres keep coming; here comes another; he says, says he, I met four people this morning, the poker face, the baby stare, the icy mitt, and the peace that passeth understanding—let this place be dedicated to X, the unknown factor, to the Missing Link, to Jo Jo the dog-faced boy, to the Sargossa Sea, to Humpty Dumpty, to Little Red Riding Hood crying for her mother, to those who never believe in Santa Klaus, to the man who turned himself inside out because he was so sleepy.

9

Steps on steps lift on into the sky; the lengths count up into stairways; let me go up for the Redeemer is up there; He died for me; so a Spanish Indian was speaking—and he asked, When the first French Jesuit looked from Yavapai four hundred years ago, did he murmur of a tall altar to go on a mile-long rock shelf down there on a mesa? did he whisper of an unspeakably tall altar there for the raising of the ostensorium and the swinging of censers and the calling up of the presence of the Heart of the Living Christ? And he went on, Where the Son of God is made known surely is a place for the removal of shoes and the renewal of feet for the journey—surely this is so.

10

Came a lean, hungry-looking hombre with Kansas, Nebraska, the Dakotas on his wind-bitten face, and he was saying, Sure my boy, sure my girl, and you're free to have any sweet bluebird fancies you please, any wild broncho thoughts you choose to have, when you stand before this grand scrap pile of hats, hammers, haciendas, and hidalgos. He went on, Yes, let this be dedicated to Time and Ice; a memorial of the Human Family which came, was, and went; let it stand as a witness of the short miserable pilgrimage of mankind, of flame faiths, of blood and fire, and of Ice which was here first and will be here again—Faces once frozen you shall all be frozen again—the little clocks of Man shall all be frozen and nobody will be too late or too early ever again.

11

On the rim a quizzical grey-glinting hombre was telling himself how it looked to him—the sun and the air are endless with silver tricks—the light of the sun has crimson stratagems—the changes go on in stop-watch split seconds —the blues slide down a box of yellow and mix with reds

that melt into grey and come back saffron clay and granite
pink—a weaving gamble of color twists on and it is any-
body's guess what is next.

A long sand-brown shawl shortens to a glimmering tur-
quoise scarf—as the parapets and chimneys wash over and
out in the baths of the sunset and the floats of the gloam-
ing, one man says, There goes God with an army of ban-
ners, and another man, Who is God and why? who am I and
why?

> He told himself, This may be
> something else than what I
> see when I look—how do I
> know? For each man sees him-
> self in the Grand Canyon—
> each one makes his own Canyon
> before he comes, each one brings
> and carries away his own Canyon-
> who knows? and how do I know?

12

> If the wind has a song, it
> is moaning: Good Lawd, I
> done done what you told me
> to do.
>
> When the scrapers of the
> deep winds were done, and
> the haulers of the tall

waters had finished, this
was the accomplishment.

The moon goes down here
as a dark bellringer doing
once more what he has done
over and over already in
his young life.

Up on a long blue platform
comes a line of starprints.

The drums of the sun never
get tired, and first off
every morning, the drums of
the sun perform an intro-
duction of the dawn here.